DATE DUE

APR 0 3 1997	APR 0 8 1998	DEC 1 6 1998
APR 1 8 1997	MAY 0 6 1998	
APR 2 0 1998		
4/8/16		

GAYLORD　　　　　　　　　　PRINTED IN U.S.A.

HOOVER INSTITUTION PUBLICATIONS

ADOLF HITLER

His Family, Childhood and Youth

ADOLF HITLER

His Family, Childhood and Youth

by

BRADLEY F. SMITH

THE HOOVER INSTITUTION ON WAR,
REVOLUTION AND PEACE
STANFORD UNIVERSITY
STANFORD · CALIFORNIA

The Hoover Institution on War, Revolution and Peace, founded at Stanford University in 1919 by the late President Herbert Hoover, is a center for advanced study and research on public and international affairs in the twentieth century. The views expressed in its publications are entirely those of the authors and do not necessarily reflect the views of the Hoover Institution.

© 1967 by the Board of Trustees of the Leland Stanford Junior University
All rights reserved
Library of Congress Catalog Card Number: 66-25727

First printing 1967, The Netherlands
Second printing 1968
Printed in the United States of America

To Mary, Maggie and Leslie

PREFACE

This study of Hitler's early years has three objectives. First, it is an attempt at a chronological development of the major events of these years which can be considered a partial biography. Second, it represents a consolidation of all available source materials, including previously unpublished accounts. Third – and this is certainly the objective least clearly attained – it is an effort to note the events and conditions in Hitler's formative years which left clear marks on his character and personality.

The techniques employed in this study are those of the historian rather than those of the psychoanalyst or the sociologist. At a number of stages, where it has seemed desirable or essential to borrow from other disciplines (for example, one aspect of Hitler's personality virtually requires consideration of conflicting medical opinions concerning the possible effects of a childhood disease; other instances, in which appraisals by trained psychiatrists are similarly useful, are more numerous), such materials are presented as part of the historical record rather than as evidence of the author's competence in disciplines far removed from his own.

The record itself, however, is fascinating enough to stand without embellishments. To some extent, it may be called scanty: Hitler's Boswells ultimately were heard from but not until after his rise to power, and the intervening lapse in time and the remarkable transformation of their subject from youthful failure to mighty leader of the German Reich combined to lessen both their objectivity and their accuracy. None of their reports can be accepted without reservation, but, considered in conjunction with Hitler's own account and such humble but usually indisputable guideposts as school reports and police registration files, they help to form a picture of the young Hitler.

One difficulty remains. There is little in this portrait which fits the perspective in which Hitler is now commonly viewed. Few historical figures have earned his position as a man other men feel a kind of compulsion to explain, for certainly no individual has done more to disturb the conscience of our era – perhaps our century – by his proven ability to lead a civilized nation into barbarities which challenged all established legal and moral concepts.

Yet in the deeds of the man as a youth there are few discernible traces indeed of evil genius. Instead of evil there is a groping futility, perhaps an occasional note of defiance, but predominantly a desire to escape from the world of hard realities into a world of romance colored by majestic art and sonorous music. Young Hitler dislikes his sisters and rejects his father – more indirectly than otherwise – but loves his mother. While his tendency is to stand outside society, he has friendships which include some members of nationalities and religions he later proclaimed "tainted" and marked for mass extermination. There is no report of a deliberately cruel act. Perhaps the nearest approximation is his consistent failure in secondary school, a failure partially motivated by his resentment of his father's attempts to discipline him. When failure becomes a pattern and the person injured thereby is no longer his father but himself, until late adolescence his response is still only verbal complaint; his actions are nothing more than further withdrawals which seem almost conscious invitations to the next disaster.

This is not, then, the portrait of the adult monster as a monster child. The young Adolf Hitler invites our sympathy. He is a very human little boy and youth, whose chief faults are his laziness and his passion for romantic games. He is someone we all know because we all have felt similar urges and experienced many of the same frustrations. To be sure, the monster perhaps can be glimpsed as Hitler the child becomes Hitler the young man, but this is largely a contribution of hindsight. Even in his early twenties, following his only success in the years prior to World War I – his escape from the total poverty and humiliation of his life in the *Obdachlosenheim* to the frail security of painting picture postcards in the reading room of the *Maennerheim* – he is still an essentially

ACKNOWLEDGEMENTS

I would like to express my appreciation to a number of people who read this volume and provided helpful advice. Portions of the manuscript were read by Dr. Ruth A. Frary, Dr. Gerald Gumeson, Dr. Richard H. Anderson, and Professor Werner T. Angress. Mrs. Agnes F. Peterson, Curator of the Western European Collection at the Hoover Institution on War, Revolution and Peace, was especially generous with her time and suggestions in guiding the author to valuable source materials in the Institution. Thanks are also due to Mr. Ward Smith, who edited the complete manuscript, and to Mrs. Arline Paul, head of the Hoover Institution's Reference Division, for her kindness and forebearance in handling interlibrary loan problems. Acknowledgement is made to Europa Verlag for permission to reproduce the picture from Franz Jetzinger's *Hitlers Jugend*.

B.F.S.

TABLE OF CONTENTS

Guide to Frequently Cited Sources   15

I. Hitler's Father, Alois Schickelgruber–Hitler   17

    Photographs   20

II. The Hitler Family   35

III. Adolf Hitler's Early Childhood   50

IV. The Later Childhood   65

V. The Early Youth   90

VI. The First Years in Vienna   116

VII. The Later Vienna Period, February 1910 to June 1913   133

VIII. The Youth and the Man   152

Appendix I: The Alteration of the Name and the Jewish
    Grandfather Story   157

Appendix II: Hitler in Vienna: The Description in *Mein Kampf*,
    and the Writings of Hanisch, Honisch, and Greiner   161

Bibliography   168

Index   177

GUIDE TO FREQUENTLY CITED SOURCES

HA – *Hauptarchiv der NSDAP*. Microfilm copies at the Hoover Institution, Stanford, California.

NA – The National Archives, Arlington Material.

L of C – The Library of Congress, "German Materials."

Bloch – Bloch, Dr. Edward (as told to J. D. Ratcliff). "My Patient Hitler," *Colliers*, Vol. 107, No. 1 (March 15, 1941), No. 2 (March 22, 1941).

Coldstream – Coldstream, John P. *The Institutions of Austria* (Edinburgh, Arch. Constable, 1895).

Daim – Daim, Wilfried, *Der Mann, Der Hitler die Ideen Gab. Von den religioesen Verirrungen eines Sektierers zum Rassenwahn des Diktators* (Munich, Isar Verlag, 1958).

Ferber – Ferber, Walter, *Die Vorgeschichte der NSDAP in Oesterreich: Ein Beitrag zur Geschichtsrevision* (Konstanz, Verlagsanstalt Merk u. Co., 1954).

Goerlitz and Quint – Goerlitz, Walter and Herbert A. Quint, *Adolf Hitler, eine Biographie* (Stuttgart, Steingrueber-Verlag, 1952).

Greiner – Greiner, Josef, *Das Ende des Hitler Mythos* (Vienna, Amalthea Verlag, 1947).

Hanisch – Hanisch, Reinhold, "I was Hitler's Buddy," *New Republic*, Vol. 98, No. 1270 (April 5, 1939), No. 1271 (April 12, 1939), No. 1272 (April 19, 1939).

Heiden, *Der Fuehrer* – Heiden, Konrad, *Der Fuehrer*. Translated by Ralph Manheim (Boston, Houghton Mifflin, 1944).

Mein Kampf – Hitler, Adolf. *Mein Kampf*. Translated by Ralph Manheim (Boston, Houghton Mifflin, 1962).

Table Talk – *Hitler's Table Talk, 1941-1944*. Translated by Norman Cameron and R. H. Stevens (London, Weidenfeld and Nicolson, 1953).

Jetzinger (G) – Jetzinger, Franz, *Hitlers Jugend: Phantasien, Luegen – und die Wahrheit* (Vienna, Europa Verlag, 1956).

Jetzinger (E) – Jetzinger, Franz, *Hitler's Youth*. Translated by Lawrence Wilson (London, Hutchinson, 1958).

Die Ahnentafel – Koppensteiner, Rudolf, *Die Ahnentafel des Fuehrers* (Leipzig, Zentralstelle fuer deutsche Personen- und Familiengeschichte, 1937).

Kubizek – Kubizek, August, *The Young Hitler I Knew*. Translated by E. V. Anderson (Boston, Houghton Mifflin, 1955).

Pichl – Pichl, Eduard, *Georg Schoenerer*, (6 Vols. in 3) (Berlin, Gerhard Stalling Verlag, 1938).

Rabitsch – Rabitsch, Hugo, *Aus Adolf Hitlers Jugendzeit. Jugenderinnerungen eines zeitgenoessischen Linzer Realschuelers* (Munich, Deutscher Volksverlag, 1938).

Zoller – Zoller, Albert (ed.), *Hitler Privat. Erlebnisbericht seiner Geheimsekretaerin* (Duesseldorf, Droste-Verlag, 1949).

I

HITLER'S FATHER, ALOIS SCHICKELGRUBER-HITLER

On June 17, 1837, a forty-two year-old peasant woman, Maria Anna Schickelgruber, gave birth to a boy in the tiny agricultural village of Strones, north-west of Vienna in the administrative district of Zwettl. The baby was registered in the baptismal record of the neighboring town of Dollersheim by the local priest under the name of Alois Schickelgruber, illegitimate son of Maria Anna Schickelgruber, father unknown.[1] This terse entry in the records of a country priest in lower Austria marks the informal beginning of the family line which culminated in the birth of Adolf Hitler in 1889. After many changes of fortune, and even a change of name, Maria Anna Schickelgruber's son Alois became the father of Adolf Hitler. In trying to probe deeper into the origins of the family, it is impossible to get behind the baptismal entry of 1837; Alois' father, i.e. Adolf's paternal grandfather, was and is unknown. The family history begins abruptly with a peasant mother and her illegitimate son.

Maria Anna Schickelgruber, or Schicklgruber, as the name was sometimes spelled, was born in Strones in April 1795. She was one of eleven children of the proprietor of peasant holding #1 in Strones, Johann Schickelgruber. Of her ten brothers and sisters, only six survived infancy. Their lives followed a pattern familiar to that of poor peasants throughout Europe. One of the boys, Josef, took over the farm, but ran into financial difficulties, and the land passed out of the hands of the family.[2] Another brother, Franz, ended as a hard-drinking, happy-go-lucky day laborer in the neighborhood of

[1] *Jetzinger* (G), pp. 17-18; *Jetzinger* (E), pp. 17-18.
[2] *Die Ahnentafel*, p. 39.

Scheibbs. Aside from Maria Anna's illegitimate child, only two of Johann Schickelgruber's children produced a line of direct descendents. Josefa went to the village of Fuenfhaus near Vienna, married in 1826, and mothered a number of children who carried on as minor officials and tradesmen for several generations. Another brother, Leopold, also had several children. The family had already lost contact with this branch by the middle of the 1870's, although it was reasonably certain that some members were still alive.[3]

It is not surprising that little is known of Maria Anna between her birth in 1795 and the birth of her illegitimate son in 1837. Poor peasant girls left few marks in records of the early nineteenth century. It is possible that, like her sister Josefa, she went off to the city and took the customary position as maid in a bourgeois household in Vienna or one of the provincial cities. On the other hand, she may have stayed in Strones and found domestic employment on an irregular basis.[4] After 1817, the family apparently fell on hard times. In that year, her father turned over the family land to the eldest son, Josef, only to see it lost shortly thereafter. Old Johann ended life as a poor cotter. Maria Anna may have shared in the general impoverishment, for when Alois was born she was not residing with her father, but in Strones, house #13, with the family of Johann Trummelschlager. Trummelschlager and his wife also served as the godparents of little Alois.[5]

Following the birth of Alois, Maria Anna and the baby moved into the house where her father was staying, Strones, house #22. They remained there without any discoverable change in their condition until Alois was nearly five. Then, surprisingly, at the age of forty-seven, Maria Anna married. The bridegroom was a fifty-year-old journeyman mill worker named Johann Georg Hiedler, Hitler, or in another variant spelling, Huettler. Johann Georg had been born to a peasant family in the village of Spital, northwest of Strones in the district of Weitra, near the present border of Austria and Czechoslovakia. He had lived the life of a wandering mill worker, with

---

[3] Records of Bezirksamt Hernals, October 18, 1862 – Heirs of Mathius Schickelgruber; Letter Alois Hitler to Alois Veit, September 17, 1876. *L of C* and File 17A, *HA*.
[4] *Die Ahnentafel*, p. 39; *Jetzinger* (G), p. 17.
[5] *Die Ahnentafel*, pp. 39 and 44-45.

changing addresses and fortune but few responsibilities. In 1823 he married a peasant girl in the town of Hohensich, but she must have died, for he later took to the road again. In 1842, his residence was listed at Duernthal, where he supposedly was a journeyman miller, but at the time of his second marriage he was actually living with Maria Anna and her father in Strones #22. The household consisted of the new bride; the bridegroom; the bride's father, seventy-eight-year-old Johann Schickelgruber; and the bride's illegitimate son, five-year-old Alois.[6]

The prospects for a lively, happy boyhood for little Alois in this environment were bleak, but he was rescued by the intervention of the Hiedler family. On the initiative of either Johann Georg's brother, Johann Nepomuk Hiedler, or his mother, Anna Maria Hiedler, Alois was removed from Strones to the Hiedler family home in Spital. This move presumably occurred in the early 1840's perhaps at the time of Maria Anna's marriage in 1842.[7] Alois' mother, grandfather, and stepfather did not accompany the boy to Spital, moving instead to the village of Klein Motten near Strones. On January 7, 1847, Maria Anna died in Klein Motten, and in November, her father also died there. Only Alois and Johann Georg Hiedler remained of the wedding household of five years before, and it is not clear what happened to Johann Georg after the death of his wife. He may have remained in Klein Motten, gone back to Duernthal or taken lodging in another of the countless villages he had wandered through while pursuing his trade. The only exact reference to him after 1847 shows that he returned to his home village of Spital prior to his death in 1857.[8]

In the meantime, little Alois had taken his place in the household of Johann Georg's brother in Spital, house #36. In 1845, Alois' new family consisted of the master of the house, forty-year-old Johann Nepomuk Hiedler, peasant owner and proprietor, his wife, Eva Maria Hiedler, born Decker, and his mother, seventy-seven-year-old

---

[6] *Die Ahnentafel*, pp. 39 and 45.
[7] Jetzinger asserts that Johann Nepomuk came and took Alois soon after the marriage in 1842, but he is vague, cites no documents and habitually guesses. It is possible that Alois went to Johann Nepomuk's household as late as the time of his mother's death in 1847. *Jetzinger* (G), p. 19; *Jetzinger* (E), p. 25.
[8] *Die Ahnentafel*, p. 39.

Anna Maria Hiedler, whose husband had been dead for many years. She had many privileges in the household on the basis of the legal settlement by which the family property had gone to Johann Nepomuk, and she probably played a part close to that of *mater familias*. Alois thus passed from an environment dominated by older men to one dominated by older women. But Johann Nepomuk, and the members of his household were very unlike his drifting, shiftless brother. Johann Nepomuk was a hard-working, conscientious family man who, from all indications, provided Alois with a good home. For the first time, the boy received his share of love and attention and was encouraged to develop his abilities. Perhaps even more important, he found himself in the company of other children. Johann Nepomuk and Eva Maria had three daughters, Johanna, Walburga, and Josefa, who were, respectively, seven, five, and three years older than Alois. The relationship between the girls and the newcomer seems to have been friendly.[9]

Alois spent the formative years of childhood in Johann Nepomuk's house, remaining with the family until the early 1850's. He was an orphan, and there was no legal connection between himself and the Hiedler family. He was the illegitimate son of the wife of Johann Nepomuk's brother, a tenuous thread on which to build a child's home. The bond was made a little closer by the fact that the mother of Johann Georg and Johann Nepomuk was still alive and in Nepomuk's household with Alois and the rest of the family. There is also the shadowy figure of Johann Georg himself, who may have been residing in Spital at this time. Even so, the Hiedlers' obligation to Alois was voluntarily assumed and remained moral, not legal. After his marriage to Alois' mother, Johann Georg had not adopted the boy, leaving him simply his wife's illegitimate son. Although illegitimacy was frowned upon by the authorities, especially in the Catholic Church, it was common in the Austrian countryside. In some districts, forty per cent of the births were illegitimate. The figure for Lower Austria as late as 1903 was still twenty-four per cent.[10] An illegitimate child in a peasant household therefore, was not an unusual phenomenon and did not involve the family in any serious

[9] *Die Ahnentafel*, p. 46; *Jetzinger* (G), p. 44; *Jetzinger* (E), pp. 33-34.
[10] Arthur J. May, *The Hapsburg Monarchy, 1867-1914* (Cambridge, Mass., 1951), pp. 173-174; Geoffrey Drage, *Austria-Hungary* (London, 1909), p. 58.

embarrassment. Whether the family's moral obligation to Alois was felt by the Hiedlers to be a family affair because of knowledge or suspicion that Johann Georg had fathered the child cannot be established. The boy was raised by Johann Nepomuk while his old mother resided in the household and while Johann Georg was still living, yet no legal action was taken to put any real or suspected closer family relationship on a firmer basis.

Despite his precarious legal status, Alois had an opportunity to develop normally within this family circle. His associations must have been reasonably agreeable, for he retained close contacts with the family throughout his life. Nevertheless, Johann Nepomuk was only a middling peasant, and there were limitations to the plans he could make for the boy's future. Even if Alois had been Johann Nepomuk's own second or third son, the most he could have expected to receive was a little schooling and, if he were lucky, some training for a trade. This is exactly what Alois obtained. After a few terms in elementary school, he was apprenticed to a neighboring shoemaker, one Herr Ledermueller in Spital #19. Following a brief period of training, he left the village while still in his early teens to pursue the trade of shoemaker in Vienna.[11]

At approximately the time that Alois was setting out on this new phase of his life, Nepomuk's household experienced a great change, which may have caused the boy to strike out on his own. In December 1854, Anna Maria Hiedler, the mother of Johann Nepomuk and Johann Georg died at 86. Three years later, on February 9th, 1857, Johann Georg himself died, cutting the last weak link between Alois and his long-dead mother. When he died, Johann Georg was listed as living in Spital #49, clearly not the Hiedler family house in which Alois had been raised.[12] Whether or not Alois had kept in continuous contact with Johann Georg in the ten years since his mother's death is not known, but, since Johann Georg died in the village of Spital,

---

[11] Report of Niederoesterreichische Landesamtsdirektion concerning "Abstammung Hitler, Adolf," Vienna, March 11, 1932. *HA*, File 17, Reel 1; *Goerlitz and Quint*, p. 18. There is a cryptic remark in *Mein Kampf*, p. 6: "The village priest had once seemed to my father the highest and most desirable ideal." The basis for this statement is not clear. At least in his later years, Alois was consistently and vocally anti-clerical.

[12] *Die Ahnentafel*, pp. 39 and 44.

some ties must have existed between Alois, Johann Georg, and Johann Nepomuk.

In the late 40's and early 50's, Nepomuk's three daughters were provided for, and the parents themselves moved into a position of semi-retirement. In 1848 the eldest daughter, Johanna, married Johann Poelzl, a peasant in Spital, and settled down in the house next door, #37. In January 1853, the second daughter, Walburga, married Josef Romeder, the son of a peasant in the neighboring village of Ober-Windhag. As part of the marriage agreement, Johann Nepomuk, then forty-six, turned over the family farm to his son-in-law. In conformity with the traditional practice of Austrian peasants, a notary was called in and a deed drawn up by which Romeder became master of the land and assumed a number of specific legal obligations to Johann Nepomuk and his wife. As was customary, Romeder granted the former master and mistress rent-free lodging as long as either of them lived. He also granted them the use of certain farm land and a section of the orchard, an area to graze stock, etc., with each obligation spelled out in precise detail.[13] Finally, if the old customs were followed to the letter, when the day to change title came, the whole family decked themselves out in all their finery as if for a festival. The former master led his son-in-law around the boundaries of the land, and as he reached each boundary stone he called down curses upon him as a warning against transgressing on his neighbors' land. To reinforce the point, he gave him a box on the ear.[14] When the circuit was complete, there was a feast and dancing to solemnize the occasion. Josef Romeder had become master of Spital peasant holding #36, and Johann Nepomuk Hiedler was merely a resident on the property, although he possessed a legal contract that guaranteed his rights and privileges.

A few years after this ceremony, Johann Nepomuk's last daughter, Josefa, married Leopold Sailer and moved to his peasant holding, Spital house #24.[15] Although Josefa was to die soon afterward (May 13, 1858), Johann Nepomuk had, on the basis of the soundest pos-

---

[13] *Die Ahnentafel*, p. 46.
[14] An engaging description of this kind of ceremony appears in Francis H. E. Palmer, *Austro-Hungarian Life in Town and Country* (New York, 1903), pp. 31-33.
[15] *Die Ahnentafel*, p. 46.

sible planning, placed his family on a firm basis for the future by the middle of the 1850's. All the girls were married and provided for, and he was able to look forward to a life of limited toil and responsibility for himself and his spouse until they died.

Meanwhile, young Alois had also made important improvements in his position during the 1850's and continued to progress rapidly in the next decade and a half. After practicing the shoemaking trade in Vienna for a short period following his arrival from Spital, he entered the ranks of the frontier guards employed by the Austrian Finance Ministry. He joined the service in 1855; by 1860, he had already reached a position equivalent to noncommissioned officer (*Finanzwach Oberaufseher*) and was assigned to duty in the town of Wels, southwest of Linz.[16] In 1860-61, he underwent special training in Vienna to obtain promotion. After passing an examination in the fall of 1861, he rose to the rank of *Finanzwach Respizienten*, the highest supervisory rank in the lower sections of the service. Following his promotion, Alois was again reassigned. In September 1862 he was serving in Saalfelden in the province of Salzburg. In 1864 he received another, more important promotion to the position of provisional assistant in the customs service, assigned to Linz. Six years later, he was elevated to the status of customs collector at the auxiliary customs post at Mariahilf near Schaerding within the administrative district of Wels, where he had served nine years earlier. Finally, in 1871 he was assigned to Braunau, the border station midway between Passau and Salzburg. He went to Braunau first as an assistant inspector of customs, and, after 1875, as a full inspector of customs.[17]

---

[16] Jetzinger (G), p. 45; Jetzinger (E), p. 36. The list of heirs of Mathius Schickelgruber made by the Bezirksamt Hernals and dated October 8, 1862 (*L of C* and *HA*, File 17A), gives Alois' address as "Finanzoberaufseher zu Wels in Oberoesterreich." Alois gave his address in a letter of September 27, 1862 as "Finanzwach Respiziert zu Saalfelden im Kronland Salzburg." *L of C* and *HA*, File 17A, Reel 1. The former address therefore must apply to a period prior to September 1862, and probably was simply carried over from the beginning of Mathius' inheritance case, i.e., 1861. This year also is used in a letter of Alois to the Veits of September 13, 1876. *L of C*, but not in *HA*, File 17A, Reel 1.

[17] Jetzinger (G), p. 46, and document opposite p. 32; Jetzinger (E), pp. 36-37. Letters, Alois Hitler to the Veits, September 27, 1862 and September 6, 1876. *L of C*; the former also in *HA*, File 17A, Reel 1.

He never became a full-fledged member of "the bureaucracy." His background was too humble, and he lacked the passport to privileged status, an academic education. On the fringe, within the walls, yet always dependent, he was, as a customs official, in an especially susceptible position to have the values of the bureaucracy stamped upon him. He succumbed to these pressures; his personality and attitudes were, above all, the product of his environment. Even his physical appearance bore the mark of his occupation and his outlook. A fairly short, heavy-set man, with deep-set eyes under heavy brows, his round face wore a flowing mustache in his youth. As he rose in years and position, he followed the example of many of his colleagues and the mustache gave way to a set of Franz Josef whiskers. Although he remained in the lower ranks of officialdom throughout his career, he was very proud of his status and his uniform. On public occasions, he could be counted on to be present in all his splendor, and always insisted that he be addressed by his correct title.[18] He had worked hard and risen far and was not always careful how he brought this to people's attention. A good example of this attitude is provided by a letter written in 1876 to a distant cousin with whom he had not corresponded for many years. Summarizing his personal life he said enthusiastically, "Since you saw me sixteen years ago when I was a *Finanzwach Oberaufseher,* I have advanced very far and have already served twelve years as an official in the customs branch." At the end of the note, below his signature, he wrote, "Official at the First Class Imperial Customs Post in the Railroad Terminal, Simbach Bavaria. Residence, Braunau, Linzergasse." Then as if recognizing that this was a bit ostentatious for a long-lost cousin, he added rather sheepishly, "This is also my address." [19]

This pride in his achievement did not adversely affect his official reputation on the job, where he was known as an efficient and devoted official who filled all requirements to the letter. One of his colleagues in the service described him as "rigid, precise, even pedantic" in the performance of his duties, adding that, characteristically, he was especially careful to be on duty every minute that the regulations

---

[18] Statement by Zollobersekretaer Hebenstreit, June 21, 1940, *HA*, File 17, Reel 1; *Jetzinger* (G), p. 71; *Jetzinger* (E), p. 51.
[19] Letter Alois Hitler to Frau Veit, September 13, 1876. *L of C*; not in *HA*, File 17A, Reel 1.

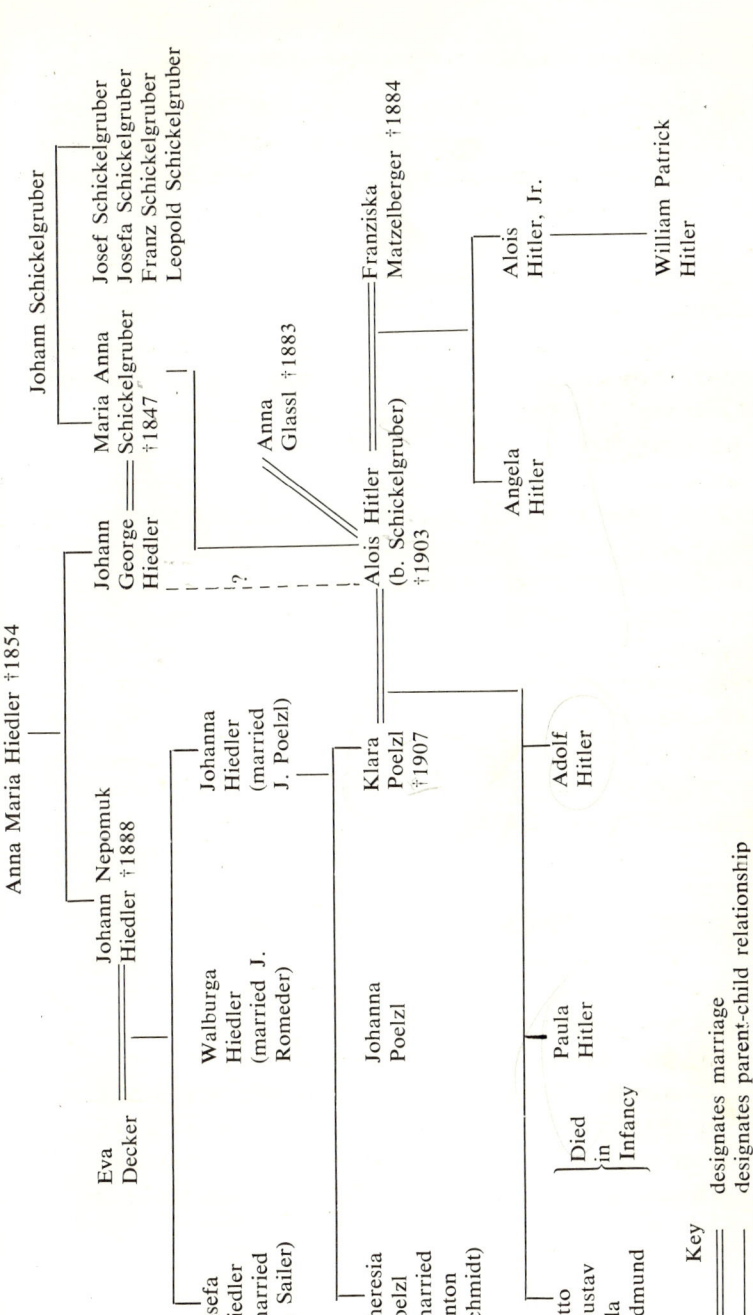

Plate 1: SOME IMPORTANT FAMILY RELATIONS OF ADOLF HITLER

Albert Reich, *Aus Adolf Hitlers Heimat*

Plate 2: ALOIS HITLER

Heinrich Hoffmann, *Hitler wie ihn keiner kennt*

Plate 3: ALOIS HITLER

Library of Congress material

Plate 4: ALOIS HITLER

Franz Jetzinger, *Hitlers Jugend*

Plate 5: THE "WRONG MAN"

Albert Reich, *Aus Adolf Hitlers Heimat*

Plate 6: KLARA HITLER

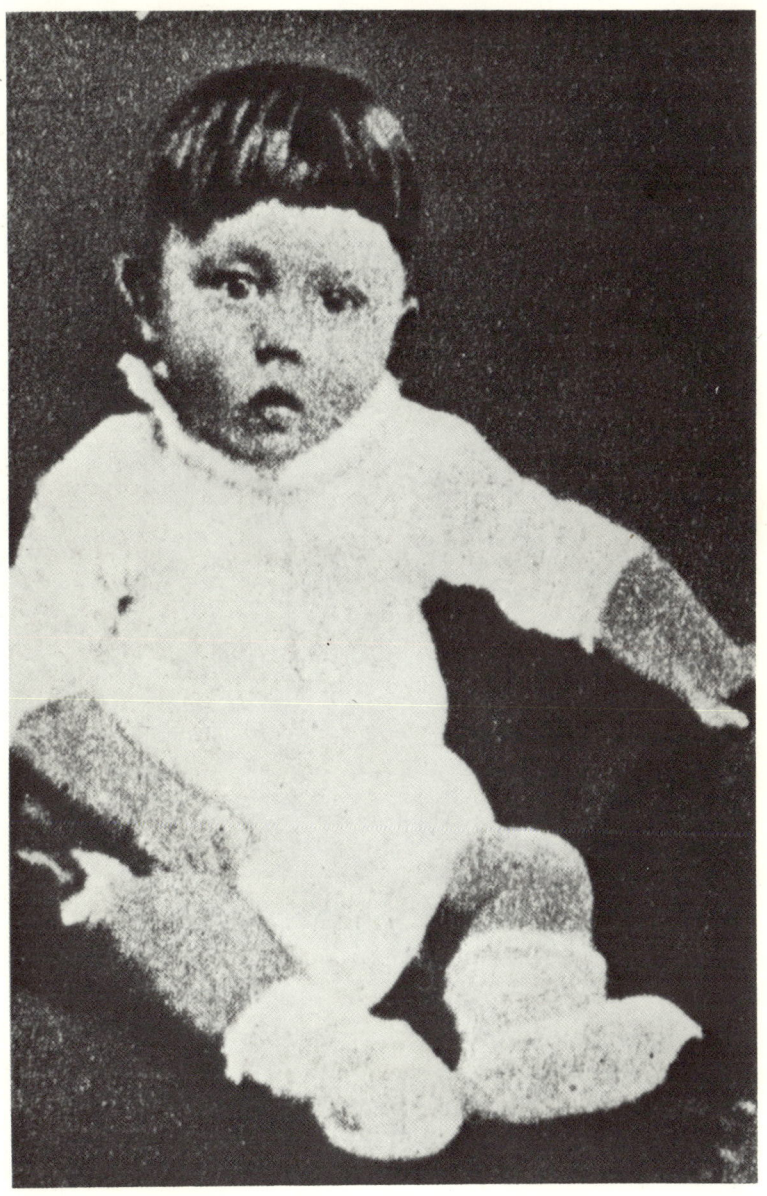

Heinrich Hoffmann, *Hitler wie ihn keiner kennt*

Plate 7: ADOLF HITLER AS A BABY

Hugo Rabitsch, *Aus Adolf Hitlers Jugendzeit*

Plate 9: Linzrealschule class in 1900-01. Hitler in top row marked by "x"

Heinrich Hoffmann, *Hitler in seiner Heimat*

Plate 10: Hitler in front of Leonding garden house, taken March 14, 1938

Albert Reich, *Aus Adolf Hitlers Heimat*

Plate 11: Hitler's uncle, Anton Schmidt, in the 1930's

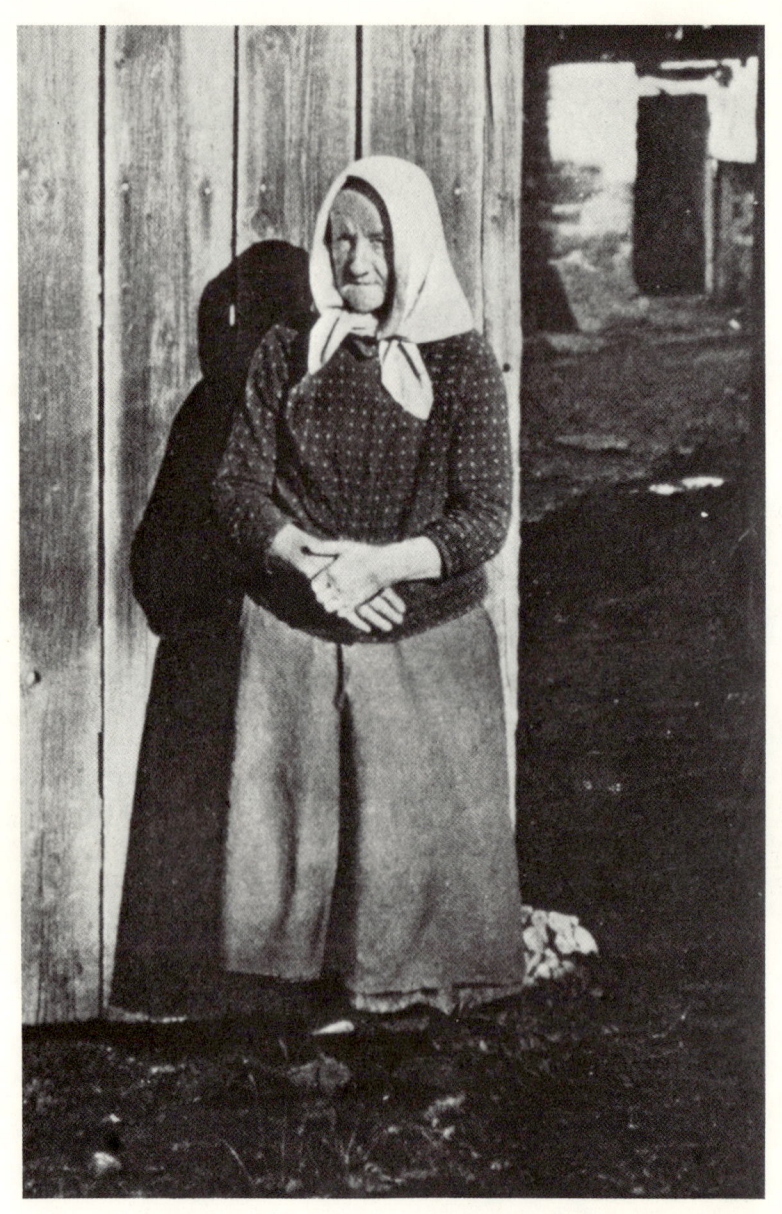

Albert Reich, *Aus Adolf Hitlers Heimat*

Plate 12: Hitler's aunt, Theresia Schmidt, in the 1930's

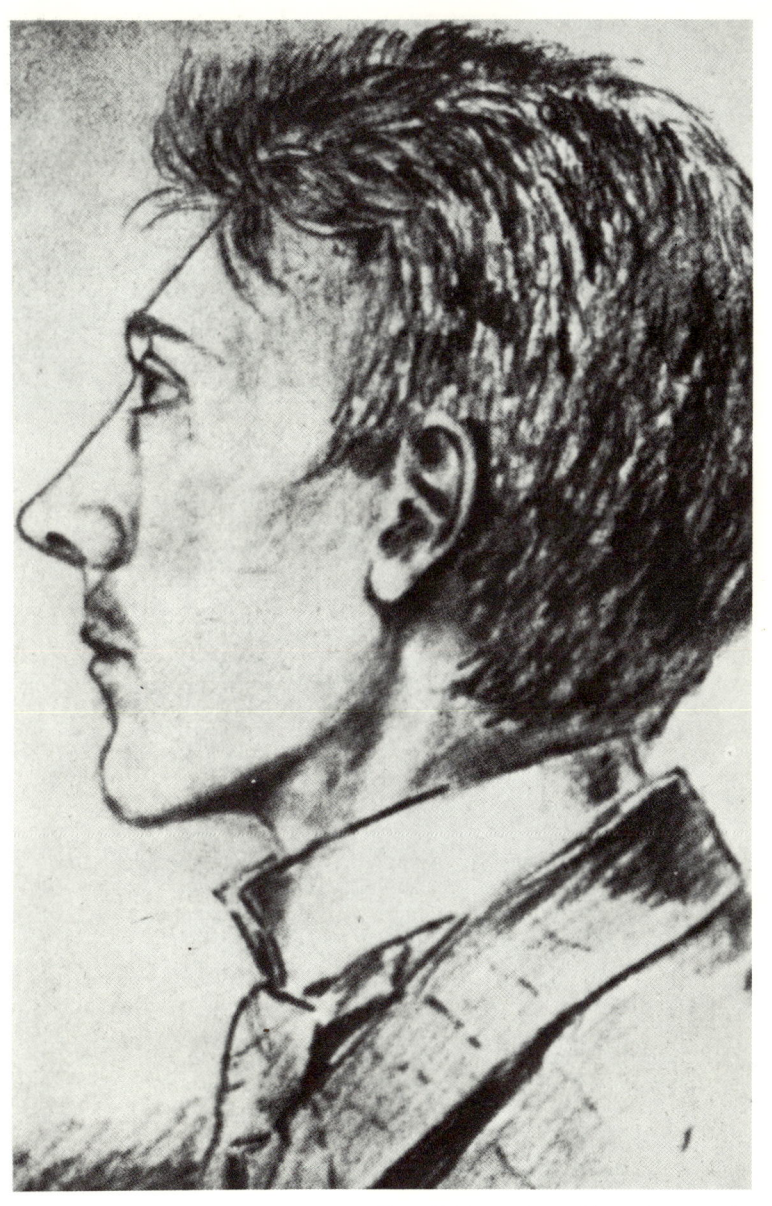

Hugo Rabitsch, *Aus Adolf Hitlers Jugendzeit Erlebnisbericht seiner Geheimsekretaerin*

Plate 13: HITLER IN 1905

demanded.[20] In later years he was able to relax a bit, but in the first thirty years of his career, strict devotion to duty dominated his life. The self-sacrifice involved in this achievement became a point of honor in the family; Alois took pains to show that his career had not been easy. In 1876, while advising his cousin on prospects for his son, Josef Veit, in the financial guards, Alois drew on some of his own experiences: "Don't let him believe that the *Finanzwach* is some kind of play, for he will be quickly disillusioned. First he is required to render absolute obedience to his supervisors at every level. Then there is much to learn, especially for one who hasn't any prior schooling. Drinkers, debtors, card players and other types that lead immoral lives cannot last. Then, of course, one must go out on duty in every kind of weather, day or night." [21] Certainly not an easy job, but Alois had not only done all the things required, he had risen above them.

This demand for recognition, this pedantry, this touch of pomposity were the least pleasant features of his personality, but there were also other, more attractive aspects. Despite his efforts to assert himself, he had genuine respect for other people's rights and real concern for their welfare. In 1876, for example, while settling the estate of a maternal uncle, he had to explain to an heir why there was so little left in the estate at the time of the death. The case was simple: Uncle Franz drank too much. "He was a great friend of common laborers," Alois wrote, "and always liked best to spend his time in the tavern. That he had not changed is shown by the fact that the 100 florins which he had set aside for the casket in his will had gone to drink. As a man lives, so does he die. But of course, that was his business." [22] The uncle's behavior was wrong but, in Alois' view, he was master of his fate, and his right to misuse his life had to be respected. Similarly, the cook in his household in the middle 1880's remembered that Alois was careful about seeing to it that others' interests and needs were not ignored. On holidays the family took pains to include her in the festivities. She remembered

---

[20] Statement of Zollobersekretaer Hebenstreit. *HA*, File 17, Reel 1.
[21] Letter Alois Hitler to Alois Veit, October 9, 1876. *L of C* and *HA*, File 17A, Reel 1.
[22] Letter Alois Hitler to Alois Veit, October 9, 1876. *L of C* and *HA*, File 17A, Reel 1.

that on one occasion, after she had finished mopping the kitchen floor, the customs official came home, took his shoes off, and walked through the room barefooted. The cook urged him not to, because he would get his feet all wet, but Alois insisted on doing it, for he said that he would not dirty a floor that she had worked so hard to clean, especially inasmuch as she had carried water up two flights of stairs to do the job.[23]

One gains the impression he was a strong man, overly conscious of his position, often condescending, yet possessing a rough code of behavior aimed at giving every man his due. He associated mainly with fellow customs men, but would drink a glass of beer in the local inn and even drank beer regularly with the cook. She once asked him if it did not trouble him to live in a house with common people, to which he replied that he did not worry much about it and would thank them if they greeted him.[24]

Whether he was being considerate or pompous, however, Alois could be rough and heavyhanded. On September 6th, 1876, he wrote his cousin Josefa Veit for the first time in sixteen years in order to arrange the inheritance mentioned above. He did not receive a reply immediately, so a week later, on the thirteenth, he started a second letter with the following sentence: "Since I still cannot believe that you would not find it worth your trouble to reply to the letter I wrote you seven days ago, the only alternative remaining to me is to believe that the letter was lost in the mails." [25] Certainly not the most charming way to renew a family relationship after sixteen years of silence! This was not an isolated incident; a man who worked with Alois in the customs service described him as "unsympathetic," "inaccessible," and "hard to work with." [26]

As an official he was a loyal servant of the government and the dynasty. As a man of modern cosmopolitan views, he championed progress and, in particular, was a passionate advocate of free public education. Education was the means by which the talented were

[23] Statement by Frau Rosalia Hoerl, recorded by Alfred Mueck, April 16, 1940. *HA*, File 17, Reel 1.
[24] Statement by Frau Rosalia Hoerl, recorded by Alfred Mueck, April 16, 1940. *HA*, File 17, Reel 1.
[25] Alois Hitler to Frau Veit, September 13, 1876. *L of C*; not in *HA*, File 17A, Reel 1.
[26] Statement by Zollobersekretaer Hebenstreit. *HA*, File 17, Reel 1.

able to rise. In bureaucratic ranks, especially, it was the source of success and power. Alois had advanced because of extra hard work and self denial – the liberal virtues – but educational deficiencies had seriously hampered him. After 1895 he was unable to advance further because of this handicap. The importance of keeping avenues for educational development open loomed large in his thoughts and ultimately became the central tenet in his personal creed.[27]

Closely related to his support of education was his tolerant skepticism concerning religion. He looked upon religion as a series of conventions and as a crutch for human weakness, but, like most of his neighbors, he insisted that the women of his household fulfill all religious obligations. He restricted his own participation to donning his uniform to take his proper place in festivals and processions. As he grew older Alois shifted from relative passivity in his attitude toward the power and influence of the institutional Church to a firm opposition to "clericalism," especially when the position of the Church came into conflict with his views on education.[28]

Alois, in short, thought and acted just as his position required. He did his duty, and added a bit extra because he had handicaps and wanted to succeed. Success required that he maintain the subtlest balance of individualism and obedience. He had to be different from his fellow officials, but not too different. He had to be dutiful, hardworking and cooperative, but also a man of initiative, ambition, and independence. In self-defense, he accentuated some of his personal idiosyncrasies and became a bit of a "character." Along with his bushy eyebrows and a taste for rumbling pronouncements, he developed a personalized jargon made up of dialect and high German, a not uncommon phenomenon among lower officials.[29] By such devices he managed to play the role his position required.

Obviously, a long-continued performance of this sort subjected Alois to conflicting pressures. He bore them successfully in his professional life, but in his personal affairs he tended to revert to the

---

[27] *Jetzinger* (G), pp. 60-61 and 70; *Jetzinger* (E), pp. 44 and 51; also the description of his family in Adolf Hitler's autobiographical statement of November 29, 1921. *HA*, File 17, Reel 1.
[28] *Jetzinger* (G), p. 71; *Jetzinger* (E), p. 51. See below, p. 69 ff., for the influence he exerted on his son's education.
[29] Statement by Frau Rosalia Hoerl. *HA*, File 17, Reel 1.

level of peasant irresponsibility symbolized by his mother. In the late 1860's, his romantic adventures led to the birth of an illegitimate child, but no marriage resulted from the affair. In 1873, perhaps on October 31st, Alois married another woman, Anna Glassl, the daughter of an official. Little is known of the marriage except that the bride, who may have been a widow, was then fifty, while the bridegroom was fourteen years her junior. It is probable that Anna Glassl was fairly well-to-do, and this may have been one motive for the marriage, despite the wide disparity in age between the partners. Alois had been accustomed to the dominance of older women throughout his childhood, so a fourteen-year age difference may not have seemed important to him. His mother had been forty-two when he was born; Johann Nepomuk's mother was an old woman when Alois lived with the family, and even Johann Nepomuk's wife, Eva Maria, was thirteen years older than her husband. It may in part have been unconscious substitution that led Alois to marry a woman so much older than himself in the year Eva Maria died.[30]

Alois' bride was seriously ill for many years. If she was not an invalid at the time of the marriage, she became one soon afterwards. Writing in September 1876, Alois says of his wife, "Unfortunately she had suffered from a chest ailment for a long time and requires very close care. Were it not for the excellent climate here [Braunau] she would never be well. It is only my position, thank God, that permits me to make her life free from suffering." [31] But if his position made her life free from physical suffering, his romantic inclinations added to her burdens. The marriage was not a happy one, and Alois' adventures seem to have been the source of the trouble. Not satisfied with the proverbial triangle, he arranged something approaching a square. In addition to installing Klara Poelzl, the adolescent granddaughter of Johann Nepomuk Hiedler, in the household as a servant girl, he simultaneously carried on an affair with Franziska Matzelberger, a girl employed in the inn in which Alois and his family lived.[32] It is not completely clear how long these affairs lasted or how he managed some of the technical details, but it is certain that they

---

[30] *Die Ahnentafel*, p. 46; *Jetzinger* (G), pp. 48-49; *Jetzinger* (E), pp. 37-38.
[31] Letter Alois Hitler to Alois Veit, September 17, 1876. *L of C* and *HA*, File 17A, Reel 1.
[32] *Jetzinger* (G), pp. 49-52; *Jetzinger* (E), pp. 38-40.

were active concurrently in the late 1870's and early 1880's. The illness of his wife and the legal obstacles to separation encouraged the continuation of this complex relationship over a number of years.

Before the final crisis in the marriage and his separation from Anna Glassl, another event occurred which markedly affected the history of the family. In the summer of 1876, Alois appeared before the parish priest in Dollersheim, whose district included the village of Spital. Supported by three witnesses, Josef Romeder, Johann Breitender, and Engelbert Paukh, he asserted that his father was actually Johann Georg Hiedler, who, after marrying his mother, had avowed his paternity of Alois and expressed a desire to legitimize him. The three witnesses, one of whom, Romeder, was Johann Nepomuk Hiedler's son-in-law, signified by crosses that Johann Georg did indeed wish to acknowledge that he was Alois' father. The priest then entered the name of Johann Georg as father and changed Alois' name from Schickelgruber to Hitler. That Alois used this spelling for his new name had no particular significance; there were many variations of the spelling within the family.[33]

Important questions arise however, concerning the means used to alter the name and the motivation for the change. There can be little doubt that deception was used. From the wording of the entry, it is clear that the priest was led to believe that Johann Georg was still alive, whereas, in fact, he had been dead for twenty years. Some suspicions may have been awakened in the priest's mind, since the wording is vague and the entry was left undated.

Legally, the adoption of the name Hitler was clearly not justified. The facts were misrepresented, and the essential factor, a living man avowing paternity, did not exist. However, once the Dollersheim priest succumbed to the pleading of Alois and his friends, the official wheels rolled on. On January 6, 1877, the governmental office in Mistelbach registered the change. Shortly thereafter, the records of the customs service also were altered, transforming Customs Official Alois Schickelgruber into Alois Hitler.[34]

---

[33] *Jetzinger* (G), pp. 23-28; *Jetzinger* (E), pp. 26-29. The spelling of the family name was not fixed until much later. Even in 1919, an army list rendered the name as "Adolf Hitler." Ernest Deuerlein, "Hitler's Eintritt in die Politik und die Reichswehr," *Vierteljahrshefte fuer Zeitgeschichte*, April 1959, p. 179.
[34] *Jetzinger* (G), pp. 23-28; *Jetzinger* (E), pp. 26-29.

There is a possibility that the name change reflected previous statements by the deceased Johann Georg Hiedler. Romeder, if not the other two witnesses, had certainly known Johann Georg, because Romeder had married Johann Nepomuk's daughter and was occupying the ancestral home of the Hiedlers in Spital when Johann Georg died in the village in the mid-1850's. An additional point is that, privately, Alois claimed as early as the fall of 1876 that Johann Georg had acknowledged his paternity. In explaining his change of name to a maternal (Schickelgruber) cousin in September, Alois stated that he had assumed the name Hitler because although he had been illegitimate at birth, his parents had later married and, together with the "acknowledgement of my father," this made him legitimate. The first time he explained the situation, the crucial phrase, "and the acknowledgement of my father," was tucked in above the line as if it was an afterthought, but, in another letter a week later, the phrase occupied its proper place in the sentence.[35] Neither this statement by Alois nor the connections between Romeder and Johann Georg make the latter Alois' father any more than the proceedings before the Dollersheim priest did, but they do indicate that the alteration was not a totally arbitrary act.

The motives behind the change of name in the summer of 1876 can be analyzed with more precision. Shame over his illegitimacy seems to have played little or no part with Alois. Far from trying to hide his illegitimacy, he openly admitted it, both before and after the events of 1876.[36] The important reasons seem to have been a desire to preserve the Hitler-Hiedler name and the requirements of a legacy. The active figure in this action was Johann Nepomuk Hiedler who had raised Alois and was understandably proud of him. Alois had just been promoted again, and was finally married, and, as far as the world knew, had settled down. He had clearly made the greatest success in life of any of the Hiedler family circle. Johann Nepomuk, on the other hand, faced uncertainties and doubts. His

[35] Letters of Alois Hitler to Frau Veit, September 6 and 13, 1876. *L of C* material; not in *HA*, File 17A, Reel 1.
[36] Letters of Alois Hitler to Frau Veit, September 6 and 13, 1876. *L of C*; not in *HA*, File 17A, Reel 1. This point is also made in an article in the *Wiener Sonn und Montagszeitung*, c. 1932, attributed to a Frau Antonie Fischer who allegedly knew Alois. Most of the information in the article is wildly inaccurate. An undated copy is in *HA*, File 17, Reel 1A.

wife had died three years before, and he had fathered no sons. One of his three daughters had already died without issue; another had only three daughters, one a hunchback. It is not known if the third family, the Romeders, had any children. Going back one generation, of Johann Nepomuk's ten siblings, six were girls and could not continue the family name. Of the four boys, two left no trace in local records and presumably died in infancy. The third brother, Lorenz, fathered only a girl who also died in infancy. The fourth brother was Johann Georg, who may or may not have produced Alois. It is probable that, though other branches of the Hitler-Hiedler family may have generated male heirs in the area of Spital, Johann Nepomuk's own branch had not, unless one could count Alois Schickelgruber.[37]

According to local rumor, Johann Nepomuk inserted a clause in his will by which he left some money to Alois if he would change his name to Hiedler-Hitler.[38] Johann Nepomuk died on September 17, 1888. Six months later, on March 16, 1889, at a time when his wife was eight months pregnant, Alois paid down 4-5,000 florins to realize his lifelong dream of purchasing a small farm.[39] Although the connection between the will, the name change, the death, and Alois' possession of a large sum of cash cannot be documented, the evidence strongly indicates that Alois did inherit from Johann Nepomuk and that the popular story that Alois changed his name to gain an inheritance is correct.[40]

The changing of his name was merely an isolated episode in

[37] *Die Ahnentafel*, pp. 39-42 and 46. Jetzinger rightly states that the dates in the *Ahnentafel* concerning Josepha are garbled. *Jetzinger (G)*, p. 44.
[38] *Kubizek*, p. 40. Kubizek couples this assertion with a date of June 4, 1876, for the name change. The source of the date is not known, but the most recent direct evidence indicates that it must be fairly close to correct. A garbled version of this relationship appears in *Greiner*, p. 31.
[39] *Ahnentafel*, p. 46; Statement by Herr Leo Weber, October 12, 1938, plus additional *Hauptarchiv* report. *HA*, File 17, Reel 1. A report of the Lower Austrian Government dates this transaction in 1888, but does not provide a month or day. This report contains many incorrect dates and appears to have been a carelessly typed copy. If the date was late 1888, it would not alter the connection made in the text, but of course a date prior to September 1888 certainly would. Report of Niederoesterreichische Landesamtsdirektion. *HA*, File 17, Reel 1.
[40] For a criticism of a very different explanation of the name change, see Appendix I.

Alois' life and not one that seems to have troubled him greatly. The incident assumes unusual importance for us because it is the origin of one of recent history's most famous names. If the change had not been made, would Alois' son, under the name of Adolf Schickelgruber, still have achieved power in Germany in later years? Alois himself seemed to have been much more concerned with other matters in the later 1870's. He was busy adjusting to the demands of his new assignment in Braunau and to other minor complications of life, ranging from a small Schickelgruber family inheritance to the effort of his nephew to solicit his aid in entering government service.[41] During this period he struck up a close friendship with another official, Karl Wesseley, who was proud of his Czech descent. The friendship with Wesseley remained Alois' most important relationship with a colleague during his duty years and lasted until his death in 1903.[42]

By far the most important event in Alois' life following his acquisition of a new name was the failure of his marriage. His wife Anna endured his infidelities until 1880, when she finally initiated legal steps to secure a separation. The decree could be granted only by mutual consent and only on the condition of aversion or incompatibility. Remarriage as long as both parties were alive was impossible for Roman Catholics under Austrian law. On November 7, 1880, all conditions being fulfilled, Anna's request for a decree of separation was granted.[43]

Following the legal separation, Franziska Matzelberger, the servant girl, emerged as Alois' consort. Franziska was a peasant girl from Weng, a little town midway between Linz and Graz, who had worked as a maid in the Gasthaus Streif where the Hitler family had been living. In 1880 Franziska was only nineteen, but she possessed enough awareness to demand that the other member of the household, Johann Nepomuk's granddaughter Klara Poelzl, leave and take up residence elsewhere. She had her way and achieved a position approximating that of a common-law wife. In January 1882 she gave birth to a

---

[41] Letters Alois Hitler to the Veits, September 1876, October 1877. *L of C*; partly reproduced in *HA*, File 17A, Reel 1.
[42] *Jetzinger* (G), pp. 50-51; *Jetzinger* (E), pp. 38-39.
[43] *Jetzinger* (G), p. 51; *Jetzinger* (E), p. 39. The legal situation is explained in *Coldstream*, p. 66.

boy who was baptized Alois Matzelberger. Fifteen months later, on April 6, 1883, sixty-year-old Anna Hitler died of consumption in Braunau, and the way was cleared for the marriage of Alois and Franziska. The ceremony took place in Braunau on May 22, 1883, with Karl Wesseley and another customs official from Simbach, Ludwig Hoezl, as witnesses. After the wedding, life went on much as before, but Alois did not repeat the mistake that may have been made in his own case. He legitimized his son, who became Alois Hitler, Jr., instead of Alois Matzelberger.[44]

Like her predecessor's, Franziska's marriage was both unhappy and short. A month after the wedding she had a second child, Angela, who was born, for some unexplained reason, in Vienna. In the following year, 1884, Franziska fell victim to a lung ailment just as Anna had before her. It was an era when tuberculosis and lung trouble were the most serious illnesses among Austrian adults. Franziska, following standard practice in such cases, tried to improve her condition with country air and a favorable climate. She took up residence in the village of Ranshofen on the edge of the forest near Braunau. Since her two small children were without care, it was necessary for someone to come into the home to look after the children and Alois. The obvious choice was Klara Poelzl, the girl whom Franziska had forced out of the house four years earlier. Strangely enough, Klara's return does not seem to have aroused any hard feeling. She frequently visited Franziska in Ranshofen and joined the ill girl's widowed mother in trying to nurse her back to health. All efforts were in vain; Franziska died of tuberculosis in Ranshofen on August 10, 1884, at the age of twenty-three.[45]

At the time of Franziska's death, Klara Poelzl was residing in Alois' quarters on the top floor of Braunau house #219, the Pommer Inn. She was his niece, his mistress, his maid, and the nurse for his children. Almost precisely at the time Franziska died, Klara became pregnant. The pregnancy provided one more reason to solve the problem of Alois' motherless children, as well as his own lone-

---

[44] Death certificate of Anna Hitler; marriage certificate of Alois Hitler and Franziska Matzelberger. *HA*, File 17, Reel 1. *Jetzinger* (G), pp. 51-52; Jetzinger (E), p. 39.
[45] Death certificate of Franziska Hitler; statement of Frau Rosalia Hoerl. *HA*, File 17, Reel 1.

liness, by the logical step of marriage between twenty-four-year-old Klara and forty-seven-year-old Alois.[46]

In spite of his extramarital adventures, Alois was still performing his duties as a customs official without suffering any professional difficulties from his irregular private life. Customs Official Alois Hitler, who should have been slowing down by this time, required an adjustment in his domestic life which would neither adversely affect his career nor infringe too much upon his personal indepenpence. Marriage with Klara, a simple peasant girl from Spital, fitted his needs exactly.

---

[46] Birth certificate of Gustav Hitler. *HA*, File 17, Reel 1.

11

THE HITLER FAMILY

If Alois Hitler had been free to do as he wished, he would not have waited a moment between Franziska's death and his marriage to Klara Poelzl. Local custom required a decent period of delay between the death and the remarriage, but Alois had never concerned himself much about what other people thought. He had remarried immediately after the death of his first wife without adverse effect, and he was ready to do so again. Klara was willing and able. Her parents favored the union, and since she was twenty-four, she no longer needed their consent. Alois' children adored their prospective stepmother, who had been in and out of their home since their birth.[1] Money presented no problem because of Alois' substantial income and secure position. Everything was easily arranged, except for one ironic detail: because of Alois' success in changing his name and becoming legitimized in 1876, the marriage had become illegal.

Klara Poelzl was the daughter of Johann Poelzl and his wife Johanna, the eldest daughter of Johann Nepomuk Hiedler. Klara had been born and raised in Spital house #37 next to the holding of Johann Nepomuk Hiedler, but by 1885 her parents had moved to house #52.[2] Alois' prospective wife was therefore not only Johann Nepomuk's neighbor; she was also his granddaughter. As a result of the legitimation and name change in 1876, Alois had become Johann Nepomuk's nephew, and the prospective bride and bridegroom of 1884 were second cousins, within the degree prohibited by the Church. The Austrian state would not permit such marriages be-

[1] *Kubizek*, pp. 29 and 33.
[2] *Die Ahnentafel*, pp. 39-40.

tween Catholics unless the marriage had been authorized by dispensation. It remains a question whether or not the couple actually had common blood; even Alois may have wondered about it. The only way he could have convinced the authorities that there was no risk to the offspring of the marriage would have been to disclose the whole story of the change of name and thus enmesh himself in even more legal difficulties. This he prudently decided to avoid.

Alois and Klara asked the religious authorities in Braunau to grant a dispensation to marry but were informed that, because of the closeness of their relationship, a papal dispensation was required. The couple then drew up an application for dispensation in which they advanced a number of arguments to persuade the authorities to favor them. The request stated that Alois was a widower with two small children who needed care and attention. The father's position in the customs service required that he be absent during the day and often at night as well. Klara had been taking care of the children regularly for a number of months, the application continued, and they were very fond of her, a good portent both for the happiness of the children and the success of the marriage. The only argument used to show that the marriage would be beneficial to Klara was the statement that the "bride is without means, and it is therefore unlikely that she will ever have another opportunity for a good marriage." This was probably an exaggeration. Even though the Poelzl family had seen better days, they were not destitute. In an age in which dowries constituted the major attraction for a husband, however, Klara was at a disadvantage if the marriage with Alois did not materialize. A more important reason for her desire to marry Alois was that, at the time of the application, she was pregnant, but that fact, of course, did not appear in the dispensation request.[3]

On October 27, 1884, the application was completed and sent to the Bishop for translation into Latin and forwarding to Rome. The Hitlers then had to endure the delay as best they could. This undoubtedly was a problem of a sort, since Klara's condition was becoming more obvious every day. To ease some of the physical strain on Klara, a young cook and maid, Rosalia Schichtl, was

[3] *Kubizek*, p. 33.

brought into the household, where she remained during the last part of 1884 and the first part of 1885.[4]

Finally, at the turn of the year 1884/1885, the dispensation arrived. In January 7, 1885, the wedding party assembled in Alois' lodgings on the top floor of house #219. The residence was an inn run by Josef Pommer, and lay just outside the old gate of Braunau in a district usually referred to as the "Salzburger Vorstadt." Aside from the bride and bridegroom and Alois' two small children, there were two customs men from Simbach present to act as witnesses, Ludwig Hoezl and Edgar Dirnhofer. Klara's younger sister, the hunchback Johanna, was also present as a witness. All the practical arrangements for the ceremony were made by the cook, Fraeulein Schichtl, who inadvertently heated the parlor to a far higher temperature than was comfortable. The wedding ceremony passed off without incident, except for Alois' periodic teasing of Fraeulein Schichtl about the high temperature of the room. After the wedding, Fraeulein Schichtl prepared the meal for the couple and their guests, but it was no feast and there was no honeymoon. Before the wedding day had passed, Alois was back on duty at the customs station at Simbach.[5]

For the next four years, the Hitlers continued to reside in the Pommer Inn. Braunau was then a little border community of approximately 3,500 people. The town was seventy-eight miles south-east of Munich, on a secondary route to Vienna. By train the trip from Braunau to the Bavarian capital took between four and five hours. Some trade and a few tourists passed through the town, but it was primarily a center for the agricultural districts between Passau and Salzburg. The buildings of Braunau were constructed along the banks of the river Inn and gave the impression of being strung out along the bed of the stream. The dull line of medium-sized buildings was broken only by the *Stephanskirche*, with its large baroque cupola. The town changed little, was ingrown, and was too small to permit many secrets, especially those carrying any hint of scandal.[6]

[4] Statement by Frau Rosalia Hoerl (maiden name Schichtl). *HA*, File 17, Reel 1.
[5] Wedding certificate for Alois Hitler and Klara Poelzl and statement by Rosalia Hoerl. *HA*, File 17, Reel 1.
[6] *Goerlitz and Quint*, p. 21; *Baedekers Oesterreich* (Leipzig, 1907), p. 129; Albert Reich, *Aus Adolf Hitlers Heimat* (Munich, 1933), pp. 14-21.

At the time of his marriage to Klara, Alois had been living in the town for fourteen years. He had lived there with his first wife until their separation, keeping Franziska as his mistress. She had produced one illegitimate child there before their marriage. Shortly after this event, she had left the town for a rest cure and never returned. Before Franziska died, Alois lived openly with his cousin Klara. Because she had been a member of the household in earlier years, her face was familiar to local gossips. During the four months she had to wait for a dispensation to marry her cousin and lover, every day's delay made it more obvious that she was pregnant. No small town could have been expected to ignore all these possibilities for gossip.

The whispers and scandalmongering could not have affected Alois overmuch. He was a thick-skinned old man who had been shocking the local inhabitants for a decade and a half without becoming noticeably sensitive to their criticisms. His position was thoroughly protected since he did not draw his living from the town but from the Imperial Government. His friends were mainly fellow officials, who, like himself, remained outside the net of the town's social system by residing in inns and other isolated living quarters. As a member of the Imperial Service, his social position had not been formed by Braunau and could not be destroyed by it; he did what he wanted to do and let people think what they liked.

Klara's position was different. A woman had few ways to protect herself from the social pressures of an Austrian small town. Klara's life outside the immediate family circle was spent in direct contact with the townspeople. She was a simple peasant girl without education and lacked sophisticated defenses against the various forms of small-town nastiness. While shopping, attending church, or exchanging polite greetings, she had to bear the burden of the family's reputation.

Yet, even as her pregnancy made her position difficult, it also had its advantages during the first months after the wedding. At least she had something to carry forward her hopes and aspirations through the standardized routine of the household. She had to look after Angela and young Alois, the children of Franziska, who were two and three years old respectively in 1885. She was aided in her housekeeping tasks by Fraeulein Schichtl, who at twenty-three was just two years younger than Klara and served as a friendly companion. Klara's family also served to relieve some of the pressures on her. She had no in-law problems; Alois had probably lost all contact with the Schickelgrubers by this time, although ten years before he had been in touch with a number of family branches and had even served as host for an unidentified Betti Schickelgruber and her family during a four-week vacation in 1876.[7] The lack of contact with the Schickelgrubers meant that Alois and Klara shared a common family – the Hitlers – and the young wife was spared the necessity of having to adjust to a new family system.

The head of the Hitler-Hiedler family was still old Johann Nepomuk Hiedler, who lived in Spital surrounded by a number of near and distant relations. Klara's mother and father, Johanna and Johann Poelzl, were also living in Spital. Klara's mother was Johann Nepomuk's oldest daughter and had been raised with Alois. The old family home was still being run by Walburga and Josef Romeder. They, too, had close ties to Alois and Klara. Walburga, Klara's aunt, also had been raised with Alois; her husband had been the chief witness at Alois' name changing in 1876. In addition Klara had two younger sisters, Johanna and Theresia, the only other survivors of eleven children. Theresia had married by the mid-1880's and was living with her husband Anton Schmidt in peasant holding #24 in Spital, the place which had originally belonged to Johann Nepomuk's third daughter, Josefa Sailer. The Schmidts seem to have had little contact with the Alois Hitlers in these years, but Schmidt was a hardworking, clever man, who managed to hold on to his land and pass it on to his son.[8] Klara's youngest sister, Johanna, was not as fortunate as Theresia. Because she was a hunchback, she had no prospects, and she was, moreover, possessed of a foul temper which made her a difficult living companion. She moved back and forth between her parents' residence, the Schmidt's and Klara's. She was the family representative at Klara's wedding and continued to spend considerable periods of time with the family in future years. At every family

---

[7] Alois Hitler to the Veits, September 6, 1876. *L of C* material. There is no record of contact between Alois and the Veit branch of the Schickelgrubers after 1877.
[8] *Die Ahnentafel*, p. 40; Report on Adolf Hitler prepared by the Niederoesterreichische Landesamtsdirektion. *HA*, File 17, Reel 1.

emergency it was always Johanna who was sent to help out, but her personality made the assistance a mixed blessing.[9]

Aside from Johanna's temper, the only real strains in the Hiedler-Poelzl family arose from the chronic misfortunes of Klara's father, Johann. He was never able to develop a farm successfully. Over the years, the family passed through a series of small holdings until Johann and his wife ended up as tenants of his son-in-law, Anton Schmidt. Johann Poelzl's problems produced a financial crisis in the family. Whatever was salvaged from the wreck went to support the hunchback Johanna, while Klara and Theresia were probably forced to struggle along with small dowries.[10] In the larger context of the Hitler-Hiedler family, Klara, therefore, represented one of the poorer branches; yet even so, she belonged, and this connection served as a major prop during the difficult months of early 1885.

On May 17, 1885, Klara gave birth to a son who was given the baptismal name of Gustav. The godparents were Johann and Johanna Prinz, distant relations of the Hitler-Hiedlers who lived in Vienna, and Maria Matzelberger from Weng.[11] The choice of Maria Matzelberger as a godparent is a jolting reminder of the strong current of peasant earthiness within the family. Maria was the mother of Alois' previous wife Franziska. She had known Klara when the two of them were nursing Franziska in Ranshofen at the time of the fatal illness. Klara and Maria seem to have become quite fond of each other at that time, and Maria's sponsorship of Klara's child might not have appeared unusual had it not been for the fact that the child was conceived at almost the precise time that her daughter was dying. Maria may have been a simple peasant, but she could not have been so simple that this had escaped her notice.[12] Still, Maria acted as sponsor for Gustav and, a year later, when a second child, Ida, was born on September 25, 1886, old Maria served as godparent for this infant too.[13] Despite all her problems with Braunau "society" and an equivocal

---

[9] Report of Frau Hoerl, *HA*, File 17, Reel 1; Jetzinger (G), pp. 38-39, 71 and 81; Jetzinger (E), pp. 47 and 54.
[10] *Die Ahnentafel*, pp. 39-40; Jetzinger (G), pp. 230-231; Jetzinger (E), p. 140. Jetzinger feels that one can apply the facts of Johanna's case to her sisters, but this does not necessarily follow.
[11] Birth certificate of Gustav Hitler. *HA*, File 17, Reel 1.
[12] Statement by Frau Rosalia Hoerl. *HA*, File 17, Reel 1.
[13] Birth certificate of Ida Hitler. *HA*, File 17, Reel 1.

position within her own family, Klara must have been able to take comfort from the comradeship of Maria Matzelberger.

On balance, however, Klara's life in the late 1880's had few pleasant features. She had all the strains of young motherhood while trying to cope with her two infants, the older children, and the household. Soon after Ida's birth, she produced a third child, who was given the name of Otto, but he died within a few days.[14] Even worse, in late 1887, both Gustav and Ida contracted diphtheria. Klara's sister Johanna took the older children to Spital while Klara tried to nurse the stricken infants back to health, but it was all in vain. Gustav died on December 8, 1887, and Ida a month later, on January 2, 1888. Both were interred in Braunau.[15] After three years of marriage, Klara had lost all her own children and was reduced to those functions that had justified her marriage in the first place – as stepmother for Franziska's children, housekeeper, and cook.

Despite the shadows that blur her personality, this woman who was to bring Adolf Hitler into the world emerges as the most compelling and sympathetic figure in the annals of the family. She lived her life under inauspicious circumstances and saw her hopes and dreams steadily come to naught over a span of twenty years. Yet in spite of all the blows she had to bear, she quietly returned again and again to fulfill her obligations humanely and conscientiously. She was a fairly large girl, almost as tall as her husband, with dark brown hair and even features. Her life was centered on the tasks of maintaining her home and caring for her husband and the children of the family. She was a model housekeeper, who maintained a spotless home and performed her duties with precision. Nothing could distract her from her round of household toil, not even the prospect of a little gossip.[16] Her home and the furthering of the family interest were all-important; by careful management she was able to increase the family possessions, much to her joy. Even more important to her than the house were the children. Everyone who knew her agreed that it was in her love and devotion for the children that Klara's

---

[14] *Jetzinger* (G), p. 57; *Jetzinger* (E), p. 43.
[15] Death certificates of Ida and Gustav Hitler; statement of Frau Rosalia Hoerl. *HA,* File 17, Reel 1.
[16] *Bloch,* p. 35; *Jetzinger* (G), p. 71; *Jetzinger* (E), p. 51.

life centered.[17] The only serious charge ever raised against her is that because of this love and devotion she was over-indulgent and thus encouraged a sense of uniqueness in her son – a somewhat strange charge to be brought against a mother.[18] The children did not share this view. Her stepchildren and her own offspring who survived infancy loved and respected their mother.[19]

Klara was conscious of her obligations and possessed the ability to adjust herself to the necessities of her situation, but she could not help but be affected by the harsh demands of her environment. Outside her home she had few close connections with other people and the few she had were mainly with family members. In her day-to-day affairs, only the Church gave her an approved activity extending beyond the narrow confines of her home. Alois insisted she attend regularly as an expression of his belief that the woman's place was in the kitchen and in church. There was no religious conviction in Alois' idea, nor did social pressures play a part; only duty and a sense of status motivated this requirement which he imposed on his wife. Happily, Klara really enjoyed attending services and was completely devoted to the faith and teachings of Catholicism, so her husband's requirements worked to her advantage.[20] Alois dominated his wife even more completely than was customary in the "authoritarian family structure" so beloved by sociologists. She owed everything to him, and, in her dependence, had nothing to counter his power. She had even been deprived of the period of give-and-take during the early years of marriage which provides maneuvering room for a wife in the most autocratic families. Alois had brought her into the household to fill a gap in the machine, and she never overcame this humble beginning. The peculiar background she shared with Alois also worked against her over the years. Even among her own close relatives, Alois was a more important figure than she. He was the most successful member of her circle, the pride and joy of her grandfather. If he was not the Prince Charming of a girl's dreams, he was an impressive catch. Marriage to him meant a step up the social

[17] *Jetzinger* (G), pp. 71-72; *Jetzinger* (E), pp. 51-52; *Zoller*, p. 46 and 115-16; *Mein Kampf*, p. 4.
[18] Stephen H. Roberts, *The House that Hitler Built* (London, 1939), pp. 3-4.
[19] *Mein Kampf*, p. 4; *Kubizek*, p. 29.
[20] Statement by Frau Rosalia Hoerl. *HA*, File 17, Reel 1.

ladder, as well as the means to gain permanent emancipation from the confines of the village.

Yet Klara was not simply taking part in a marriage of convenience. That her feelings for Alois involved something more than duty is indicated by her period as his mistress and her pregnancy prior to marriage. She seems to have had lofty and hopeful dreams about her married life which were abandoned only slowly and painfully. The relationship in which Alois was both a status symbol and a husband left the girl in a confusing and helpless position. How much this ambivalence affected her outlook can be seen in the fact that she found it exceedingly difficult to accustom herself to playing the role of Alois' wife. Try as she might, the poor girl was unable to break herself of the habit of addressing Alois as "uncle" until long after the marriage ceremony.[21]

The complexities and frustrations of her existence inevitably left scars. She once said that she had been married early in the morning and that an hour after the ceremony her husband was on duty again.[22] Although it was a slight exaggeration, this statement reflected the circumstances of her marriage. As the years went by, and her girlhood dreams lost all hope of realization, she bore the look of a disappointed woman whose best efforts had not received the reward they deserved. The unhappiness gradually increased until it was obvious to outsiders. The optimistic and happy girl of 1884-1885 was slowly transformed into a disappointed woman who did her duty and transferred all her hopes and dreams to the children.[23]

In contrast to Klara, Alois' role in the family appears to have been much more sharply delineated. Much of the insecurity and overdeveloped drive that had characterized the illegitimate peasant boy had disappeared by the time he married Klara, and in his work and social contacts he assumed the stance of a successful official. Still careful to perform his duties satisfactorily, he now worked like a man who had achieved something rather than an ambitious parvenue. He remained close to a small circle of cronies, most of whom were also in the customs service. Not all of his fellow bureaucrats found him a sympathetic character, but within his circle he was pleasant

---

[21] Statement by Frau Rosalia Hoerl. *HA*, File 17, Reel 1.
[22] *Jetzinger* (G), p. 55; *Jetzinger* (E), p. 41.
[23] *Kubizek,* pp. 31, 114-15.

enough.[24] He enjoyed the comradely evenings in the local tavern where he could enjoy a glass of beer or wine, smoke a steady stream of black cigars and expound his views. Although subsequent accounts have exaggerated this activity into drunkenness as a simple explanation for all the problems of Alois and his offspring, it is reasonably clear that during those years Alois was a moderate drinker. He loved the robust good fellowship of the tavern, but a participant at these get-togethers has stated emphatically, "I never saw him tight, and he always started back home in good time for supper." [25]

His comradely outings were all innocent and exactly what a man of Alois' age and station would have been expected to enjoy. Yet they also constituted nearly the whole of his social life. He sharply divided his official duties, his social activities, and his family contacts. Increasingly, a shadowy line appeared between Alois and his social inferiors. Despite the scandals that resulted from his romantic activities in Braunau, he was and would remain an Imperial Customs Official, and no one was allowed to forget it. The peasants, both at this time and after his retirement, looked up to him, his rough, gruff manner notwithstanding, and extended their courtesy as his due.[26]

At home he was something more than a formidable character. He was master, and he impressed this fact upon every member of the household. He alone had raised the whole lot of them and he demanded the obedience and respect that he felt they owed him. Despite his monopoly of family power he was not a tyrant, nor did he poke and pry into every feature of family life. The household was there to serve his needs while he provided the income for a better than average living and set the family tone. The bulk of his time was spent in long and irregularly timed tours of duty at the customs station; when he came home he wanted to eat and sleep without interference. When he wanted recreation he went to the tavern, but that was his own affair and did not concern the family. If, when he came home, things were out of line, his voice would generally set things right. If more was needed, then a box on an obstinate child's ear soon

---

[24] Statement by Zollobersekretaer Hebenstreit. *HA*, File 17, Reel 1; *Jetzinger* (G), pp. 60-61; *Jetzinger* (E), pp. 43-45.
[25] *Jetzinger* (E), p. 44.
[26] *Jetzinger* (E), p. 44; statement by Frau Rosalia Hoerl. *HA*, File 17, Reel 1.

set matters straight. The judgment of a friend of later years who held that "his bark was worse than his bite" was undoubtedly correct; his bluster was also bluff, but it succeeded completely.[27] The old man's dominance made him a permanent object of respect, if not of awe, to his wife and children. Even after his death his pipes still stood in a rack on the kitchen shelf, and when his widow wished to make a particularly important point she would gesture toward the pipes as if to invoke the authority of the master.[28]

The only point at which Alois shed some of his authoritarianism was in pursuit of his hobby. He was a passionate beekeeper. He also kept pet birds in the early years, but the love of his life remained beekeeping. His son, in typically exaggerated fashion, once described the beekeeping activity of the Hitler family in the following manner: "To be stung by a bee in our family was an ordinary, everyday occurrence. My mother often pulled out as many as forty-five or fifty stings from the old gentleman when he returned from clearing the hives. He never protected himself in any way; all he did was to smoke all the time – in other words, a good excuse for another cigar!"[29]

Alois seized every opportunity to talk about his bees and, according to rumor, he wrote about them for a technical journal, but there is no confirming evidence. While he was stationed in Passau in the early 1890's he kept his bees at Hailbach on the Austrian side of the border, and every evening he made the half-hour walk to take care of them. Then, on the way back, he stopped off at the local inn with his friends.[30] Earlier, during the 1880's, when he lived in Braunau, he had actually moved out of his house for three months and taken up residence in the old part of town in order to be closer to his bees, which were kept in a neighboring valley.[31] This unrestrained enthusiasm for beekeeping served to underline the main features of his personality – master at home and independent character abroad.

Alois' bees were also the thin thread which linked him to his peasant past. His dream was that some day he would be able to buy

---

[27] *Jetzinger* (E), p. 51.
[28] *Kubizek*, p. 37.
[29] *Hitler's Table Talk*, p. 608.
[30] *Jetzinger* (G), pp. 59-60; *Jetzinger* (E), pp. 43-44.
[31] Statement of Frau Rosalia Hoerl. *HA*, File 17, Reel 1.

a farm to serve as a home for his beehives. Urban life and absorption in his career never succeeded in dampening the peasant drive to acquire his own land. Finally, on March 16, 1889, shortly before the birth of Adolf, the great day arrived and he purchased a small peasant holding at Woernharts in the *Waldviertal*, not far from Spital. The property was 150 kilometers from his duty station, and it was obviously impossible for him to reside there. He seems to have planned to hold on to the land until his retirement and then turn it into the family residence. As an interim arrangement, Johanna Poelzl moved to Woernharts and, in exchange for lodging, kept the property in as good shape as her crippled condition permitted. After three years this scheme was abandoned, probably because of inevitable squabbles between the domineering Alois and his shrewish sister-in-law. On October 27, 1892, he reluctantly sold the farm.[32] This was merely a temporary setback to his farming ambitions, however; he purchased two more plots of ground before his death.

The purchase and sale of the Woernharts property provides a convenient point from which to appraise the financial condition of the family. The original purchase price of the house is not available, but Alois sold it for 7,000 florins in 1892, (approximately equal to 3,000 dollars at the turn of the century). Of this sum, only 2,000 florins was used to pay off debts which Alois contracted at the time of purchase. He received an additional 1,000 florins in cash and granted credit to the purchaser for the remaining sum of about 4,000 florins, either in the form of a mortgage or as a loan secured by other property.[33]

The transaction also indirectly revealed that the children of Alois' second marriage, Angela and young Alois, had been provided for by their mother. When Alois Senior purchased the farm, 800 florins of the money he borrowed came from the children's trust fund, but he apparently did not take it all, for the total bequest was about 1,000 florins.[34] Therefore, if this sum is excluded and allowance is

---

[32] Statement of Herr Leo Weber (made October 12, 1938) and report of *Hauptarchiv* investigator. *HA*, File 17, Reel 1.

[33] Statement of Herr Leo Weber and report of *Hauptarchiv* investigator. *HA*, File 17, Reel 1. This transaction may have some connection with Jetzinger's discovery that Johanna's savings increased in 1892. *Jetzinger* (G), p. 231.

[34] *Jetzinger* (G), p. 126; *Jetzinger* (E), p. 81.

made for the money Alois borrowed to purchase the property, he must have put down approximately 4-5,000 florins in cash when he bought the land, assuming that the property's value did not change radically between 1889 and 1892.

A number of factors undoubtedly played a part in Alois' accumulation of the 4-5,000 florins, a sum three times his highest annual salary. He had a solid income; his wife was careful about household expenditures, while he himself had a reputation for "great frugality and a sense of economy and thrift." [35] It is unlikely, however, that much of the money came from petty savings. He enjoyed a comfortable standard of living, and the family was not cramped by stringent economy. Some money came from a series of small legacies; in addition, he may have saved a portion of the dowries of his three wives. After the name change in 1876, Alois was able to inherit from two rather populous families; even though the sums were small, he was bound to inherit rather frequently. In 1862, he had inherited a few hundred florins from the estate of one of his mother's brothers, and in 1876 he obtained 230 florins from his uncle, Franz Schickelgruber.[36] Altogether, the accumulation may have reached as much as 1,000 florins by the late 1880's.

Alois' first wife, Anna, appears to have been well-to-do, and her dowry should have been large. Her advanced age at the time of their wedding awakens the suspicion that Alois' money sense played a part in the marriage. However, he may not have gained much from the union; at the time of the separation in 1880, Anna had a good opportunity to recover some of the money. Similarly, Alois' gains from Franziska's dowry may also have been minimal. The 1,000 florins in the children's trust fund probably represented a large portion of the original dowry. As for Klara, the dispensation request of 1884 emphasized that she was not well provided for, and the accuracy of this description is supported by the indirect evidence of her family's financial troubles.[37] Her sister Johanna may have received a sum as high as 1,600 florins as the equivalent of a marriage portion, but it would be hazardous to assume from this that

---

[35] *Jetzinger* (G), p. 73; *Jetzinger* (E), p. 53; Zoller, p. 46.
[36] *HA*, File 17A, Reel 1 material concerns these two inheritances as does the *L of C* material.
[37] *Die Ahnentafel*, pp. 39-40.

Klara received a like amount, because Johanna was a cripple and may have been favored in the settlement.[38] If the maximum sums from the dowries of Alois' three wives and the probable amount of small inheritances were added together, the total would still fall far short of 4-5,000 florins. During the fifteen years that intervened between Alois' first marriage and the purchase of the property, he also had suffered losses and had to pay unexpected costs, such as the medical care for his first wife, the expenses involved in Franziska's convalescence, and the illness of Klara's first two children. After balancing these expenditures against his windfall gains, it seems reasonable to conclude that Alois could have saved about 2-3,000 florins by the end of the 1880's. An additional source of funds would have been necessary to reach the 4-5,000 florins figure by 1889. The probability is, as has been argued earlier, the extra money came from the bequest of Johann Nepomuk Hiedler. This apparently was the real turning point in Alois' fortunes. Henceforth he was in continuous possession of either land or a sizeable sum of cash until the time of his own death.

The large reserve that Alois had acquired was a major element in the family's security, but it was not the basis for its social position or standard of living. Alois was a salaried official, and it was on his monthly income and his pension prospects that the family primarily depended. In the ten years between his third marriage in 1885 and his retirement in 1895, the annual family income ranged between an approximate low of 1,000 and a high of 1,350 florins (2,000-2,700 kronen). After retirement his pension was generous, consisting of his old salary in full, less pre-retirement allowances to compensate him for having to serve away from his domicile. (Within the service, assignment to the border stations was looked upon as a form of exile, and the Imperial Government paid compensation to those who claimed a home town different from that of their duty stations. Alois had been clever enough to qualify for this subsidy, but after retirement, when he was free to live where he wished, the government ceased to pay it.) After subtraction of these allowances, as well as his taxes and the interest on the houses he acquired from time to time, Alois' net income remained 1,000 florins per year.[39] Although

---

[38] *Jetzinger* (G), p. 231; *Jetzinger* (E), p. 140.
[39] *Jetzinger* (G), pp. 122-24; *Jetzinger* (E), pp. 78-79

it is difficult to state Alois' income in modern terms, an estimate of his relative financial position can be made. At the peak of his earning power, he received considerably more than the average elementary school principal, and his income placed him in approximately the center of the salaried middle class. He was far removed from the status of a great entrepreneur, but he was also well above the position of all blue collar and the majority of white collar workers. Even in retirement, Alois' financial position was excellent. In the 1890's, his pension was approximately twice the income of a factory worker. At the time of his death in 1903, his 1,000 florins income was still six times the income of a lower Austrian day laborer who worked regularly.[40]

In terms of income, assets, expenditures and standard of living, the family nearly epitomized the middle class. A steady income was backed by substantial savings, with the sure prospect of a comfortable pension and widow's and orphan's benefits if needed. Wild extravagance was not possible, but there was also no need for oppressive self-denial. All the trappings of middle-class existence, from paid education for the children to plenty of big black cigars, were readily obtainable in the Hitler household. Only Alois' age and the youthfulness of his family marred the classic picture. In retirement he was to find that raising young children on a pension was not altogether easy, because his income declined just at the point when the costs of child rearing rose. This was irritating and required some adjustments, but the family continued to receive a comfortable income.

Throughout the period between the middle of the 1880's and Alois' death in 1903, the family's security and standard of living were never in danger.[41] When Klara became pregnant again in the winter of 1888-1889, the prospect of increased expenses created no alarm in the Hitler household. Klara was apprehensive, but only because she feared another tragedy such as those which had overtaken her first three children. If her fourth child lived, his economic well-being was assured.

---

[40] *Jetzinger* (G), pp. 122-24; *Jetzinger* (E), p. 79; *Drage*, p. 68.
[41] Statement by Frau Rosalia Hoerl. *HA*, File 17, Reel 1.

III

ADOLF HITLER'S EARLY CHILDHOOD

On April 20, 1889, Klara gave birth to a boy in the family's quarters in the Pommer Inn. The child was given the name of Adolf. Like Klara's previous children, he had the Prinz couple as godparents, while Klara's sister Johanna replaced Maria Matzelberger as an additional godparent.[1] The child was sickly, and Klara lived in constant fear that he, too, would die in infancy. The baby never acquired a rugged constitution, but his mother's fears gradually abated in the succeeding months as he appeared to develop normally. Living conditions were not ideal in the small flat for a family with a baby and two active older children. Soon after Adolf's birth, the family moved to a new residence on the Linzerstrasse, where they remained until they left Braunau in the late summer of 1892.[2]

The location of Adolf Hitler's birthplace on the river Inn bordering Austria and Germany provided a basis for unlimited propaganda in later years. Hitler himself worked hard to wring every ounce of political advantage from the accident of his birthplace.[3] However, the town's influence on the "drummer from Braunau on the Inn" could not have been extensive. In later years, while still exploiting his Braunau origin, Hitler himself casually admitted that he remembered little or nothing about this period.[4]

As with other infants, it was the home itself and his relations with the members of the family that were important for little Adolf in

---

[1] Birth certificate of Adolf Hitler. *HA*, File 17, Reel 1.
[2] *Kubizek*, p. 41; *Reich*, p. 14-15.
[3] *Mein Kampf*, p. 3. Sentence number one of *Mein Kampf* is the classic example.
[4] *Mein Kampf*, **p. 4.**

Braunau. The family circle was his world, and his experiences therein constituted an important stage in his personal development. Unfortunately, a baby's vital experiences usually elude the historian: the record provides only a few vague references to his Braunau years. The really important events in shaping the man-to-be largely escape us.

Klara was wrapped up in her baby and seems to have provided him with ample love and attention. Her fears about his health may have resulted in a degree of over-protectiveness and indulgence. As he grew, he learned to take advantage of this concern to get what he wanted.[5] Despite this selfish tendency, he was very fond of his mother and a deep bond united them throughout his childhood.[6] Angela and young Alois, however, failed to play an important part in Adolf's development, and he did not have any lasting affection for either of them. A great distance also separated the little boy from his father. Alois Senior was seldom home. After working extended day and night shifts at the customs station, he filled his scanty free time with his friends and his bees. He had little interest in the details of child rearing, a task he left to Klara. He did not enjoy going home; when he joined the rest of the family, it was to achieve some specific end and not to be bothered with the children.[7]

[5] Statements by young Alois quoted in G. M. Gilbert, *The Psychology of Dictatorship* (New York, 1950), p. 18. Of course, one may question the genuineness and sufficiency of any mother's love, but the historian is bound to follow the evidence. As noted above (pp. 41-42), the statements of outside observers, and of Adolf himself, indicate that Klara was a conscientious and affectionate mother. Whether this love was sufficient for Adolf's needs only he could tell, and none of his remarks provide the basis for a penetrating judgment. This fact also has bearing on the general question of his childhood development. The kind of information that psychologists and analysts value highly in evaluating a person's childhood – details on toilet training, food preferences, ideas on compromise, etc. – are, in the main, not available for Hitler. Therefore, one must either apply the conclusions of a particular theory – for example: maladjustment in later life proves that something went wrong in the first two years – or try to explain the case on the available evidence. The historian must take the second alternative and let individual psychologists fill in the gaps as their separate schools dictate.
[6] *Zoller*, p. 46, 115-16; *Bloch*, p. 36; *Kubizek*, p. 36; *Mein Kampf*, p. 18; *Table Talk*, p. 359.
[7] This estimate of Alois' attitudes toward home and family during the early 90's was reached by comparing his opinions in the middle 1880's with those of the later 1890's. Statement of Frau Hoerl, HA, File 17, Reel 1; and *Jetzinger* (G), p. 70; *Jetzinger* (E), p. 51.

When he arrived home in an irritable mood, the older children and his wife bore the brunt of his wrath. Klara was wise enough in the ways of her husband to move the infant out of harm's way whenever the danger flags were flying. An occasional nod, smile, or rumble reached the child directly from his father. For the rest, he merely learned through his mother that Alois held the ultimate family authority.

Adolf's life in Braunau passed peacefully under Klara's loving care. There were no important changes until 1892, when Alois was promoted and transferred to a new assignment. The advance and the move were the result of important changes in Austrian tariff policy made in 1890 and 1891. In the spring of 1891, after six months of negotiations, Austria and Germany signed a new tariff agreement establishing lower duties on many products traded between the two countries. In the latter half of 1891, additional agreements established between these nations a reduced tariff zone which was extended to Italy, Switzerland, and Belgium.[8] The new duty rates and procedures required administrative changes in the Austrian customs service, since the men on duty had to be trained in the new regulations and more men were needed to oversee an increased volume of trade. The expansion of the customs service also meant opportunities for advancement. To take advantage of them, Alois had to undergo training in the new customs procedures and study for a promotion examination. For a period, he was more than usually busy and his contacts with the family decreased.

In May 1892, when Adolf was three, Alois left his family and traveled to Vienna where he remained until June 6.[9] The trip may have been to make arrangements for his advancement, but there may also have been other reasons. At approximately this same time, he borrowed the sizeable sum of 600 florins, using the Woernharts farm as security.[10] It seems logical to assume a connection existed

---

[8] Heinrich Benedikt, *Die Wirtschaftliche Entwicklung in Franz-Joseph-Zeit* (Vienna, 1958), p. 138.

[9] *Anmeldung* form of Alois Hitler, copy in *HA*, File 17, Reel 1. The original seems to have been in the Arlington material. *NA*, Micro-Copy T-84, Reel 4. This form states that Alois' family was in Braunau at this time, which confirms Jetzinger's rejection of the old story that the family lived in Gross-Schonau between 1900 and 1907. *Jetzinger* (G), p. 57.

[10] *Hauptarchiv* material on the Woernharts land purchase. *HA*, File 17, Reel 1.

between the loan and his stay in Vienna, but the details are unknown. By August he had attained his goal – elevation to the senior status of a Higher Collector of Customs.

Braunau did not have a post for a Higher Collector, so the promotion carried with it the obligatory transfer to the customs station at Passau. This city on the German side of the boundary was the most important trade center on the northern portion of the frontier between Austria and Germany.

Even in his hour of triumph, Alois had to accept an unwelcome change. Thirty years of service had ended in success, but success required that Alois and his family leave Braunau, where he had made his home for twenty years. He quickly liquidated his investment in Woernharts, selling the house on October 27th. By this time, the family had already left the Linzerstrasse and settled down in Passau.[11] The Hitlers took up residence in Passau because the customs inspection was done in that city and not on the Austrian side of the river. At the time of the move, Alois Jr., Angela, and Adolf were ten, nine, and three years old respectively. The new residence imposed no particular hardships on the children, aside from the severing of childhood friendships. It seems probable that only Alois Sr. was seriously inconvenienced. In April 1894, after only eighteen months in Passau, he was reassigned to Linz. During the next year, Klara and the children remained in Passau.[12]

The short period during which the family was together in Passau saw changes in the relative positions of the various children. Alois and Angela were maturing and could better take care of themselves, while Adolf was less able to find effective defenses against his father's power. The old man's routine had been broken by the move. The new situation forced him into closer contact with his family and provided him an opportunity to take better note of his young son's activities. Adolf, then between three and five, was at a stage when aspirations naturally resulted in ever-expanding attempts to test his strength within the family. Such preliminary evidences of confidence and a sense of initiative must have been continuously threatened by his father's attitude. Alois, who had a limited under-

[11] Material on the Woernharts land purchase. *HA*, File 17, Reel 1; *Jetzinger* (G), p. 58; *Jetzinger* (E), p. 43.
[12] *Jetzinger* (G), p. 63; *Jetzinger* (E), p. 43.

standing of children and a minimum of interest in their development, was not one to appreciate a boy's attempts at self-expression. Adolf began to encounter increasing numbers of sobering confrontations with his father from which he was less and less able to slip back into a protected position.

In the early summer of 1893, Klara became pregnant again. Her condition undoubtedly reduced her effectiveness in acting as a shield for the boy. During this time, he was particularly exposed to paternal attention. Much of Klara's worry about her previous pregnancies assuredly returned at this time and further clouded the relations between mother and son.

Klara gave birth to a boy on March 24, 1894. The appearance of this child, who received the name of Edmund, immediately cost five-year-old Adolf what was left of his privileged position as mother's darling and the baby of the household.[13] The situation called for the boy to make a rapid adjustment which should have produced closer ties between father and son or more independent responsibility to compensate for the loss of his protected position. Responsibility had not been forced upon him consistently up to this time. Edmund's birth provided the perfect circumstances under which to make the change, but at the last moment Adolf escaped again. On April 1, 1894, one week after the birth of Edmund, Alois was transferred to his new post at Linz, and left for the new assignment. The family, however, apparently fearing the risks of traveling with the new baby, stayed behind in Passau.[14] For twelve months the family lived apart from the father, who made only occasional visits to maintain the lines of authority. During the year, everyone in the family was busy in Passau; Klara had her new baby to care for, while Angela and young Alois were involved in the last phases of their elementary education. Adolf was busy, too, doing exactly as he wished with almost total freedom. Everyone was too occupied to watch him; he was too young for school, and his awesome father was living fifty miles away. Instead of renewed demands for conformity, he had been presented with the gift of freedom.

For one whole year, Adolf lived in a five-year-old's paradise,

[13] Birth record of Edmund Hitler. *HA*, File 17, Reel 1; *Jetzinger* (G), p. 57; *Jetzinger* (E), pp. 56-57.
[14] *Jetzinger* (G), p. 88; *Jetzinger* (E), p. 37.

playing games and roughhousing with the children of the neighborhood. Miniature wars and fights between cowboys and Indians appear to have been his favorites, and they were to continue as his major diversions for many years. Since Passau was in Germany, war games would have pitted French against German in the spirit of 1870, yet there was no particular importance in the nationality of the victims. Europe was full of heroic little boys who massacred all national and ethnic groups impartially. This year of childhood combat was important in Hitler's life not because it was spent on German soil and added a Bavarian touch to his speech, but because it was a year of escape into almost complete freedom.[15] At home he began to assert himself more and probably displayed the first signs of consuming anger when he did not get his way. Outside, play, without limit to action or imagination, reigned supreme.

Happy as the year was, it could not last forever. The reckoning came in April 1895, when the family was reunited in Linz. In February 1895, Alois had purchased a house and nine acres called the *Rauscher Gut* in Hafeld near Lambach, approximately thirty miles southwest of Linz. The family settled on the farm,[16] and Adolf was abruptly required to make a transition from freedom to new responsibilities. This was undoubtedly a serious challenge for the boy to meet, as it would be for any child of six, but it was only the beginning of limitations on his independence. A month after his arrival in Hafeld, he was enrolled in school for the first time at the little country school at Fischlam bei Lambach, which he entered on May 1, 1895.[17]

On June 25, 1895, Alois retired after forty years of service and came home to the *Rauscher Gut* to devote himself to a life of leisure and beekeeping.[18] It must have seemed the golden moment he had sought for years. Finally he could do what he wished and play the gentleman farmer to his heart's content. He was only fifty-eight at the time, and although retirement at this early age had been justified on the basis

---

[15] *Mein Kampf*, p. 126; Jetzinger toys with the idea that the German character of Passau exerted a special influence on Adolf. *Jetzinger* (G), p. 88; *Jetzinger* (E), pp. 56-57.
[16] *Jetzinger* (G), pp. 65-67; *Jetzinger* (E), pp. 47-48.
[17] Munich police report of 1924. *HA*, File 1760, Reel 25A. Statement on earlier schooling in Leonding school records. *HA*, File 65, Reel 13A.
[18] *Jetzinger* (G), pp. 64-67; *Jetzinger* (E), pp. 47-48.

of unidentified medical problems, he acted and thought of himself as a healthy, rugged individual.

The situation was quite different from Adolf's point of view. He found his life suddenly confined in a narrow circle of activities demanding responsibility and discipline. For the first time, he was steadily and systematically forced to conform. His time was divided between the order and regimentation of school and the obedience required at home by a father who was almost always present. Although the boy did not yield without some tests of temper and will, he soon capitulated and did as he was told. In school he appeared to be a cut above the peasant children who were his schoolmates. He quickly adjusted to the routine and did very well throughout his two-year stay in the Fischlam school, receiving the highest mark (1) in his subjects and deportment.[19] At home, he was surrounded by the three siblings, with little Edmund occupying the place of security that had once been his. Here, too, with no means of escaping authority, he outwardly submitted, but there were reservations. He was still able to manipulate his mother to a degree, and his temper could explode at any time against anyone.

Aside from periodic angry outbursts, Adolf's only release from the sudden imposition of paternal and school authority came in the hours he spent in the open countryside, an ideal setting for playful struggle with Indians, cowboys and soldiers. Escape into the open air served as a link to the glorious year of freedom and independence now gone.[20] At this stage, while the boy was six or seven, play performed a necessary role in his life and succeeded in easing some potentially dangerous barriers to his adjustment. Slowly over the subsequent years, however, the play increased in intensity and importance for Adolf, until in adolescence it became a form of dreamy escape into fantasy. In Hafeld, everything was still under control, but play patterns established at that time would lead to future difficulty.

In 1896 the demands imposed on seven-year-old Adolf increased.

---

[19] Munich police report of 1924. *HA*, File 1760, Reel 25A; *Goerlitz and Quint*, p. 22.
[20] Ludwig Wagner, *Hitler Man of Strife*, translated by Charlotte La Rue (New York, 1942), p. 22.

On January 21, Klara gave birth to a daughter, Paula.[21] The boy was thereby pushed farther out of babyhood and along the road which would make him a miniature adult. There were now five children in the house, ranging in age from fourteen years to a few days. Everywhere Alois looked, there were children under foot. He was no longer able to issue general directives and await their execution. With seven people under one roof, it was necessary for him to be involved in the rough-and-tumble of everyday family life. The old man fled the turmoil as often as he could, leaving behind the echoes of his rumbling and roaring, to the sanctuary of the local inn, where he was able to find relaxing companionship, papers to read, a chance to chat over a soothing glass of wine or beer. As the weeks followed one another in unending succession with nothing to break the routine and no hope of permanent escape from the chaos at home, his drinking seems to have increased.[22]

Somehow all his hopes and dreams about retirement had worked out wrong. Alois had been a restless soul all of his life, pushing onward, advancing himself and his family, and constantly seeking something new. He had moved frequently, and even when he had stayed in a duty station for an extended period, as at Braunau, he had resided in inns and temporary quarters as if attempting to preserve the atmosphere of movement. All of this had been justified by the great dream: at the end of his career there would be an arcadia in which he would be a gentleman farmer in the peace and tranquility of the countryside. Security and stability would prevail while he tended his bees and puttered in his garden.

As a dream, the picture was alluring, but its translation probably had no chance of success under ideal conditions, and the situation in Hafeld was far from ideal. The noisy, troublesome children were ever-present, the farm a far more serious undertaking than Alois had anticipated. Nine acres presented weighty obstacles to successful cultivation by a man whose farming experience lay thirty-five years in the past. His strength was limited, and he had only the

---

[21] *Jetzinger* (G), p. 57; *Jetzinger* (E), p. 43.
[22] Wagner, pp. 22-23; *Jetzinger* (G), p. 66; *Jetzinger* (E), pp. 60-61; Hans Frank, *Im Angesicht des Galgens. Deutung Hitlers und seiner Zeit auf Grund eigner Erlebnisse und Erkenntnisse* (Munich, 1953), pp. 330-31. Jetzinger discounts his drinking, while Frank stresses it.

children to help him. His beehives hardly made a dent in the nine acres; the remainder of the property was neither productive nor profitable. His savings were tied up in land which yielded nothing, while the value of the property actually declined due to neglect. He could renew his efforts at least to break even, but this meant a life of drudgery in the midst of yelling, scrambling children. The *Rauscher Gut* had turned into something very different from a rural paradise.

The disappointments and obstacles encountered in Hafeld made Alois more crotchety and irritable. His moods increased family tensions and made life more burdensome for everyone. The oldest child, fourteen-year-old Alois, was the first to succumb. In 1896 he left home. His departure caused a violent controversy with his father; the old man stipulated that at his death young Alois would only inherit the amount required by law.[23] Alois Jr. was a cantankerous individual who was to drift through life a failure. He worked as a waiter for a while, and was jailed for theft in 1900 and 1902. In 1907 he was a waiter in Paris and two years later turned up in Ireland, where he married and started a family. In the 1920's he was living in Germany, and in the course of this sojourn he was jailed again, after which he seems to have returned to England. When his half-brother, Adolf, emerged as an important political figure in the 1930's Alois, never loath to exploit a stroke of fortune, appeared in Berlin, where he opened a cafe which became a meeting place for lower Nazi party leaders. In this era, Adolf ignored him, and even forbade the mention of his name in his presence.[24]

At the time the younger Alois left home, however, the relationship could not be dismissed so lightly. After his departure, Adolf became the chief target of his father's anger. All the old man's toil and sacrifice had been wasted on the older son. Adolf, now the oldest boy in the household, had to assume added responsibility at a time when he already was hard pressed to meet the demands of home and school. Alois' ambition led him to promote the competitive virtues in his children, but at the same time he required absolute

---

[23] *Jetzinger* (G), p. 40; *Jetzinger* (E), p. 42. The legal implications are explained in *Coldstream*, p. 73.
[24] Heiden, *Der Fuehrer*, p. 43; "Hitler vs. Hitler," *Time*, Vol. XXXIII, No. 15 (April 10, 1939), p. 20; Otto Dietrich, *Hitler*, translated by Richard and Clara Winston (Chicago, 1955), p. 221.

subordination to his authority. This demand for a combination of self-reliance and obedience was a common source of conflict in the middle class of half a century ago. The conflict was pronounced in Alois' case because of his early retirement and the immaturity of many of his children. He was especially vulnerable to pressures created by conflicts in his value system, and his resulting restlessness and moodiness compounded the difficulties of his seven-year-old son.

Nothing the old man attempted succeeded in making the situation more agreeable for himself or his dependents. The farm, the family, and his private goals all ran into unforeseen snags. Even as he was trying to adjust himself to play the required role, the world outside was changing in ways which further enraged and embittered him. His era and the people who stood for the things he believed in were passing from the scene, banished by powerful new forces. The non-German populations of the western empire were increasing their power and importance in parliament, while the German vote was splintered between the traditional parties and a host of new political organizations. In the increasing bitterness of nationality conflicts, German national consciousness also intensified, but no leader was able to provide a unifying organization or ideology. To strengthen their position and defend German interests, party leaders resorted to a wide range of tactical maneuvers. Two of these must have been particularly offensive to Alois: the increase in Church influence personified by Lueger's Christian Socialists, and the Badeni language decrees which attempted to mollify the Czechs by permitting use of their language in the administration of Bohemia and Moravia. Alois' opposition to "clericalism" was intense, but not less so than his devotion to the ideal of a centralized imperial administration, exclusively German in language and largely German in personnel. The Badeni language decrees struck at the roots of the institution with which he most closely identified himself. They not only meant decentralization; they also hurt German interests, since most Czech civil servants were bilingual while few Germans spoke Czech.

The Badeni language decrees were ultimately revoked, but not before they had unleashed a storm of German national protest which shook many people out of their political apathy. Certainly, they made it difficult for a man like Alois to remain optimistically unconcerned while the German position in Austria was seriously threatened. These events and the reactions they created occurred during the years that the Hitler family lived in Hafeld. They provided a discouraging counterpoint to the souring experience with the farm and retirement. Alois also became convinced that he could not obtain a decent education for his children in backward Hafeld.[25] Confused, frustrated and angry, he threw in his hand in July 1897, three months after the Badeni language decrees were issued. He sold the Hafeld farm and took up residence in the town of Lambach.[26]

During the first months in Lambach, the family lived in temporary quarters at #58 (the later *Gasthof Leingartner*). In the early part of 1898, they moved into a set of rooms on the second floor of a mill run by a miller named Zoebl. The mill was still being used, with Zoebl working in the forward part of the ground floor and a blacksmith named Preisinger practicing his trade in the rear. The Hitlers lived in the mill for approximately a year, over half the time they resided in the town.[27] Lambach was a little settlement of 1,700 inhabitants, but it probably appeared comparatively large after the years on the farm. Little change occurred here in the pattern of the family's life, however, largely because Klara took charge of the household with her customary efficiency.

The new surroundings and the relief from the financial losses in Hafeld seem to have encouraged Alois temporarily, and the first months in Lambach may have found him easier to live with. Before long, however, the old problems of restlessness, frustation and irritability returned and increased. The close quarters and the increasing assertiveness of his offspring made Lambach an even less congenial environment than Hafeld. There was no farm or beehives to which Alois could flee. The tavern, therefore, saw too much of him, but even this was not enough to insure peace for the children. The little

---

[25] *Reich*, p. 16.
[26] *Jetzinger* (G), pp. 68-69; *Jetzinger* (E), p. 48. Part of a newspaper series on Hitler's youth "Aus Adolf Hitlers Jugendland" by Firtz Chelius, which is preserved in *HA*, File 17, Reel 1A, begins at this point. It appeared in a Rhenish newspaper in April 1933 [?] and contains some solid facts mixed with omission and error.
[27] *Goerlitz and Quint*, p. 22; "Aus Adolf Hitlers Jugendland." *HA*, File 17, Reel 1A.

tots, Paula and Edmund, were bothersome, but safe enough under Klara's protective wing. Angela, fourteen at the time of the family's arrival in Lambach, was preparing for the role of mother and household organizer; she was able to slide in alongside Klara and achieve immunity from the sharpest clashes with her surly father. Only Adolf had no secure haven. He was still too young to stand on his own feet, yet too advanced to enjoy the security of Klara's apron strings.

At ten, Adolf, although still a constant victim of his father's discontent, appears to have devised ways of making life bearable. His responsibilities as the oldest son may have served as an outlet for a growing need to participate in the adult world. He seems to have been spared the intense feelings of jealousy and guilt which often assail children at this age.[28] He continued his schooling at the relatively modern elementary school in Lambach, and his record there remained excellent. His father, who enjoyed singing, seems to have provided the incentive for the boy to take voice lessons at the choir school in the local monastery.[29] During this period Adolf temporarily thought of becoming a monk, but the mood passed quickly. Such ambitions could receive no sympathy from his father; they also clashed with his own aggressive and competitive temperament.[30] Even while dreaming of a monastic life, he was caught by a priest in the act of smoking a cigarette, the great boyhood crime.[31] The indiscretion caused problems at school, but it is unlikely that it made serious trouble at home. Alois appreciated smoking more than he did priests. Neither this incident nor the passing attraction of the religious life was important in Adolf's development. In Lambach as in Hafeld, it was on the childish campaign trail or the make-believe scalping expeditions that he came to life. No matter what the game, he took his place as an enthusiastic participant.[32]

The frustrations and conflicts experienced by Alois made commu-

---

[28] *Erikson*, pp. 225-26.
[29] *Mein Kampf*, p. 6; *Jetzinger* (G), p. 73; *Jetzinger* (E), p. 53.
[30] *Mein Kampf*, p. 6. The existence of a stylized swastika above the door of this monastery once caused a great flurry of interest, but it was a coincidence and played no part in Hitler's development. Heinz A. Heinz, *Germany's Hitler* (London, 1934), p. 18; "La premiere rencontre d'Hitler avec la croix gammee...," *Illustration*, November 4, 1933, pp. 322-23.
[31] *Reich*, p. 17.
[32] "Aus Adolf Hitlers Jugendland." *HA*, File 17, Reel 1A.

nication between father and son increasingly difficult. Alois took out some of his difficulties on his son, and the youngster, unable to express his anger at his father, probably repressed his problems, turning to childhood games as a means of acting out some of this aggression. Nothing in the record indicates a crisis in family relations at this stage, and a change was in the offing.

Once again, Alois gave up in the face of an unpleasant situation. In November 1898 he purchased a one-story country house on a half-acre adjacent to the cemetery wall in the village of Leonding on the outskirts of the small provincial city of Linz. On February 23, 1899, the family moved into the new house. Four days later Adolf was enrolled in his third elementary school.[33]

The acquisition of the Leonding property, Alois' third effort to discover a stable life in retirement, proved successful at last. He settled down as owner of the property and continued to reside there until his death in 1903, while the rest of the family, less dominated by wanderlust than the head of the household, made the Linz area their home. This was especially true of Adolf, who grew up in Leonding-Linz and never overcame the influence of the town. One of his secretaries, speaking after the war, said: "Even in March of 1945, I have seen Hitler stand for endless periods in front of a wood model representing the rebuilding and extension of the city of Linz. In such moments Hitler forgot the war; he lost the marks of tiredness, and for hours he told us of the detailed changes that he planned to make in his home city." [34]

To a lesser extent, Alois also put down roots in Leonding-Linz. The half-acre of land permitted him to resume his dabbling with bees, but without the heavy costs that had turned Hafeld into a liability. He eased into a routine of puttering in the garden, punctuated by a morning visit to the *Gasthaus Stiefler* and an evening get-together there or in one of the other inns in the area.[35] He attained a degree of genuine contentment, but his nature was too explosive for him to be able to settle down to a completely passive existence. He continued to be unhappy about the events of the day

---

[33] *Jetzinger* (G), pp. 69 and 90, *Jetzinger* (E), pp. 50-51. "Aus Adolf Hitlers Jugendland." *HA*, File 17, Reel 1A.
[34] *Zoller*, p. 57.
[35] *Jetzinger* (G), pp. 69 and 73; *Jetzinger* (E), pp. 51-52.

and never attempted to hide his opposition to the course of politics or to what he considered the excessive power of the Church.[36]

Alois' better adjustment did not bring any lessening of his determination to dominate his family. Klara and the children were left with no doubts concerning who was in control. His best friend in Leonding, Josef Mayerhofer, later said of him: "He was strict with his family, no kid gloves as far as they were concerned; his wife had nothing to smile about." Mayerhofer emphasized, though, that the rough exterior was partly bluff and that the children were not physically abused. "He never touched him [Adolf]. I don't believe that [he beat him], but he often scolded and bawled at him. 'That miserable urchin!' he used to say, 'I'll bash him yet!' But his bark was worse than his bite. The boy stood in awe of him, though." [37]

The boy was wary and not a little fearful (with good reason), but he learned to stay at a distance and move carefully. In school, he followed the now established routine, compiling an excellent record, without a blemish in either conduct or class assignments.[38]

Occasionally, when Alois was especially out of sorts or Adolf was imprudently forward, the orderly relationship made possible by youthful caution broke down, and an unpleasant confrontation ensued.[39] But beyond the walls of the pretty garden house, the boy played on with few signs of concern about the future or the world around him. Always it was the old cycle of wars and Indian conflicts, pursued with little alteration except for the different companions of his new environment. Whether the frequent changes in residence and school exerted a harmful influence on his emotional development is difficult to say. His outward behavior did not indicate any serious problem, but the question cannot be disposed of easily. Throughout his early childhood, the numerous moves were paralleled by continuous shifts in the routine of the family and the treatment of the children. Alois' attitude ranged from aloof unconcern to quarreling meddlesomeness. Klara passed back and forth between

---

[36] *Jetzinger* (G), p. 71; *Jetzinger* (E), p. 51; M. W. Fodor, "Austrian Roots of Hitlerism," *Foreign Affairs*, July 1936, p. 687.
[37] *Jetzinger* (G), p. 70; *Jetzinger* (E), p. 51.
[38] Munich police report of 1924. *HA*, File 1760, Reel 25A.
[39] *Dietrich*, p. 14. The conflict described herein may refer to adolescence rather than childhood.

overprotectiveness and a withdrawal occasioned by pregnancy or obedience to Alois' insistence upon iron discipline. Sometimes, as in Passau, the boy was utterly free; on other occasions he was rigidly controlled. During much of the earlier period he was lost among the other children, but in Lambach he was suddenly thrust forward as the family's heir apparent.

This random, transient manner of life imposed heavy burdens on a young child. All schools of child psychology agree that a clear, continuous, dependable, and purposeful system of love and guidance is of the utmost importance in the healthy development of a child.[40] The young Hitler simply did not have this kind of family environment. Nevertheless, that he was able to hold the external features of his life together in a way that allowed him to function effectively both at home and at school suggests a rather unusual degree of youthful self-confidence and tenacity. On the other hand, character traits cannot completely escape environmental influences, and the boy still faced difficult obstacles to adjustment.

Adolf's undoing was the impossibility of making time stand still. He was due to finish elementary school in the spring of 1900, and at that time the basic decisions about his future education and career would have to be made. Already, he was edging into adolescence with its exciting but often painful problems. Given a background of longstanding opposition to his father's outlook, the chances for a successful transition along lines his parents might favor were problematical. Just as the time came when these questions would have to be faced, Adolf's little brother Edmund died of measles on February 2, 1900.[41] The whole family passed through a phase of shock. As it receded, one fact emerged clearly: Adolf was the last of the boys – the only individual capable of carrying on the upward march of the family. In the preceding months, decisions about his future had seemed important, but not critical. After Edmund's death, all this changed. The responsibility for preserving the family name and vindicating all his father's efforts devolved upon him.

---

[40] This is a central thesis of Erikson's *Childhood and Society*. Erikson, *passim*.
[41] Edmund's death certificate. *HA*, File 17, Reel 1.

IV

THE LATER CHILDHOOD

In 1900 Adolf Hitler was an active lad of eleven, suspended between childhood and adolescence. His class picture shows a boy of medium height with a thin though normally developed frame. Straight black hair crowned a rather angular face, and the trademark of later years, the dangling forelock, was already present. By occupying the central position in the group and striking an heroic pose, young Hitler managed to stand out among his fellows. Self-assured, perhaps even cocky, he made it perfectly clear that the *Volksschule* did not pose many difficulties for him.[1] Gliding lightheartedly through his class work, he had ample time for the boyhood games which were the mainstay of his life. He was the major instigator of all forms of rough-and-tumble amusement, and promoted more than his share of deviltry. "I was really anything but 'good' in the ordinary sense of the word," he says of this period in *Mein Kampf*. "The school work was ridiculously easy, leaving me so much free time that the sun saw more of me than my room. ... I thank heaven that a portion of the memories of those happy days still remains with me. Woods and meadows were the battlefields on which the 'conflicts' which exist everywhere in life were decided." [2]

From the beginning of his stay in Leonding, Adolf took a prominent place among the village children. In addition to his accomplishments in the classroom, he enjoyed the prestige accruing from his family's social position. His residence in a whole series of towns and attendance at two schools also gave him some flavor of a man

---

[1] Illustration, Plate 8.
[2] *Mein Kampf*, pp. 8-9.

of experience. When the children turned to the games which determined their own pecking order, Adolf again showed to advantage, for he was highly skilled in originating and carrying out enthralling play projects. Since these games – Indian wars and the like – had been a major device through which he released adjustment tensions, it was only natural that he gradually came to excel at them. The children of the village so admired his abilities that he quickly became, as he later described it, "a little ring leader." [3]

At this time (1899-1900), the Boer war broke out, and Adolf and his mates became rabid partisans of the Boers.[4] The South African conflict provided the inspiration for numerous games in an atmosphere of exotic adventure. At approximately the same time, Adolf found intriguing books in his father's library that furnished additional ideas to be carried into play. He was absorbed by a large pictorial volume on the war of 1870 which became the model for endless campaigns on the battlefields of Leonding.[5] Adventure stories also gripped his imagination. His first favorites were the tales of James Fenimore Cooper, and later, those of Cooper's German counterpart, Karl May. May's melodramas, which in Germany slowly took on the status of classics, were the creation of an ex-convict whose literary endeavors bordered on fraud.[6] Although he attempted to create the impression, both in and out of his books, that he possessed deep knowledge and experience of Indian life, May had never been in America, and his ideas about the country and the Indians were confused. His works, however, served as effective stimuli to the imagination, because they were themselves so completely imaginary. An endless procession of noble Indians and Yankees – plus the necessary villains – range through his pages amid large amounts of gush and gore. The books possess a certain soaring magic. Adolf was captivated by old Shatterhand and his companions.

Children in the isolated and conservative towns and small cities of central Europe found the free and wide-ranging adventures described by May appealing. Without his guidance it would have been difficult

[3] *Mein Kampf*, p. 6; Munich police report, 1924. *HA*, File 1760, Reel 25A.
[4] *Mein Kampf*, p. 158; "Aus Adolf Hitlers Jugendland." *HA*, File 17, Reel 1; *Rabitsch*, pp. 12-13.
[5] *Mein Kampf*, p. 6.
[6] Klaus Mann, "Cowboy Mentor of the Fuehrer," *Living Age*, November 1940, pp. 217-22.

for youngsters to hear the echo of rapid and exciting changes in the world from the quiet backwaters of their own towns and homes. Since most parents and teachers held that May was an unhealthy influence (his tales were well laced with brutality and violence), an avid young reader could simultaneously enjoy the derring-do and twit the establishment. Adolf's pursuit of fantasy and adventure was a perfectly normal direction of taste at the age of ten or eleven. Besides, the stories had a practical value: they were a mine from which he could extract material to be used in games with other children.

Yet if Hitler's infatuation with May was normal in the last years in *Volksschule*, it took on more serious overtones in later years. For Hitler never gave up Karl May. He read him in adolescence and as a young man in his twenties. Even as Reich Chancellor, he continued to be fascinated by him, rereading the whole series on the American West.[7] Furthermore, he never attempted to disguise or hide his enjoyment of, and admiration for, May's books. In the *Table Talk* he extolls May and describes how he enjoyed his work. He talked about him with nearly everyone – his press chief, his secretary, his servant and his old party comrades.[8]

What is so significant about this is that it was so atypical. Hitler very seldom described features of his childhood and development simply for their own sake. Nearly every story he told had an immediate point or was useful as a weapon in argument. He was reticent about revealing his debt to books or writers, especially those important to him in childhood and youth. One searches in vain through his writings and conversations to discover what he read and its effect upon him. Only May is acknowledged, and he is displayed without embarrassment or apology. It therefore seems safe to conclude that the childhood infatuation with May was a sincere, important, happy and, to his mind, normal phenomenon. That he clung to it so tena-

---

[7] Ward G. Price, *I Know These Dictators* (New York, 1938), p. 18; *Daim*, p. 248, note 38; Walter Goerlitz, *Adolf Hitler* (Goettingen, 1960), p. 23.
[8] *Table Talk*, p. 316; *Dietrich*, p. 149; *Zoller*, p. 46; Hans Ziegler, *Adolf Hitler Aus Dem Erleben Dargestellt* (Goettingen, 1964), p. 76; Karl Wilhelm Krause, *Zehn Jahre Kammerdiener bei Hitler* (Hamburg, n.d.), p. 51. Professor Mosse has suggested that May's writings could be fitted in with some features of *voelkisch* thought. George L. Mosse, *The Crisis of German Ideology: Intellectual Origins of the Third Reich* (New York, 1964), p. 174.

ciously, as the only clear and exposed thread to his childhood, suggests that it was a satisfying and necessary carry-over into a period when his early adjustments failed to solve the challenges of adolescence. The continued fascination with May suggests further that his elementary school years were comparatively happy and that his adolescence involved more problems than he was able to handle without a childhood prop.

The Austrian system of education, with true Germanic precision, decided at exactly what point a youth should turn away from childhood. Until the age of eleven, most boys found themselves in a position similar to Adolf's, attending a *Volksschule* with a heterogeneous group of children their own age. During these five years, little effort was required for those with above average ability. There was something almost carefree about the *Volksschule* atmosphere, perhaps to compensate in advance for the stringent discipline which would be imposed in succeeding years. At the age of eleven, this phase was abruptly terminated. The child was informed that he must put away childish things and face decisions that would determine the course of his education. Four alternate paths were laid out before him and his parents. The first choice was to leave school with only five years of *Volksschule* training. This course almost inevitably condemned the youngster to life as a day laborer, unless a combination of toil and luck brought a spot in a small office or a marginal skilled trade. A second possibility for the *Volksschule* graduate lay in the direction of specialized craft courses that trained journeymen and offered master's status to the fortunate. Both of these routes led to the lower orders of society, and in Adolf's case, either would have meant a loss of social position. Adolf and his parents were too conscious of their status to tolerate any such development. Neither of the above choices was considered, therefore, in the calculations concerning his future.

The two remaining alternatives consisted of a four-year term in the lower *Realschule* or in the *Gymnasium*, the two forms of secondary school designed to prepare a student for higher education. The *Gymnasium* emphasized classical education, while the *Realschule* was considered a center for more modern studies. Some overlap inevitably existed between the two schools, but, in general, the *Realschule* emphasized technical and scientific studies and tended to favor modern over ancient languages. No future occupation was absolutely barred by attendance at one institution rather than the other, but the *Gymnasium* was the accepted route into the professions, while the *Realschule* opened the door to a technical or engineering career. If a student deviated from the accepted pattern he could expect an arduous future. To reach the bureaucracy, for example, the normal choice would have been the *Gymnasium*, followed by the study of law at the university. The *Realschule* student might, in unusual cases, also enter the university's legal faculty, but it would have been more natural for him to complete a specialized course and enter the bureaucracy in a technical capacity. The *Gymnasium* provided certain advantages in social status, but the *Realschule* often led to more profitable careers. In any case, the significant choice facing eleven-year-olds divided those who attended either type of secondary school from those who did not. This was a major step in the formal separation of the haves from the have-nots. The Hitlers clearly affirmed that they belonged to the haves.

Between the spring of 1900, when he completed *Volksschule*, and September of the same year, when the new school term began, Adolf's educational program had to be established. Since his brother Edmund had just died, the entire hope for the family's future had fallen upon his shoulders. Technically speaking, the point at issue was merely the selection of a school, but this also raised the questions of curriculum and plans for an occupation. Alois held strong opinions on all these questions and had no intention of abdicating his authority. As his son later realized, this was partly motivated by his concept of authoritarian family control, but it also derived from his sense of duty. "It would have seemed intolerable to him to leave the final decision in such matters to an inexperienced boy having, as yet, no sense of responsibility." [9] Adolf's future involved an important family decision; Alois always made the important family decisions.

Concerning the question as to whether the boy should attend a *Realschule* or a *Gymnasium*, Alois quickly decided in favor of the *Realschule*. The *Gymnasium* was too old-fashioned for him. To a self-made man, humanistic studies appeared impractical and irrele-

---

[9] *Mein Kampf*, p. 8.

vant. The *Realschule*'s emphasis on modernity and technical excellence better suited his views, and its curriculum included a number of subjects, such as drawing, which he thought should be encouraged. Adolf was showing interest in drawing both in and outside the classroom, and his father felt that the *Realschule* would develop whatever artistic talents he possessed. In part at least, the *Realschule* decision met the boy's interests and enthusiasms, and Alois held more than a distant hope that something practical and profitable might result.

None of these considerations seem to have made any deep impression on Adolf, who was initially neither especially enthusiastic nor noticeably hostile. The decision in favor of a *Realschule* rather than a *Gymnasium* was a matter of indifference to him. The situation became serious only when Alois began to consider the fine points of his class program and the selection of an ultimate career. "It was his basic opinion and intention," Hitler wrote in *Mein Kampf,* "that, like himself, his son would and must become a civil servant. It was only natural that the hardships of his youth should enhance his subsequent achievement in his eyes, particularly since it resulted exclusively from his own energy and iron diligence. It was the pride of the self-made man which made him want his son to rise to the same position in life, or, of course, even higher if possible, especially since, by his own industrious life, he thought he would be able to facilitate his child's development so greatly." [10]

The virtues of the civil service were proverbial in the Hitler household. It was necessary that one child should be prepared for the bureaucracy, almost as noble sons once were destined for army and Church. Yet, when the actual decision had to be made, the old man ran into unexpected resistance. A serious conflict erupted between father and son because the boy refused to cooperate in Alois' plans. He claimed that he had no interest in an official's life; nothing his father could propose, through either commands or blandishments, succeeded in changing his stand. The struggle between father and son gradually became more serious. Alois became increasingly bitter and intransigent. And Adolf's whole manner of life was profoundly changed. During the years in *Realschule* (1900-1905), he emerged

[10] *Mein Kampf,* p. 7.

as a solitary, resentful, and uncooperative youth who sullenly went through the motions at home and failed in school. After compiling an excellent record in *Volksschule*, he slipped from one mediocre term to another, either failing completely (1900-1901) or barely skating by. The whole experience deeply affected his later development. It barred his way to higher education and left him with a full measure of unhappy confusion and resentment about himself, his family and his future.

The significance of this five-year period necessitates a careful examination of the facts in the case and the possible causes. The major source of information is the comparatively lengthy description in *Mein Kampf*. According to this account, the struggle began suddenly when Adolf directly rejected his father's career plans. A contest of wills followed in which Alois won the nominal victory by forcing the boy to go to school, but Adolf held on to his determination not to become an official. In the ensuing months (Hitler fails to mention that his grades in *Realschule* were unsatisfactory from the beginning) Alois tried to awaken the boy's interest in administrative work and did his best to paint alluring pictures of bureaucratic life. But Hitler says he merely "yawned and grew sick to my stomach." Eventually he brought forward a counterproposal: he wanted to become "a painter, an artist." However, the first time he mentioned this to his father, Alois rejected it emphatically: an "artist, no, never as long as I live." Finally, Hitler claims, in order to force his father to agree to an artist's career, he threatened "to stop studying altogether." When Alois failed to yield, he silently "transformed my threat into reality." [11]

This description obviously presents the young Hitler in the best possible light, for it portrays the conflict as an important confrontation between two responsible and mature people. It coincides exactly with Hitler's picture of himself as a hard and determined man who had managed to rise a long way by 1924 (when *Mein Kampf* was written) and would go on to final victory. At the same time, it is the basis for the picture of the frustrated artist who went into politics with the resolve to save Germany. Most important, it explains away his poor grades in *Realschule* and his slow maturation while at the

[11] *Mein Kampf*, pp. 9-10.

same time it makes his adolescence appear heroic – a difficult task for any politically conscious autobiographer. In fact, the story served the later Fuehrer's purposes so well that one may well ask whether or not he invented the whole episode.

Several items of evidence make it probable that a struggle over Adolf's career did in fact occur. Alois' determination to make his last son an official coincides with what we know of his outlook and manner of doing things. That Adolf decided on an artist's career during his youth is certain. The essential conditions for a conflict were, therefore, present. It should also be noted that the father was a veritable model of resolute and obstinate behavior, who had already had a serious struggle with his oldest son, Alois Jr. Furthermore, it is obvious that at some point Hitler's stubborn determination, so marked in subsequent years, must have come into the open. This issue may well have been the catalyst. An incident from a later period shows that the conflict remained very real for him. During lunch, on May 10, 1942, a conversation arose at headquarters about children's problems in school. Hitler stated that parents made an important error when they demanded that a child be good in all subjects. He added:

Parents make it worse when they try to prepare a child for a profession prematurely and then, when it doesn't work, they immediately begin to talk of a lost or misguided son. His [Hitler's] parents wished to make him enthusiastic about an official's life at the age of thirteen and dragged him to the customs office in Linz – a real bureaucratic cage – in which the old men squatted beside each other like monkeys. Since they had not considered that such a picture would awaken horror and hate rather than enthusiasm, from this point on he was left with disgust for the life of an official.[12]

---

[12] Henry Picker (ed.), *Hitlers Tischgespraeche im Fuehrerhauptquartier 1941-42* (Stuttgart, 1963), p. 324. Jetzinger denies that there was any conflict over schooling or career, believing that the whole account in *Mein Kampf* is an invention to account for Adolf's poor school record. He states that Alois could not have chosen the *Realschule* for a prospective bureaucrat. Granting that it was unusual, the choice was not impossible and was justified by the points given in the text, plus the fact, which Jetzinger ignores, that Alois had made a comfortable living without legal training. In any event, the type of school had no intrinsic importance in the conflict between father and son except that the choice of school opened up the career question. *Jetzinger* (G), pp. 98-99.

This is as strong confirming evidence as one can hope to find in a question of this kind. A conflict may be accepted as reasonably certain. This does not mean, however, that Hitler's account is faithful in all details or that he placed it in a meaningful setting. He was unable to explain why the struggle developed the way it did. In describing his decision to become an artist, he frankly says, "How it happened, I myself do not know, but one day it became clear to me that I would become a painter, an artist." [13] To get beyond spontaneous revelation as a cause of the conflict and the abrupt personality shift, it will be necessary to examine two possible explanations, one medical and one psychological.

A German physician has recently advanced the opinion that Hitler suffered from epidemic encephalitis.[14] This disease, usually contracted in childhood in association with a severe head cold or influenza, may produce middle brain damage, pass through a period of remission, and finally emerge in the form of parkinsonism in later life. In Hitler's case, the appearance of something approximating parkinsonism from the age of 53 until his death prompted the suggestion of possible epidemic encephalitis. Epidemic encephalitis may produce a dramatic change in character and personality soon after contraction of the disease, which might account for Hitler's sudden failure in school and accompanying personality troubles.

However, a number of considerations make this hypothesis highly speculative. The diagnosis was not based upon an examination of Hitler. The Fuehrer's own physicians earlier advanced a number of possible explanations other than parkinsonism for his later physical symptoms, including physical exhaustion, lack of exercise, overstrain, and drugs. Medical people who also did not see the patient but who based their opinions on secondary descriptions, discussions with the attending doctors or motion pictures have suggested other possibilities, including hysteria and parkinson's disease (*paralysis agitans*).[15] Due to the imprecise nature of the evidence, none of these alterna-

[13] *Mein Kampf*, p. 9.
[14] Johann Recktenwald, *Woran hat Adolf Hitler gelitten?* (Munich/Basel, 1963).
[15] The most important account of Hitler's later health is in Hugh Trevor-Roper, *The Last Days of Hitler* (New York, 1947), pp. 58-66. Recktenwald makes no direct reference to this material, much of which is difficult to reconcile with his diagnosis.

tives can be convincingly sustained or completely disproven. This is especially true of parkinson's disease, because, in addition to the specific malady (*paralysis agitans*), the major symptom – the tremor – may also appear in a wide range of other illnesses, including an advanced syphiloid condition and a form of epidemic encephalitis. Of these possibilities, the only one that has immediate bearing on Hitler's childhood is epidemic encephalitis, which is especially dangerous for children. Even though there is no record of severe illness, a child may contract the disease, manifest the personality change, then undergo remission – the absence of surface symptoms – for decades, only to display evidence of severe middle brain damage in later life.[16] This pattern roughly corresponds to phases of Hitler's development over a span of forty-five years, but the only satisfactory way to confirm the hypothesis would be by a thorough medical examination, especially in the later stages of the disease, or a very careful autopsy. Neither of these was conducted. The psychotic states that may accompany the disease are not pathognomonic; they are so varied, and can overlap so many other conditions, that it is not possible to diagnose encephalitis on the basis of the psychotic symptoms alone. Furthermore, one must also assume that the features of Hitler's behavior, described by contemporary observers, are in fact organic psychotic symptoms and not techniques the Fuehrer used to dominate his subordinates and visitors. For example, pupillary abnormality may be a late encephalitic symptom, but there is also strong evidence in Hitler's case that he used his famous "magical" eyes to dominate or transfix visitors in order to get them to do what he wished.[17] The number of questionable assumptions, such as this,

---

[16] Recktenwald refers to the possibility that Edmund's death from measles may have involved complications and that Adolf may have contracted epidemic encephalitis as a result. *Recktenwald*, pp. 100-102. That epidemic encephalitis occurs more frequently with measles than other childhood diseases is doubtful. One form of measles encephalitis (acute hemorrhaic encephalitis of Strümpell) has a very different history from that of epidemic encephalitis. The other form of measles encephalitis (demyelinating or allergic type of encephalitis) may resemble true epidemic encephalitis, but it is not insidious and is unlikely to have escaped medical attention.

[17] In the midst of one of his military conferences, Hitler remarked that he had to allow time for a meeting in which he had to "hypnotize" Quisling. It is difficult to escape the conclusion he knew exactly what he was doing. Helmut Heiber (ed.), *Hitlers Lagebesprechungen* (Stuttgart, 1962), p. 862.

which must be made to sustain the diagnosis of epidemic encephalitis makes it a doubtful explanation for Hitler's development. It seems more reasonable to look to the personal and family pressures that were exerted upon him for an explanation.

As noted earlier, in *Volksschule* Adolf showed strong signs of repression which was relieved by an escape into fantasy. During the *Realschule* stage, when he was called upon to assert himself more and take on additional responsibility, this defensive response simply made matters worse. Instead of trying to ease his son's adjustment problems, the father relied on his arbitrary dominance, and attempted to force the boy to conform to his wishes. This demand for rigid control on Alois' part was in flat contradiction to the adult role the boy was supposed to assume. Adolf was ordered to identify with his father, accept his values and adopt his educational and career plans. Psychological studies with adolescents have shown that this kind of arbitrary and authoritarian treatment is an excellent way to lessen a boy's identification with his father.[18] In the end, Adolf did not repudiate his father's goals; he repudiated his father. As he later said, "I did not love my father and therefore feared him more."[19] In a relationship based solely on fear and force, it was only natural that the boy would be badly confused. He had to evolve whatever defenses he could against the cold and empty relationship with his father.

Adolf seems to have faced additional difficulties rising from a delayed maturation. There are a number of indications that both physically and emotionally he developed rather slowly. In his *Volksschule* class picture he appears equal if not superior to his peers in physique and poise, but in his first *Realschule* picture he seems com-

---

Dr. H. D. Röhrs, a Hitler sympathizer and apologist, rejects Recktenwald's diagnosis of epidemic encephalitis and blames Dr. Morrell's ministrations for Hitler's apparent late parkinson symptoms. Röhrs points out many of the weaknesses in Recktenwald's case, especially the speculations about Hitler's childhood, but his object is to preserve Hitler's image from the taint of mental illness. H. E. Röhrs, *Hitler, Die Zerstoerung einer Persoenlichkeit*, (Neckargemünd, 1965).

[18] Donald E. Payne and Paul Henry Mussen, "Parent-Child Relations and Father Identification among Adolescent Boys," in *The Adolescent: A Book of Readings* (New York, 1960), p. 399.

[19] Zoller, p. 46.

paratively smaller and less significant.[20] One of his *Realschule* teachers remarked that his behavior in school was characterized by "innocuous pranks of a kind not uncommon amongst immature school boys." [21] Hitler's own descriptions of these adventures – though sharply overdrawn for dramatic effect – emphasize the kind of attention-getting devices frequently used by late-maturing youngsters.[22] This tendency also appears in Adolf's continued fascination with children's games – cowboys and Indians – which went on all through the *Realschule* years. Sexually he seems to have matured even more slowly, adding strong elements of puritanic repression that led to a muted and frustrated development. His fears and the barriers he built up around them did not initially produce overt complications, for he tended to withdraw and gain release from tension through intensive play. As he grew older, however, he resorted to sham courting devices. He attempted to make contact with girls by carrying packages for them when they walked with their mothers, or by making funny faces at them in church. When he succeeded in speaking to them or making them laugh, he quickly broke off the contact and went on to some other form of childish amusement.[23] This sexual repression apparently continued throughout his whole adolescence.[24]

The *Realschule* itself compounded Adolf's problems. It was more difficult than the *Volksschule* and required a new departure in interest and effort. Since he had at least normal intelligence and had been accustomed to excel without applying himself very much, it was easy to slip into difficulty before he realized what was happening. Once he had taken his place near the bottom of the class, an

---

[20] See photographs, Plates 8 and 9.
[21] *Jetzinger* (G), p. 106; *Jetzinger* (E), p. 69.
[22] *Table Talk*, pp. 189-95, 674, 697-98; *Zoller*, p. 47; Paul Mussen, John Conger, Jerome Kagan, *Child Development and Personality* (New York, 1963), pp. 518-19.
[23] *Zoller*, p. 48.
[24] Hitler's sexual repression is discussed in *Goerlitz and Quint*, p. 37; Douglas M. Kelley, *Twenty-Two Cells in Nuremberg* (New York, 1961), p. 153; *Daim*, pp. 221-25. The factual basis for Kurth's ideas is incorrect, but she reaches a similar conclusion. See Gertrude M. Kurth, "The Jew and Adolf Hitler," *Psychoanalytic Quarterly*, 1947, pp. 15-29. Likewise, Kubizek's description of Stephanie, even if imaginary, indicates Hitler's outlook, *Kubizek*, pp. 56-69. Also see *Hanisch*, pp. 297-98.

even greater effort was required to make up the lost ground. Here the debilitating effect of his slow maturation and the poor relations with his father made recovery more difficult. It was much easier to acquiesce in failure and to comfort his battered ego with dreams about a glorious future as an artist.[25] All the features of his life pointed in the same direction: the most effective solution to his problems was withdrawal. He became the shadowy youth who just got by – never in sufficient trouble to excite serious concern, but never effective at anything he attempted. He skirted the demands of his family but was unable to penetrate the circle of his school comrades. He stood alone, an unhappy and resentful youngster.

From the time he entered the Linz *Realschule* on September 17, 1900, Adolf's life was occupied with school routine. He made the trip from Leonding to Linz daily, sometimes by foot, in which case the journey required an hour and a half each way. More often, he took the local suburban train. The *Realschule* was in a rather gloomy building in the center of the little city of 60,000. Linz was the provincial capital of upper Austria, dominated by a middle class that strove to give it the measure of beauty and modernity appropriate to a real city. Communities like Linz suffered from the overpowering attraction of Vienna, and local boosters had to work hard to make the town appear progressive. There was an electric streetcar line, then a key status symbol, and a municipal opera house which served as a cultural center. If one arrived in Linz from Vienna or Munich, the urban affectations of this sleepy, provincial town were all too obvious, but if one came from Lambach, Hafeld, or Leonding, it possessed the confusion and excitement of a real city. In the year that Adolf entered the *Realschule*, the first auto tour from Paris to Vienna went through Linz, a sign that the capital of upper Austria was a place of some importance.[26]

The *Realschule* student from Leonding found Linz interesting, but he had little opportunity to explore. As soon as classes ended, he started out for Leonding alone. Upon his arrival he could count on

---

[25] Children with repeated school failures tend to set low goals or unrealistically high ones. Paul Mussen, et. al., *Child Development and Personality*, p. 491.
[26] *Baedeker*, pp. 119-20; *Goerlitz and Quint*, p. 24; *Rabitsch*, pp. 8-9, 82-83, and 147.

an eager reception from the younger village children who were anxious to resume their play with him.[27] Here he was the undisputed master, and the old round of conflicts and games continued as if there was no *Realschule* and no problem of maturity. When left to his own devices, he played and read as he had done before, with only a few new activities. He spent time painting and drawing and may also have had a passing contact with Wagner's music.

There were repeated difficulties between father and son. In addition, Adolf's relations with his sisters cooled, which is not surprising in a twelve-year-old. However, he retained his low opinion of them even during his years of power, when he dismissed them as "stupid geese."[28] The bonds that tied him to Klara were not severed so easily. Edmund's death increased her concern for the remaining children. She tried to hold them as tightly as possible, but she was unable to interfere effectively in the conflict between Adolf and his father. The boy was withdrawing. It became increasingly difficult to keep the lines of maternal communication open.

The academic side of Hitler's first year in *Realschule* was at best spotty. His diligence was "variable," and he failed both mathematics and natural science. Though he was enthusiastic about drawing outside of school, his classroom work in this subject was merely "adequate," rather than "outstanding." The drawings of the leading art students were hung in the drawing classroom to serve as examples for boys in future classes, but none of Hitler's found their way there.[29] He did not excel in any subject, and this, combined with his failure in two courses, did not permit him to advance to the second form.

During the year 1901-1902 Adolf repeated the first two semesters of *Realschule*. His work improved somewhat, and he managed to obtain passing grades in his courses along with favorable marks in diligence and conduct.[30] He was still working far below capacity, however, and his improvement did not occasion any relaxation of tension at home or increase his enthusiasm for school. In 1902-1903, he struggled through the second form of *Realschule*, but again the

---

[27] Jetzinger (G), pp. 100-101; Rabitsch, p. 30; Heinz, p. 27.
[28] Zoller, p. 46.
[29] Rabitsch, p. 74; Jetzinger (G), pp. 101-102; Jetzinger (E), pp. 65-66.
[30] Jetzinger (G), pp. 101-102; Jetzinger (E), p. 66.

results were mediocre. His conduct and diligence were "variable," and he failed mathematics again. He was allowed to stand a special examination in this subject in the late summer of 1903, and, after passing it, was permitted to advance to the third form in 1903-1904.[31]

If Adolf's record was poor, so were most of his impressions of the school and its staff. With few exceptions he disliked his teachers, finding them unsympathetic and dull. He was particularly unhappy about their appearance, which he later described as sloppy, "with dirty collars, unkempt beards and the like." [32] This opinion, reflecting some middle-class fastidiousness, combined with his low performance to lessen teacher interest in him. To the teachers, Adolf appeared a "cantankerous" and "lazy" lad who did not cooperate and resented reproof. His pranks were not appreciated, but they were not serious enough to be characterized as delinquency. The school records do not reveal anything unusual, and a police investigation, carried out at the time of his trial in 1924, failed to turn up any mention of serious trouble. The investigators emphasized that the rumors then current in Germany which portrayed Adolf as a wild troublemaker in *Realschule* were definitely false. What Hitler remembered as heroic encounters had grown enormously over the years. Considering the ineffectiveness of most of his childhood plans, the delinquency tales probably represented the things he had wanted to do but lacked the necessary freedom and courage to carry out.[33]

Despite his uncooperative attitude, one of his instructors took a special interest in him. Professor Huemer taught German and French and was the advisor to Hitler's class in 1902-1903. Unfortunately, Adolf did poorly in both of his subjects, and the professor never got beyond a few tentative attempts to reach him.[34] Profes-

---

[31] *Jetzinger* (G), pp. 101-102; *Jetzinger* (E), p. 66.
[32] *Picker*, p. 273.
[33] *Jetzinger* (G), p. 105; *Jetzinger* (E), pp. 68-69; Munich police report, 1924, *HA*, File 1760, Reel 25A; *Table Talk*, pp. 189-95, 674, 697-98; *Zoller*, p. 47.
[34] Huemer's case is complex. In 1924 he wrote a very unflattering summary of Hitler which he sent to Hitler's lawyer during the treason trial. *Jetzinger* (G), pp. 104-106; *Jetzinger* (E), pp. 68-69. After Hitler triumphed in Germany, he backtracked and said polite but empty things about him. Huemer letter, *NA*, T-84, Roll 4, File 4. Finally he resorted to the most fawning and humiliating glorification of the Fuehrer. *Rabitsch*, pp. 58-65. On the other

sor Poetsch, a history teacher, succeeded in awakening his interest in history, although he had no special concern for the boy himself. Poetsch used vivid descriptions and imaginative constructions to awaken his young charges' curiosity about the heroes and events of the German past.[35] Adolf was enthralled by the stories, even though they did not stimulate him to produce good grades in history. All he acquired was a taste for historical romance, which he considered the genuine article; this enthusiasm was easily absorbed into his world of dreams and play. A light sprinkling of romantic history enhanced the wars and Indian campaigns that raged in Leonding nearly every afternoon. The great figures of German myth and romance were especially appealing, and their attraction was enhanced by the compositions of Richard Wagner. Adolf saw his first Wagnerian performance at the Linz opera house during his second *Realschule* year and was soon addicted to the music and drama of the master of Bayreuth.[36]

Adolf's feelings about politics during his *Realschule* years are especially important in tracing the course of his career. As an established political figure in the 1920's, Hitler stated, in a deceptively simple manner, that he had taken an important political step when he "became a nationalist" in secondary school.[37] Together with most of the boys in his class, he supported the cause of German rights and privileges, seizing every opportunity to proclaim devotion to the cause of "Germandom."[38] However, the question of German "nationalism" in Austria at the turn of the century was much more complicated than might be imagined from Hitler's description. During the 1880's, the nationality struggles within the Empire had in-

---

side, however, when the Hitler family doctor, who was a Jew, needed help after the *Anschluss*, only two prominent people came forward to aid him. One of these was Huemer. "Bericht zur Sache Dr. Bloch," *HA*, File 17, Reel 1.

[35] *Mein Kampf*, pp. 14-15. After the *Machtergreifung*, the story circulated that Poetsch had become a recluse. *Rabitsch*, pp. 53-54. Jetzinger accepted this and added that he withdrew in order to cut all connections with Hitler. *Jetzinger* (G), pp. 107-108; *Jetzinger* (E), p. 70. The last point is incorrect; the record of correspondence between Poetsch and Hitler between 1929 and 1939 is in *HA*, File 15, Reel 1.

[36] *Mein Kampf*, pp. 16-17.
[37] *Mein Kampf*, p. 10.
[38] *Heinz*, pp. 28-29; *Mein Kampf*, pp. 12-13.

tensified and led to the formation of powerful German national organizations. At the local level, especially in mixed language areas, cultural protective associations came into existence. The *Schulvereine* and the *Schutzvereine* were the most important of the large organizations, but gymnastic societies and shooting clubs also played a part. Naturally enough, the schools performed an important role in the activities of the Germanic organizations. Secondary schools, such as Hitler's *Realschule,* as well as institutions of higher education, became the strongholds of those who sought a German monopoly of education.[39]

During the late 1890's the crisis over the Badeni language decrees intensified these organizational efforts and endowed them with a bitter crusading tone that seeped into every corner of German Austria. Such conditions created an ideal climate for the dreams of glory of adventuresome schoolboys, and the children responded by providing constant demonstrations of their loyalty to Germandom. The school authorities had to tolerate these activities, since suppression would have exposed them to the kind of criticism that most institutions wish to avoid. Additionally, most faculty members were sympathetic to the organizations defending German culture because its preservation was a sacred cause for them too.[40]

The position of the schools was made more difficult because some nationalist organizations favored extreme solutions. Under the leadership of Georg von Schoenerer, the extremists enjoyed a certain vogue, especially in the area of Vienna. Schoenerer, an able fanatic, had political skill, but his combative personality led to dissension within the *Alldeutsche* or Pan-German movement, which he founded. By the mid-1890's, German nationalists were divided between the *Deutsche Fortschrittspartei*, which accepted both Austria and Jews; the more radical *Deutsche Volkspartei* which was mildly anti-Semitic but accepted Austria; and the *Alldeutsche* or Pan-Germans, who wished to kill Austria and were already racial anti-Semites.[41] As if this was not chaotic enough, Schoenerer attempted, in the late 1890's,

---

[39] Paul Molisch, *Geschichte der deutschnationalen Bewegung in Oesterreich von ihren Anfaengen bis zum Zerfall der Monarchie* (Jena, 1926), pp. 81-87, 112-13, and 118-22; *Ferber*, pp. 13-14.
[40] *Mein Kampf*, pp. 12-13; *Rabitsch*, pp. 34 and 47.
[41] Molisch, *Geschichte*, p. 179; *Ferber*, p. 10.

to force his followers to break with the Catholic Church and join the Protestants, who were supposedly more loyal to German nationalism. The demand that the Pan-Germans also participate in this *Los von Rom* movement produced another split in the ranks of the German radicals; in 1901 a new Pan-German movement, independent of Schoenerer, was established under one of the master's lieutenants, Karl Wolf.[42]

The proliferation of parties and factions hopelessly split the vote and insured that no German party which stressed nationalism could effectively guide policy in the Austrian parliament. Prior to 1907, the champions of German nationalism were dependent on a rigidly controlled suffrage law that withheld the ballot from the lower classes. Each of the national parties managed to collect enough votes in the various German districts to survive, but by the turn of the century the *Alldeutsche* had suffered mortal defeats in Vienna and lower Austria, where it remained little more than a political curiosity. Only in Bohemia, where mixed ethnic districts and a Czech resurgence threatened German supremacy, did the *Alldeutsche* have any mass appeal after 1900.[43]

In the solid German areas, such as Linz, the extreme nationalist groups had no chance of winning an important share of power at the turn of the century, even with an electorate restricted to the propertied classes. Schoenerer received some polite applause as one of the forerunners of the German cause, but few "reasonable and respectable people" joined his organizations or voted for his futile candidates. Schoenerer, and later Wolf, too, maintained token organizations in communities like Linz. They generally ran or authorized little extremist papers like the *Linzer Fliegende Blaetter*, a weekly, or the *Alldeutsche Blaetter*, which appeared twice a month. How-

---

[42] Ferber, pp. 27-28; Eduard Pichl, *Georg Schoenerer* (Berlin, 1938), Vol. VI, pp. 383 ff.; Heinrich Schnee, *Georg Ritter von Schoenerer: Ein Kaempfer fuer Alldeutschland* (Reichenberg, 1943), pp. 80-81; Rudolf Kuppe, *Karl Lueger und seine Zeit* (Vienna, 1933), p. 303.
[43] Rudolf Sieghart, *Die Letzten Jahrzehnte einer Grossmacht. Menschen, Voelker, Probleme des Habsburger-Reichs* (Berlin, 1932), pp. 303-304; *Kuppe*, p. 310; Henry Cord Meyer, *Mitteleuropa in German Thought and Action, 1815-1945* (The Hague, 1955), pp. 39-40; *Pichl*, Vol. IV, pp. 111-13, and Vol. V, pp. 82-83; and Kurt Schuschnigg, *My Austria* (New York, 1938), p. 50.

ever, the Pan-Germans, in whatever faction they happened to appear, were less a political party in Linz than a cult of devotees.[44] In the eyes of adolescent schoolboys, though, the situation was somewhat different. The devotion of the *Alldeutsche* to symbols and childish games could not help but touch a young man's heart. The cornflower was selected as the symbol of Schoenerer's movement because it was the favorite of the old Emperor of Germany, William I.[45] Wearing the cornflower was a safe way to indicate that one's Germanic heart yearned to cross the border. When the Austrian national anthem was played, the Pan-German supporters customarily sang the Reich German lyrics (*Deutschland ueber Alles*); the music of the two anthems was the same. The Pan-Germans' concern for the purity of race and language led them to advocate the revival of linguistic and social forms which they thought were old Germanic. They tried to substitute Germanic terms for Latin and adopted a Germanic calendar. Within their ranks, the Germanic "Heil" became the standard greeting and toast.[46]

Most of this was adult nonsense and gave the *Alldeutsche* members the appearance of antiquarian cranks, but their outlook was tailored to the adolescent mind. Many of Schoenerer's enthusiasms paralleled interests which young Adolf developed in these years. The Pan-Germans venerated Wagner as a nationalist hero and were primarily responsible for the creation and extension of the Wagner cult as part of the German nationalist program.[47] Schoenerer also supported the Boers and even attempted to establish an embargo on Austria's meager shipments of war material to Britain during the South African

---

[44] Pichl, Vol. VI, pp. 132 and 548; Schnee, *Schoenerer*, pp. 82-83; Gustav Adolf v. Metnitz, *Die Deutsche National-Bewegung 1871-1933* (Berlin, 1939), pp. 42-43; Georges Weil, *Le Pangermanisme en Autriche* (Paris, 1904), pp. 226-44; Robert A. Kann, *The Multinational Empire: Nationalism and National Reform in the Habsburg Monarchy, 1848-1918*, 2 vols. (New York, 1950), I, p. 100.
[45] Pichl, Vol. II, p. 430.
[46] Pichl, Vol. IV, pp. 546-47; Ferber, p. 25. An interesting example of this activity appears in Pichl. All his months are written in old Germanic. As he explains in the preface, this was intended to reduce foreign contamination, especially that of Latin and the Catholic Church. The page numbers of the preface are, humorously enough, in Roman numerals. *Pichl*, Vol. I, p. xviii.
[47] Pichl, Vol. IV, pp. 586-87; Schnee, *Schoenerer*, pp. 17-20.

conflict.⁴⁸ The *Alldeutsche*, like others who shared the emerging *voelkisch* ideology, also stressed general concepts with a special appeal for young people. Rejecting the uncertainties and changes that characterized modern life, they glorified the eternal verities represented by home, soil, Germanic culture and the *Volk*. The need for a social and political program which would "root" men in this true Germanic life was a constant theme in their propaganda. This version had genuine appeal, especially for adolescents looking for self-awareness and established goals in a rapidly changing society which provided few clear guideposts. One could immerse oneself in the *Volk* and find the sure footing and fixed relationships upon which to build a clear sense of identity and purpose.⁴⁹

During his *Realschule* years, however, Hitler did not undertake a systematic study of *Alldeutsche* aims, nor did he consciously commit himself to the program of any political party.⁵⁰ He merely absorbed many of the symbols, attitudes and enthusiasms that the *Alldeutsche* favored. These features were extreme and totally impractical in the eyes of most adults but they appealed to him. Through them, he could rebel and make his mark while enjoying a measure of safety on the fringes of radical nationalism.

A belief in German national superiority and the emphasis on blood as the carrier of this primacy played an important part in Hitler's thinking. During his secondary school years he acquired an emotional commitment to this idea, although, as yet, he had no theory of racial or national differences. The closely related position, also advocated by the Pan-Germans, that all Germans belonged in one Reich, left important marks upon him, though it is doubtful whether he had any concrete idea of the vast and revolutionary changes implicit in this belief.

Incidentally, Adolf's anti-Habsburg sentiments provided another means of picking at his father. Alois supported nationalist causes, but only to the degree that they established firm defenses around

---

⁴⁸ Pichl, Vol. V, pp. 123-24.
⁴⁹ An extended discussion of the *voelkisch* ideology and "rootedness" appears in Mosse, pp. 16 ff.
⁵⁰ Hitler's description indicates this. *Mein Kampf*, pp. 13-14. Later he stated that he sympathized strongly with Pan-Germanism before he came to Vienna but that he really studied it for the first time in the capital.

German privileges, especially in the imperial service. Even then, he was not a fanatical opponent of the claims made by other nationalities. Ethnic and religious prejudice did not color his personal relations; his best friend was a Czech. What Alois could not tolerate, as a devoted subject and servant of the crown, was the suggestion that the Habsburg realm be destroyed and that the Austrian Germans become dependent on the Prussians, whom he thoroughly disliked.[51] When his combative and obnoxious son discovered Alois' vulnerability in this area, the boy must have been secretly pleased. A few well-timed anti-Habsburg remarks, or prominent displays of the cornflower, could penetrate the old man's defenses just as well as a miserable school record or hints about an artist's career.

In contrast to the ultra-nationalist doctrines of the *Alldeutsche,* which profoundly effected Adolf, its counterpart, the *Los von Rom* movement, made little impression upon him. He was skeptical about the Church from an early date and persistently annoyed his religious instructor in the *Realschule,* but this had a minimal influence on his home life.[52] His father had long been suspicious of the Church and cool towards religious influences in the schools; he found it difficult to crush the boy's game of baiting the priest. However, neither Adolf nor his father accepted the positive side of the *Los von Rom* movement, which called for a conversion to Protestantism.[53] The Linz criminal police, when tracking down rumors about Hitler's youth, emphasized that he had not played a part in the *Los von Rom* movement while in Linz.[54]

With Adolf positively affected by racial nationalism but largely

---

[51] Without substantiating evidence, except the fact that Alois was anticlerical, some writers have assumed that he supported Schoenerer. *Fodor,* p. 687; *Goerlitz and Quint,* p. 28; and *Daim,* p. 191. Anticlericalism was not a monopoly of Schoenerer's group. Other parties, such as the Progressives and the *Deutsche Volkspartei,* held the same position. Schoenerer's Pan-Germanic and anti-Semitic position ran counter to Alois' whole life and career. The direct evidence against Alois' being a supporter of Schoenerer is in *Jetzinger* (G), pp. 60 and 73; *Jetzinger* (E), pp. 44 and 53. Wesseley, Alois' Czech friend, remained close to him all of his later life and was one of his pallbearers.
[52] *Rabitsch,* pp. 66-67; *Table Talk,* pp. 188-92; *Greiner,* pp. 46-49.
[53] In Vienna, Hitler sounded pro-Lutheran (see below, p. 139), but later he was much more sympathetic to Catholicism. *Table Talk,* pp. 89, 142 and 412-13.
[54] Munich police report, 1924. *HA,* File 1760, Reel 25A.

unaffected by the *Los von Rom* movement, the question of his relation to organized anti-Semitism arises. Anti-Semitic movements had been active in Austria since the early 1870's, and had managed to intertwine their activities and doctrines with those of radical German groups. Prior to the late 1880's, there were a handful of racial anti-Semites and a few who attacked the Jews on religious grounds, but the mainstream of anti-Semitism consisted of those who struck at liberal capitalism by hitting at its hinge point, the Jews. The anti-Semitic movements came to life after the crash of 1873 and undercut the liberals' political position. This forced the liberals to slow down their attacks on the traditional powers, especially the Church. Anti-Semites demanded, and in part received, palliatives to soften the effects of capitalist competition on the lower middle class. Once these successes had been registered, the broad popularity of political anti-Semitism began to abate.[55] The political aspirations of the Slavic groups, which increased sharply in the 1880's and early 1890's, also contributed to the weakening of political anti-Semitism. In the regions of greatest national rivalry, the German radicals were afraid of losing the support of German Jews.[56] Economic and political anti-Semitism slowly atrophied as liberalism declined and the capitalist system was weakened. During its heyday, this form of anti-Semitism had not hesitated to use murderous propaganda against the Jews and had succeeded in awakening a large amount of anti-Jewish hatred. There were no pogroms, however, and the movement lost its most violent overtones after the social and economic conditions on which it rested had been altered. Exceptions to the latter statement can be found, such as the vulgar Jew-baiting *Deutsche Volksblatt,* which carried on in Vienna far into the twentieth century, but these were

[55] P. G. Pulzer, *The Rise of Political Anti-Semitism in Germany and Austria* (New York, 1964), pp. 127-89. *Drage*, pp. 588-89; Kann, *Multi*, I, pp. 101-103; *May*, pp. 59-68; Oscar Karbach, "The Founder of Political Antisemitism: Georg von Schoenerer," *Jewish Social Studies*, January 1945, p. 15; Max Grunwald, *Vienna* (Jewish Communities Series, Philadelphia, 1936), pp. 423-25. Molisch, and, to a degree, Mayer, hold that the anti-Semitic movements were triggered by the nationality struggles rather than the crash of 1873. Molisch, *Geschichte*, pp. 140-42; Sigmund Mayer, *Ein Juedischer Kaufmann, 1831 bis 1911, Lebenserinnerungen* (Leipzig, 1911), pp. 279-80.
[56] Oscar Jazi, *The Dissolution of the Habsburg Monarchy* (Chicago, 1929), p. 174; *Metnitz*, p. 112; Paul Molisch, *Politische Geschichte der deutschen Hochschulen in Oesterreich von 1848 bis 1918* (Vienna, 1939), p. 122.

local phenomena, no longer in the mainstream of events. Beneath the surface, of course, the era of social and economic anti-Semitism had left a large, but temporarily quiescent, pool of prejudice against Jews.[57]

Even as the first wave of organized anti-Semitism began to recede, another and more violent current emerged. The same Schoenerer who had fathered the Pan-Germanic movement attempted to play down economic, social and confessional questions in favor of an attack on alleged racial characteristics of Jews. Racism was on the upswing at the end of the century as a scientific explanation of biological and social phenomena. Popular agitators throughout the West were quick to seize upon race as a scientific, materialistic justification for their theoretical arguments. What Schoenerer said in Central Europe was not very different from white supremacist and Anglo-Saxon arguments then prevalent in America.[58]

Prior to the turn of the century, Vienna was the major campaigning ground of the racial anti-Semites. After 1904-1905 they became ineffective in the capital, and, following the lead of the extreme German nationalists, they transferred their main operations to Bohemia. In upper Austria, specifically Linz, racial anti-Semitism never acquired a broad appeal. The area was almost unanimously German and only indirectly touched by the economic and ethnic struggles which gripped so much of the Empire. Similarly anti-Semitism, in its social and economic phase, had never been as important there as it was in Vienna. During periods of excitement, the people of Linz went along with slogans imported from Vienna. Small groups of radicals were ready to proselytize for the Pan-Germanic and anti-Semitic cause at all times. But it should be emphasized that the latter were distinctly in the minority in the early twentieth century.[59]

Hitler claimed that he was not an anti-Semite in Linz and that his family, being cosmopolitan and liberal, distinctly frowned upon anti-

---

[57] Karbach, p. 28; Sigmund Mayer, *Die Wiener Juden, 1700-1900* (Vienna and Berlin, 1918), pp. 473-79.
[58] Three recent studies have investigated various features of the emergence of a *voelkisch* and racial anti-Semitic ideology in Central Europe in the period before World War I. Fritz Stern, *The Politics of Cultural Despair* (New York, 1965); *Pulzer*; and *Mosse*.
[59] Pichl, Vol. VI, pp. 132 and 548; Schnee, *Schoenerer*, pp. 82-83.

Semitism as a mark of backwardness and lack of education.[60] He further asserted that he had found references to what he called "religious quarrels" unpleasant, if not revolting, due to his own liberal and tolerant outlook.[61] The description of the family attitude coincides well with what we know of Alois' convictions, but Adolf's account of his own views was probably exaggerated. A boy who knew him intimately in Linz claimed that he was distinctly anti-Semitic prior to his departure for Vienna in 1907.[62] Adolf apparently picked up some traces of social anti-Semitism at the *Realschule* or through his reading and play. It seems likely that it was the outgrowth of schoolboy snobbery, plus a few echoes from the radical anti-Semitic propaganda of Schoenerer's friends. The vast majority of the students with whom Hitler went through *Realschule* were German Catholics, but there were a few Jews, Czechs and Protestants. A breakdown of the school records in this period shows one Italian, one Serb, four Czechs, and 323 Germans. There were 299 Catholics, 14 Protestants, one Greek Orthodox, and 15 Jews. In Adolf's class, 1B, during the spring of 1902, there were 28 Catholics, five Protestants, and six Jews; all the students were listed as being German nationals.[63] Under the circumstances, some classroom anti-Semitism was possible, perhaps even natural. Hitler may have cultivated this antipathy until it became a generalized distaste, perhaps unconsciously reinforced by the peripheral currents of anti-Semitic propaganda. However, he was probably not a political nor even an ideological anti-Semite. He was not committed to anti-Semitic theory nor to any anti-Semitic organization, and, as yet, he remained almost completely ignorant of racial anti-Semitism.

[60] *Mein Kampf*, p. 51. Hitler uses the term "cosmopolitan" to denote a liberal lack of prejudice. This was a word commonly applied to the opposition by the anti-Semites. *Pichl*, Vol. III, p. 106. Hitler stated also that he was not anti-Semitic in Linz in his defense speech in 1924 (*Adolf Hitlers Reden* [Munich, 1934], p. 96) and in his autobiographical sketch of 1921. *HA*, File 17, Reel 1. The old assumption that an anti-Semitic child signified an anti-Semitic family is disposed of in Nathan W. Ackermann and Marie Jahoda, *Anti-Semitism and Emotional Disorder: A Psychoanalytic Interpretation* (New York, 1950), p. 84.
[61] *Mein Kampf*, p. 52.
[62] *Kubizek*, p. 79, qualified by *Daim*, pp. 37-38.
[63] Linz *Realschule* records. *HA*, File 653, Reel. 5. Obviously there is no correlation between "good and bad contacts" with Jews and the growth of anti-Semitism. See *Ackermann*, p. 83.

During his first years in the *Realschule*, Adolf drifted, indirectly affected by the political forces which surrounded him but primarily concerned with his own problems. Despite his inner torment and inability to master his father or school, life in the Hitler household was secure and tranquil. On January 3, 1903 the situation suddenly changed.

His father had not been in good health for a few years, following a severe attack of influenza in December 1901, and a lung hemorrhage in August 1902. Little alteration had been made in his manner of life, though. On the morning of January 3rd, he had gone off to the Gasthaus Stiefler as usual. He had just taken his glass of wine, after scornfully rejecting the newspaper handed to him because it was "too black," i.e., clerical, when he collapsed. He was moved into an adjoining room, and a doctor was summoned, but he arrived too late. The 65-year-old Alois died almost immediately.[64]

---

[64] *Goerlitz and Quint*, p. 34; *Fodor*, p. 687; *Jetzinger* (G), p. 72; *Jetzinger* (E), p. 52.

V

THE EARLY YOUTH

In the days immediately following Alois' death, Klara and the children had to take care of all the numbing chores which mark the end of one era and the beginning of another. The formal announcement of death was printed and sent to relations and acquaintances. A long, laudatory obituary appeared in the Linz paper. The funeral itself was costly and ostentatious enough to usher out an Imperial Customs Official. The body was interred in the Leonding cemetery under a stone which bore a portrait of the deceased and an inscription:

> Here rests in God
> Alois Hitler
> Higher Customs Officer and Householder
> Died 3 January, 1903, in his 65th year.[1]

The formal arrangement for the funeral and burial was merely the first of the problems facing Klara. Her husband's estate had to be settled, the pensions arranged, and the legal position of herself and the children clarified. Under the standing regulations of the customs office, she received a lump-sum payment at the time of Alois' death of 605 kronen (302½ florins). She was also entitled to draw an annual pension half as large as her husband's and a yearly payment of 240 kronen for each child under twenty-four who was not self-supporting. Excluding the lump-sum payment, Klara received a first-year pension of 1,930 kronen for herself and the three children. This

---

[1] *Jetzinger* (G), p. 73; *Jetzinger* (E), pp. 52-53; "Aus Adolf Hitlers Jugendland." *HA*, File 17, Reel 1A. A copy of the announcement is in the Veit family material, yet there is no indication of a contact between the two families during the preceding twenty-six years. *HA*, File 17A, Reel 1A.

THE EARLY YOUTH 91

was approximately 500 kronen less than the family had received while Alois was alive, and in view of reduced expenditures, probably resulted in no decline in its standard of living.[2]

The arrangements with the customs office were completed in a routine manner, but the settling of the estate involved complications. Under the law, Klara, a mere female, could act as guardian only in concert with a second, male, guardian. To meet this requirement, Alois' old friend, Josef Mayerhofer, was appointed guardian of the children.[3] Mayerhofer and Klara set aside part of the estate as legacies payable to the children at the age of eighteen. Alois Junior, who was eligible for immediate payment, received the minimum required by law, 305 kronen, from his father, and the additional 1,000 kronen that his mother, Franziska Matzelberger, had left for him. Adolf, Paula, and Angela each received 652 kronen from their father, and Angela, the only other child old enough to receive immediate payment, also obtained the 1,000 kronen that Franziska had left her. The bequests for young Alois and Angela seem to have been met by using available funds, but the money due Adolf and Paula was covered by a lien on the family home. Four years earlier, Alois had paid 7,700 kronen for the house, of which 5,200 kronen had been paid in cash and 2,500 carried as a mortgage. None of the mortgage had been retired, so Klara's capital consisted of approximately 3,700 kronen (5,000 kronen, less 1,300 kronen due Adolf and Paula), assuming the value of the house had not diminished.[4] The family emerged from the legal proceedings in a solid position, with sizeable sums set aside for the children, and an adequate income backed by comfortable reserves.

Alois' death was, of course, much more than a financial problem. After the family had struggled through the technical difficulties, the real adjustment still lay before them. They had to feel their way amid bruised emotions and the sudden and startling discovery, made a dozen times a day, that Alois was gone, and things would never be the same. We do not know what scars were left on Klara and the girls by Alois' passing, nor do we have reasonable grounds for speculation, but significant changes occurred in the framework of

[2] *Jetzinger* (G), pp. 124-25; *Jetzinger* (E), pp. 79-81.
[3] A summary of the legal situation appears in *Coldstream*, p. 72.
[4] *Jetzinger* (G), pp. 126-27; *Jetzinger* (E), pp. 81-83.

Adolf's life. The great force which had determined the conditions under which he lived was gone. He immediately gained more freedom and saw his position within the family enhanced. Klara did not allow Alois' ideals and goals to perish completely. She used his memory as her strongest support in guiding the boy, but her pleading and urging was a pale shadow of the old patriarch's mandates. All Klara really wanted, in contrast to the set program of her husband, was for the boy to finish school, make something of himself, and be happy.[5]

For his part, Adolf was little more than a composite of pleasurable games and dreams bound together tenuously by the desire to stand up against his father and show that he could be powerful, determined, and, if occasion demanded, cruel. Suddenly, all that remained of his father were memories and a name. This ghostly father was inaccessible, and the pleasure to be gained by thwarting him was gone. However, in a peculiar, intangible form, he was still there. He lived on in Klara's admonitions and in the boy's memory, which perhaps contained a few pangs of conscience. Adolf still refused to carry out his wishes. He muddled along in the old way, pointlessly failing and dreaming, with no purpose and little hope.

In the semester that followed Alois' death (Spring 1903), a new arrangement was made for Adolf's schooling in order to get him through a difficult adjustment period without further damage to his academic record. Klara placed him in a home for schoolboys (*Kostplatz*) in Linz, where he lived during the week and then came home to Leonding on the weekend. Adolf was polite but reserved to the woman who ran the home, a Frau Sekira, and also to the five children who stayed there. He never broke through the formal form of address (*Sie*) with any of them, and spent most of his time reading and drawing.[6] In school his record, as usual, was barely passing, and he failed mathematics, which meant that he had to take another makeup examination in the fall in order to advance to the third class.[7]

[5] *Kubizek*, pp. 37, 108-109.
[6] *Goerlitz and Quint*, pp. 34-35; *Jetzinger* (G), p. 103, rejects this account, but cites no evidence for his rejection except to refer to the class picture of the *Realschule* which does not seem very relevant.
[7] *Jetzinger* (G), p. 102; *Jetzinger* (E), p. 66.

The completion of one more mediocre school year, coming as it did on the heels of Alois' death, must have cast a gloomy shadow over the prospect of a summer in Leonding. Klara and her children packed all the vacation necessities in two great trunks and set off by train for the family home in Spital. Sister Theresia and the rest of the Schmidt family were still residing in house #24, and it was there that Klara and the children spent the summer.[8] Schmidt's holding had become the center of the Hiedler-Poelzl clan in Spital. In addition to the Schmidts, Klara's mother resided there, together with the third sister, the hunchback Johanna.[9] Spital #24 was an old-fashioned peasant farm which Schmidt had turned into a mildly profitable undertaking. He had several fields and a little woodland. The Hitler children found it an ideal setting in which to run off tensions created by their father's death. Companionship with her mother and sisters provided Klara with an opportunity to recover from her emotional losses and to prepare for her new life as a widowed mother when she returned home.

The country atmosphere did not bring any great change in Adolf's activities. He spent the bulk of his time reading, drawing, and playing with the young Schmidt children. He liked the woods but did not appreciate field work, which he managed to avoid in favor of his private amusements.[10] Apparently neither his mother nor the Schmidts attempted to interfere with him. By this time, he had shed most of his need for companionship, becoming as he later said, something of a "solitary," [11] who did not require other people to interest or amuse him.

Still, Spital was a pleasant spot in which to pass the summer; the vacation probably ended all too quickly. The arrangement had been successful, and the family returned to Spital for the following

---

[8] Statements by Johann Schmidt and Maria Schmidt (October 16 and October 23, 1938), and report on Hitler by Niederoesterreichische Landesamtsdirektion. *HA*, File 17, Reel 1.
[9] *Die Ahnentafel*, p. 40.
[10] Statement by Johann Schmidt. *HA*, File 17, Reel 1.
[11] *Table Talk*, p. 360. Hitler also impressed others as a solitary youth. Bloch, p. 36; Heinz, p. 28. Some observers have considered this an essential feature of his makeup. Roberts, pp. 7-8; Medicus, "A Psychiatrist Looks at Hitler," *New Republic*, April 26, 1939, pp. 326-27.

three summers. Adolf went back alone in 1908.[12] But in 1905, the summer's end meant that the boy had to make the unpleasant trek back to school. He successfully completed the makeup examination in mathematics in September, and went on to the third term of *Realschule*. While he was enduring the preliminaries of the school year, his half-sister, Angela, was making preparations to leave the household. On September 14, 1903, she married an assistant tax collector named Leo Raubal, who was stationed in Linz. The marriage was hardly a matter of great joy to Adolf, who was uncertain whom he disliked more, Angela or Raubal.[13] There was some consolation for him in the fact that Angela's marriage actually improved the financial condition of the Hitlers. With her departure, their gross income declined by only 480 kronen a year, leaving a comfortable 1,690 kronen for Klara and the two children.

During the year 1903-1904, life in the Hitler household seems to have flowed along with a minimum of worry and excitement. Adolf continued to slip by in school. His mother's fears about his poor record remained, but he had been on the edge of failure for three years, and there had been no serious consequences. As a third-year student, however, with more know-how and freed from the danger of paternal interference, he was emboldened to make a nuisance of himself. He constantly baited his teachers, particularly the unfortunate man providing religious instruction. An increasing interest in sex led him to the adult part of a wax museum for some three-dimensional enlightenment. He also saw his first motion picture in a small theater near the southern railroad station in Linz.[14]

From Klara's point of view, the most important event of early 1904 was, most likely, Adolf's confirmation, which occurred on May 22, 1904. An old friend of the family, Emmanuel Lugert, who had served as one of Alois' pallbearers, acted as sponsor. The confirma-

---

[12] There is direct evidence that Hitler was in Spital in 1903, 1905 and 1908. Maria Schmidt says he was there every year after 1903, and the account in the text follows that statement. Statement of Maria Schmidt. *HA*, File 17, Reel 1. Whether he was there or not in 1904, 1906 and 1907 is not a critical issue.

[13] For his dislike of Angela see *Zoller*, p. 46. For his dislike of Leo see *Kubizek*, p. 30. A sketch of the main events of Angela's life appears in *Jetzinger* (E), p. 42.

[14] *Table Talk*, pp. 188, 191 and 195.

tion took place in the Linz Cathedral. After the ceremony, Lugert and his wife took Adolf to their home for lunch, followed by a drive in a carriage and pair. Since Adolf was so prosperous that he already possessed two watches, Lugert bought him a special prayerbook and gave him a savings bank book with a small deposit in it. However, the boy failed to respond to the Lugerts' approaches and remained sulky and noncommital. Throughout the service and the later ride he continued to scowl and behave unpleasantly. When the party returned to Leonding, he was met by a gang of yelling boys, and ran off immediately "charging around the house playing Indians." [15] Little wonder that the Lugerts went away feeling that he was a rather strange fifteen-year-old.

During the school year 1903-1904, Hitler compiled another mediocre record. This time he failed French, and a makeup examination in this subject awaited him in the fall. The family made the trip to Spital again during this summer and followed the same pattern of activities as during the previous year. Back in Leonding in September, Adolf took the makeup examination prepared by his French instructor, Professor Huemer. Since Huemer was still traveling in France at the time of the examination, the tests were actually administered by a Professor Groag. Adolf received a passing mark, but only on condition that he not return to the Linz *Realschule* for the fourth term.[16] The years of dallying and passive resistance had finally caught up with him, or so it seemed.

His mother immediately enrolled him in the neighboring *Realschule* at Steyr. Since this school was fifty miles from Leonding, Klara rented a room for him in the house of a family named Cichini at Gruenmarkt # 19 in Steyr. Soon after his conditional pass in the French examination (September 1904), he left home and moved into the house on the Gruenmarkt.[17] Some of the students in the new *Realschule* made life difficult for the newcomer, viewing him with suspicion as an outsider. Hitler disliked the town and later described it as "conservative and clerical." He was fond of his land-

---

[15] Jetzinger (G), pp. 115-17; Jetzinger (E), pp. 74-75.
[16] Jetzinger (G), p. 102; Jetzinger (E), p. 66. Letter of Prof. Huemer, April 28, 1935, *NA*. T-84, Roll 4, File 3.
[17] *Table Talk*, pp. 193-94; statement by Gregor Goldbacher. *HA*, File 17, Reel 1.

lady, however, and struck up a friendship with a boy named Gustav, who also lived with the Cichini family. The change in schools did not improve his grades during the first semester. To at least one of his teachers, Professor Goldbacher, he appeared shy and withdrawn, and a bit depressed. The professor attributed this, as well as his low achievement, to the fact that this was his first time away from home and mother.[18] During the first semester he failed German, mathematics, and stenography, but received good marks in gymnastics and free-hand drawing. The rest of his subjects were divided between "adequate" and "satisfactory." His diligence was described as "variable" and his handwriting as "displeasing." [19]

The overall record during the first semester in Steyr, coupled with his mediocre achievement during four years at Linz, placed Hitler in a difficult situation. Unless he made marked improvement in the second semester, he faced more makeup examinations and the possibility of having to repeat the year. Worse still, he was approaching another important hurdle in the educational system. After completing the fourth year of *Realschule*, his record would be evaluated to see whether he should be admitted to an *Oberrealschule*, the next rung up the ladder.

As his record stood in the winter of 1904-1905, a strong effort would have been required to enable him to pass the fourth-year courses. A near miracle would have been necessary to make him eligible for *Oberrealschule*. These chill facts seem to have made some impression on him. In the second semester, his work improved markedly, even though he did not completely emerge from his torpor. At the end of the semester, he again received "excellent" in gymnastics and drawing, while his grades improved in diligence, religion, German, mathematics, geography, and history. Whereas he had failed mathematics and German in the fall, he passed in the spring. He also passed a singing course, which replaced stenography in the spring curriculum. Although his grade in physics fell during the second semester, it was still passing. Only geometry and geometric drawing fell from pass to fail. The overall record was much better, but he still faced a makeup examination in geometry and was

---

[18] Statement by Gregor Goldbacher. *HA*, File 17, Reel 1.
[19] Heiden, *Der Fuehrer*, p. 49. His handwriting remained poor, as he knew. *Table Talk*, p. 191; *Zoller*, p. 18.

THE EARLY YOUTH

not allowed to graduate, much less advance to *Oberrealschule*.[20] The train trip from Steyr to Linz must have been a long and painful one in July 1905. When he arrived back home, he went not to the familiar garden house in Leonding, which his mother had sold on June 21st, three weeks before his return, but to a rented flat at Humboldtstrasse #31, in Linz. The selling price of the Leonding property had been 10,000 kronen, leaving a net profit of 2,300 kronen over the price Alois had paid seven years before. After all encumbrances were removed, Klara retained a lump sum of approximately 5,500 kronen.[21] This improvement in the family's financial condition may have helped to offset some of the disappointment over Adolf's failure in Steyr. During their stay in Spital on the now customary vacation with the Schmidts, Adolf either contracted a disease or an existing condition became more serious. He was a patient under the care of a Dr. Keiss in the neighboring town of Weitra.[22] In *Mein Kampf*, Hitler stated that he suffered from a lung infection during this period. Such an ailment would not have been unusual; there is a long record of such illnesses in the Hitler family. Adolf's cousin, Johann Schmidt, later remembered that during this summer Klara brought her son a large cup of warm milk every morning, which he drank in his room. Such treatment suggests that Adolf was suffering from a respiratory ailment and that the traditional countermeasures of nourishing food, rest, and country air were being applied. By the time the summer was

---

[20] Heiden, *Der Fuehrer*, p. 49. Statement by Gregor Goldbacher. *HA*, File 17, Reel 1. Jetzinger prints only the first semester record for this year, and thus gives the impression that Hitler's work was worse than it actually was. *Jetzinger* (G), p. 103; *Jetzinger* (E), p. 67. *Wagner*, p. 37, provides a chronicle of Hitler's deficiencies in Steyr, allegedly based on a teacher's notebook for 1905-1906, but Hitler was not in Steyr that year.
[21] *Jetzinger* (G), pp. 127-29; *Jetzinger* (E), pp. 82-83; *Rabitsch*, p. 17, is two years early on the move to the Humboldstrasse.
[22] Heiden, *Der Fuehrer*, p. 51. Statement of Johann Schmidt, *HA*, File 17, Reel 1. Jetzinger is at great pains to prove that Hitler's statement of his sickness in *Mein Kampf* (p. 18) is false and that he had no serious illness. Although Hitler certainly misrepresented the case, Jetzinger's counterargument is also weak. None of his evidence comes from the summer of 1905, and the statement by Johann Schmidt, which was unknown to Jetzinger, makes a strong case for some illness. *Jetzinger* (G), pp. 148-51; *Jetzinger* (E), pp. 89-90.

over, his cousin recollected, the boy was much improved and the family returned to their new residence in Linz.[23]

Shortly after they got back, Adolf traveled on to Steyr to take the geometry examination. His instructor, Gregor Goldbacher, held the examination on September 16, 1905, and Adolf completed it satisfactorily.[24] This apparently satisfied all of the essential deficiencies in his record and made him eligible to graduate from lower *Realschule*. Had he followed the usual course at this point, he would have entered an *Oberrealschule*, or gone to a technical school. If he had applied for admission to *Oberrealschule* and his record had been found deficient, remedial work and a later petition for reconsideration would have been normal. Yet, aside from the fact that he quit school in the fall of 1905, we know very little about his course of action. In *Mein Kampf* he claimed that his illness was so serious that Klara decided to withdraw him from school. However, health did not prevent him from taking his final examination at Steyr, and the two boys closest to him in 1906 failed to note any signs of serious illness. Others with whom he came in contact, however, described him as pale and sickly.[25] The only picture of him from this period is a sketch made by a fellow pupil at Steyr, which makes him look thin, with drawn cheeks, and an overall sickly appearance.[26] His weak constitution, aggravated by the summer's chest trouble in Spital, may have been a contributing factor in the decision to quit school, although it assuredly was not the sole cause.

It is possible that his mother attempted to get him admitted to a higher institution, such as an *Oberrealschule*, but was refused. His poor record was a formidable obstacle to any kind of further education. By playing on this fact and that of his illness, he may have persuaded her that his schooling should end. He had not liked school

---

[23] Statement by Johann Schmidt. *HA*, File 17, Reel 1. Such illnesses were very common in Austria, *Drage*, p. 57.

[24] Statement by Gregor Goldbacher. *HA*, File 17, Reel 1.

[25] *Jetzinger* (G), p. 150; *Jetzinger* (E), pp. 89-90. Dr. Bloch, who treated his mother in 1907 and also acted as Adolf's doctor in the same period, had no knowledge of a serious lung ailment. Bloch also denied that he was sickly, though he described him as sallow and frail looking. *Bloch*, p. 36. Bloch's acquaintanceship came two years after the time at issue and is not decisive, but the statement of a neighbor that Adolf had serious lung trouble in 1907 is even more suspect. "Adolf Hitler in Urfahr!" *HA*, File 17, Reel 1.

[26] See photograph, Plate 13.

and had succeeded in thwarting the system and his parents by refusing to cooperate. After five years of repeated poor performances, he knew so little about the material in the curriculum that tremendous effort would have been required for him to do satisfactory work. When he tried harder, as in the spring of 1905 in Steyr, it still was not enough to counterbalance the great gaps in his preparation.

His departure from school was not a joyous event, however. On at least one occasion, in the circle of his advisers and servants, the Fuehrer of the Greater German Reich recalled the circumstances that surrounded his departure from the *Realschule* in Steyr. He stated that after the examinations he had received a certificate, and then joined some of the other boys for a party over a quart of local wine. They stayed out all night, and when he returned to his lodgings at dawn "in a lamentable state," he discovered that he had lost his certificate. "What could I have done with it," Hitler thought, "and what was I to show my mother? I was already thinking up an explanation: I had unfolded it in the train, in front of an open window, and a gust of wind had carried it off." But then he reconsidered and following the advice of his landlady, applied for a duplicate certificate rather than attempt to deceive his mother. Hitler's description continued, "The director [of the *Realschule*] began by keeping me waiting for a long time. My certificate had been brought back to school, but torn into four pieces, and in a somewhat inglorious condition. It appeared that in the absent-mindedness of intoxication I had confused the precious parchment with toilet paper. I was overwhelmed. I cannot tell you what the director said to me, I am still humiliated even from here." [27] How much of this complicated and embarrassing story is true it is impossible to say. Parts of it were certainly distorted, but the focus on the faulty certificate and the concern over Klara's reaction appear genuine enough. The deep feeling of humiliation indicates that he left Steyr with a keen awareness of defeat and mortification.

By the end of September 1905, Hitler had slipped back into Linz and taken up residence in his mother's flat, a badly lost sixteen-year-

---

[27] *Table Talk*, pp. 194-95. A slightly different account appears in *Zoller*, p. 49. That this incident remained in his secretary's memory betokens the intensity of the experience for Hitler, and also confirms the general reliability of Zoller.

old. He had a room to himself, and this provided a sanctuary in which he could nurse his wounds and start building up defenses again. According to one story, his mother took pity on him and sent him to an art school for a few months to let him try to carry out the plans he had espoused for so long. He was enrolled in a private school, run by a Professor Groeber, on the Bluetenstrasse in Munich. A writer in the early 1930's claimed that he had seen a picture of the students in the school and that Hitler was among them.[28] If this was true, the experiment lasted only a few months before Adolf was once more back in Linz. The Fuehrer never referred to this alleged stay in Munich, perhaps because he wished to preserve the story of the frustrated artist who dramatically entered Germany on the eve of the Great War.

In any event, by the early winter of 1905, Adolf was firmly planted in Linz without occupation or plan for study. The great battle over his career had been won. He had thwarted his dead father and amassed a miserable academic record that made it nearly certain he would never enter the ranks of the bureaucracy. Yet what a price he had paid for this victory! He was neither a man nor a child. Little more than a year earlier he had been playing Indians in Leonding. He was not completely well, nor was he very sick – certainly not sick enough to persuade an unbiased observer that he needed a long vacation at home. When asked what he wanted to be, he would reply, "a great artist." [29] That is, he wanted to be a painter. Or was it an architect? How either was to be accomplished on the basis of his school record he had no idea. It was all so jumbled and difficult to unravel that Adolf did his best to ignore it.

He made only one important decision. That was to stay at home, reading, drawing, and dreaming. Comfortably established in the flat on the Humboldtstrasse, he could afford to indulge himself. He

---

[28] *Heiden*, p. 51. The only source of this story is Heiden, who is in general very accurate. His interpretations are often debatable, but his facts are seldom completely wrong. Jetzinger claims Heiden is often wrong (*Jetzinger* (G), p. 150), but it is difficult to see how he reaches this conclusion. Greiner rejects the story of Hitler's art study in Munich on the grounds that the Hitlers lacked money, but this is completely erroneous. *Greiner*, p. 135.

[29] An example of this appears in "Adolf Hitler in Urfahr!" *HA*, File 17, Reel 1.

tolerated the presence of young Paula and his mother in his sanctuary because he could not get away from them without making the nauseating decision to leave home and go to work. However, they were not allowed to interfere, though his mother paid the bills and his sister cleaned up after him. All that Hitler needed to make his world complete was a bosom companion who would consider himself an "artist," be enthusiastic about Wagner and architecture, and agree to play Sancho Panza for young Adolf. In the fall of 1905, such a companion walked into his life in the person of August Kubizek, the son of a Linz upholsterer. Kubizek wanted to become a musician and, like Adolf, to submerge himself in the game of being an artist. His general submissiveness and the effort of his parents to direct him to a solid trade alone deterred him. A chance meeting with Hitler at a Wagner performance in the Linz Opera House began a friendship which offered each of the partners exactly what he wanted. Kubizek wished to be led, and in the eighteen-month-older Adolf he saw something more than a lost ex-*Realschule* student. To Kubizek, Adolf seemed a tower of strength and determination, one who could hold violent opinions and condemn the humdrum life of the entire provincial middle class, including upholsterers and Imperial officials.[30]

On his side, Adolf needed time to piece together the outward form of his life after the disasters in school. Kubizek's eagerness to have him play master recalled an earlier period in which he had dominated the neighborhood children in Leonding. In both cases he needed a pliable audience through which to project his ideas and plans. With Kubizek, Adolf found his pleasant drifting focused more consistently in the realm of artistic adventure. Slowly a new Hitler began to emerge. Of medium height, thin and nearly consumptive in appearance, he temporarily lost the drooping forelock and gained a thin

---

[30] *Kubizek*, pp. 1-7. Kubizek's account must be used with great care, as Jetzinger constantly points out in his own book. Kubizek unquestionably tailored his remarks to the audience. In 1938 one of the rather cautious investigators of the *Hauptarchiv* had a conversation with Kubizek, and in the description of the talk he said, "I can only say that the insight into the young Hitler provided by his childhood friend is simply astounding. Even then all the incomprehensible greatness of the Fuehrer was present." "Notizen fuer Kartei," *HA*, File 17, Reel 1. This is a somewhat different impression than the one Kubizek was to convey in the 1950's.

adolescent mustache. During the day, he seldom left the house, remaining in his room through most of the daylight hours. When evening fell and it was time for a stroll or a visit to the opera, he appeared faultlessly dressed, complete with cane, ready to take his place among the better people of Linz.[31]

His life of idleness and ease reinforced his sense of social standing. His father had tried to develop his class consciousness, in part to drive him forward. In the process, Adolf developed a sense of superiority toward members of the lower classes.[32] Class consciousness failed as a spur, but, in the midst of his idle adolescence, he used it to justify his manner of life. Though technically idle, he was still a member of the middle class. Furthermore, he was preparing to become an artist and was, therefore, not bound by the dreary obligations which applied to common people.

Kubizek and Hitler, bound by a kind of unspoken fraternal vow, determined to devote their lives to art. Their hours together were spent formulating designs for the future. Sometimes they planned Adolf's career as a painter and Kubizek's life as a pianist and composer, interspersed with digressions into the world of letters so that the older boy also could be a writer. The central dream, however, was "Adolf the Architect," since he had by now switched his aspirations from painting to architectural drawing. Hitler made room for Kubizek in his architect's dreams by constructing imaginary villas which Kubizek was to occupy after he became a success in his own field.

Kubizek, although he wanted to follow, still labored under serious handicaps in the partnership. He had to work in his father's shop and also go to school; the work was physically exhausting, dirty, and marred by distinctly lower class overtones. Kubizek's attendance at school represented in the eyes of his companion all that was humdrum and degrading. Adolf was not burdened by any comparable outside activities, and his gentlemanly status remained pure. After spending the day sketching and daydreaming, he would meet Kubizek

---

[31] *Kubizek*, pp. 7 and 9. Bloch also states that he was "neatly dressed" during this period. *Bloch*, p. 36.
[32] *Greiner*, pp. 25-26. In *Mein Kampf*, Hitler himself refers to his comfortable middle-class childhood environment. *Mein Kampf*, pp. 22-23. One of the first to discover this period of idleness in Hitler's background was Price, but he claimed it lasted five years, which is too long. *Price*, p. 47.

brimming over with ideas and enthusiasm. The two boys would then spend the late afternoon or early evening wandering through Linz and its environs. As they went, they carried out the mental demolition of old buildings that did not please them so that Adolf would have room in which to create new and more glorious structures. This kind of play became the center of Hitler's existence. As Kubizek later said, "He gave his whole self to his imaginary building and was completely carried away by it." [33]

Along with imaginary construction, the opera provided an additional center of enthusiasm for Hitler and his friend. Here Wagner played the key role with extravagant visual displays and a preoccupation with the shadowy power of the German myths. The boys thoroughly enjoyed the music, but for Adolf, Wagner also served as a stimulus to incessant brooding and dreaming. Some performances had the effect on him of religious experiences. On such occasions, he would leave the theater deep in introspective fantasies.[34] But, despite the intense emotion called forth by Wagner, his operas could not hold Adolf's attention for long. When daylight came, the imaginary building projects rolled on again. Great bridges, blocks of houses, castles, villas, a monastery and an opera house appeared in Hitler's mind or took form on paper. Their style followed the ponderous, monumental pattern later dubbed "Nazi classical."

Throughout all the ups and downs of his later career, Hitler retained his love for architectural sketching, and his subject matter and style remained approximately the same. Perhaps it is not accidental that all of the projects that Kubizek describes, as well as the Fuehrer's later plans for his home city, involved the destruction or drastic remodeling of noteworthy existing structures. It was as if he sought revenge against Linz, the scene of his frustrations, by destroying its landmarks and changing its face.[35]

There were other, more obvious, danger signs in this phase of Hitler's development. He followed his dreamy and irresponsible

---

[33] *Kubizek*, p. 84. Hitler never overcame his ambivalence concerning architecture and painting. *Zoller*, p. 55. The intense seriousness of these episodes is shown in Kubizek's description of their dreams about winning a lottery. *Kubizek*, pp. 92-96.
[34] *Kubizek*, pp. 98-101.
[35] *Kubizek*, pp. 82-98.

manner of life in Linz for two full years after leaving Steyr, until well past the age of eighteen. The pattern of his behavior coincided almost exactly with the earlier play-escapism of the Leonding period. One effect was that many of the adjustments necessary for sexual maturity were delayed by this new dream world. Adolf was concerned with only one girl in Linz, and this was a one-sided romance, in which Adolf never tried to speak to the girl. Together with Kubizek he strolled by her home, gazed at her from a distance and poured out his anguished heart in solitary monologues. Gradually, he began to build her imaginary villas, until she, too, was safely insulated from reality.[36]

The perils inherent in this withdrawal may have been recognized by his mother. Many things she did for him can be seen as gentle urgings to get him to break with his preoccupations. She paid for the clothes which turned him into something of a dandy, perhaps in the hope that this would serve as a bridge to wider social horizons. If this was her plan, it failed completely. The clothes merely served as symbols of independence and self-sufficient isolation.[37]

Similarly, in May 1906, Klara allowed Adolf to take an extended trip to Vienna, and, as usual, defrayed expenses. He stayed at least a month (May 7 to June 6), and, though he may have lodged with friends, the trip still probably cost her around 100 kronen. As an exercise in re-direction it was a disaster. The four surviving cards which Adolf sent to Kubizek from Vienna contain nothing but enthusiastic comments on Wagner and Viennese architecture, together with a few cryptic notes which Kubizek claims referred to Hitler's elusive girl friend in Linz. The cards also show that his first excursion to a great city carried him away on new flights of fancy. He was enraptured by the monumental buildings of the capital, and described them with such words as "mighty majesty," "dignity," and "grandeur." Any building to which these words could be applied immediately became in his eyes a work of art. The cards also revealed that his spelling and punctuation were well below the standard

---

[36] *Kubizek*, pp. 56-69. Jetzinger succeeds in eliminating any factual importance from the Stephanie episode. *Jetzinger* (G), pp. 146-48; *Jetzinger* (E), pp. 105-108.
[37] *Kubizek*, pp. 108-109.

one would expect of a seventeen-year-old who had completed four years in secondary school.[38]

Soon after his return to Linz, it was time for the family to make its summer trek to Spital, a somewhat sadder journey in 1906 because Klara's mother had died at the Schmidt's in February.[39] The stay in Spital was uneventful, and in the late summer the family was back in Linz, where the Hitler-Kubizek duo resumed. In October, Klara assumed the expenses of a new enterprise. Kubizek had been taking piano lessons from a Josef Prevratsky (whose name had been changed to Wendt by the 1930's). Adolf also began to take lessons from him at a cost of five kronen per month. As a music student, Hitler was conscientious and cooperative, but Prevratsky found him reserved, "almost timid." He took lessons for only about four months, ending on January 31, 1907. He quit in part because of his dislike for the dull routine of scales, but mainly because Klara became seriously ill at the turn of the year, and the family had to reduce expenses.[40]

Klara first consulted a doctor on January 14, 1907. When her condition was found to be serious, she was admitted to the Convent hospital in Linz on January 17th. On the following day she underwent an operation for *sarcoma pectoris*, a malignant growth in the breast. She was the patient of Dr. Edmund Bloch of Linz, but the operation was performed by Dr. Karl Urban, a local surgeon. The operation was seemingly successful. After remaining in the hospital for nineteen days, she was released and was not seen by Bloch again until March 15th, nearly two months after the operation. In April, her condition seems to have become serious once more; she visited Bloch six times during the month, and four more times in May. During the summer, she may have shown a temporary improvement because, aside from three visits in July, she had no contact with the doctor between June and the end of August.[41]

---

[38] *Kubizek*, pp. 102-106; *Jetzinger* (G), pp. 151-56; *Jetzinger* (E), pp. 90-93. A passing reference to this trip appears in *Mein Kampf*, p. 19.
[39] *Die Ahnentafel*, p. 40.
[40] *Kubizek*, p. 195. Prevratsky's acount book, and statement by him dated November 17, 1938. *HA*, File 17, Reel 1.
[41] Statement by Dr. Karl Urban, *HA*, File 17, Reel 1; statement by Dr. Edmund Bloch, *HA*, File 17, Reel 1; Hospital Records, and Bloch's account book, *HA*, File 65, Reel 13A. The description given in Bloch's article in-

Klara's illness affected the life of the family in many ways. Aside from her suffering and the decision to terminate Adolf's piano lessons, the expenses of the operation and convalescence were moderately high. The cost of the operation and the hospital amounted to approximately 150 kronen, and 60 kronen was paid to Bloch for house visits during the spring and summer.[42] Apparently Klara's sister, Johanna, joined the family during these months and helped to run the household while the mother was bedridden. During May or June, for no known reason, the family moved again, taking a flat in an imposing stone apartment building in Urfahr (Bluetengasse 9). This was a suburb of Linz across the Danube and was connected to the city by a large bridge. The streetcar line provided a convenient link to the main part of town. In the new residence, Adolf had his own room and a view of a central courtyard.[43]

It is not clear whether the Hitlers took their customary trip to Spital in the summer of 1907. If they did, it might explain the drop in frequency of Klara's visits to the doctor during these months. In any event, by September, she was going to the doctor more regularly. She saw Bloch six times during this month, and it must have been clear, at least to her, that she was not showing any improvement. Moreover, she had to consider her financial position and the future of the children. She had a large sum of money left in September 1907, but she faced mounting medical bills and surely realized that if her illness was prolonged the family finances would suffer. Two of her children, Angela and young Alois, had left home and were no longer her financial responsibility, but Paula, only eleven, would have

---

cludes many inaccuracies. *Bloch*, pp. 36-39. By the time the article was written, he was an old man, who had been worked over by the Gestapo and pumped by the *Hauptarchiv* people before leaving Austria. It should be stated that the representatives of the *Hauptarchiv* were comparatively kind to him ("Die Sache Bloch," *HA*, File 17, Reel 1), as he himself later stated. *Bloch*, p. 73. The vague account he gave to the *Hauptarchiv* agrees fairly well with the later article, but the latter was more drawn out and hence more inaccurate. By this time he had lost his memory for detail, and, in any case, was discussing many things he had never known. *Kurth*, footnote 28.

[42] Dr. Bloch's account book, *HA*, File 65, Reel 13A.

[43] Dr. Bloch's account book, *HA*, File 65, Reel 13A; *Jetzinger* (G), pp. 171 and 176; *Jetzinger* (E), p. 100. Rabitsch has a good description of the Bluetengasse but, again he dates the move two years too early. *Rabitsch*, pp. 18 and 31.

to stay with her mother as long as possible, eventually to pass to the care of Angela. Until then, Johanna could do the housework and take care of Paula. Several helpful and interested neighbors in the apartment building were available to aid in emergencies.[44]

But what of Adolf? His mother's illness notwithstanding, the pattern of his life altered only slightly. During the day, he occupied himself painting and drawing. Toward six in the evening, he would leave the house for a stroll or meet Kubizek to go on one of their expeditions. When he returned, he read in his room until late at night, punctuated by hours of nervous pacing.[45] Political ideas, including Pan-Germanism and anti-Semitism, appear to have played a smaller part in his speculations than in the *Realschule* period. Kubizek was not interested in politics, so Adolf had to pursue this interest alone or abandon it and concentrate on music and art. German nationalist politics had become calmer during these years in Linz, and Adolf seems to have put a corresponding damper on his own enthusiasms, especially his social anti-Semitism. His mother was under the care of a Jewish doctor, Dr. Bloch, and Adolf was also treated by him. The boy appreciated the efforts Bloch made on behalf of his mother and seems to have been genuinely fond of him. During one of his trips to Vienna, either in the spring of 1906 or the fall of 1907, Adolf sent Bloch an elaborate card containing his "heartiest good wishes." In early 1908, after his mother's death, Adolf again sent him a special card, this time a New Year's greeting that included his best wishes and offered thanks for what Bloch had done.[46] Adolf probably retained during this period his prejudice against Jews and a sympathy for Pan-Germanism, but it is difficult to believe that he was a raging racist or that his prejudices were as intense as they had been in the *Realschule* years.

At this time Adolf was more clearly vegetating than during any previous period of his life. Although over eighteen, he had never had a

---

[44] Dr. Bloch's account book, *HA*, File 65, Reel 13A; "Adolf Hitler in Urfahr!" *HA*, File 17, Reel 1.
[45] "Adolf Hitler in Urfahr!" *HA*, File 17, Reel 1.
[46] The Gestapo reached Bloch and confiscated the cards before the *Hauptarchiv* got to him, but he had kept a copy of the texts. "Notizen fuer Kartei," *HA*, File 17, Reel 1. Some secondary information appears in Bloch's statement in the same file. See also *Bloch*, p. 70. Only one biographer of Hitler picked up the Bloch story and that was *Wagner*, p. 54.

job and showed no inclination to get one. Klara, the neigbors, and other members of the family all failed to persuade him to go to work. To their pointed questions about employment, Adolf always replied with his "plans" for an artist's career.[47] By September 1907, with Klara's condition growing worse, something obviously had to be done. Presumably in the absence of other alternatives, since this could not have been entirely welcome, his mother allowed him to obtain his patrimony, approximately 650 kronen, and go to Vienna to apply for the painting course at the Art Academy. He had withdrawn his money from the Mortgage Bank of Upper Austria during the summer.[48]

The atmosphere surrounding Adolf's move to Vienna was marked by dreamy good cheer, despite Klara's condition. He was not going off determined to make his way in the world, but to return to the scene of the happy times he had enjoyed with Wagner and architecture the year before. His devotion to painting was not as serious as he later pictured it in *Mein Kampf*. Even in his play activities it lacked any decided advantage over architectural planning or Wagner.[49]

Adolf went to the capital in late September, or early October of 1907, and rented a room at Stumpergasse #29, a private house owned by a Polish woman, Frau Maria Zakreys. The house was in the southwest quarter of the city, just three or four blocks from the *Westbahnhof*, where he had alighted from the Linz train. He had sufficient money from his patrimony to live for a year, and his mother certainly did not withhold from him the 240 kronen she was authorized to draw on his behalf from the customs service.

Hitler did not take time to get his bearings in the city, but took the lodgings near the train station and then ran to the Art Academy to take the admissions examination. The examination was given only once a year, during October. If he had missed it, he would have had to wait until 1908.[50] He apparently thought he could breeze through the examination while a magic wand filled in all the gaps in his studies. He was quickly set right. The result of the test, as recorded in the classification list of the Academy stated: "Adolf Hitler, Brau-

---

[47] "Adolf Hitler in Urfahr!" *HA*, File 17, Reel 1.
[48] *Jetzinger* (G), pp. 172-173; *Jetzinger* (E), p. 101.
[49] *Kubizek*, p. 84.
[50] *Kubizek*, p. 115; Heiden, *Der Fuehrer*, p. 52.

nau a. Inn, April 20, 1889, German Catholic. Father Civil Servant. 4 Classes in *Realschule*. .... Test Drawing Unsatisfactory." [51] The shocking effect of this report was still very much alive in Hitler seventeen years later when he wrote *Mein Kampf*: "I was so convinced that I would be successful that when I received my rejection, it struck me as a bolt from the blue." [52] Unable to accept the decision, he requested, and obtained, an interview with the director of the Academy in order to find out why he had been rejected. According to Hitler, the director actually managed to persuade him that he did not possess the necessary talent for painting, but only by sweetening the pill with lavish praise for his architectural abilities. He went away brooding about his failure and the comments on his architectural ability. "Downcast, I left von Hansen's magnificent building on the Schillerplatz, for the first time in my life at odds with myself. For what I had just heard about my abilities seemed like a lightning flash, suddenly revealing a conflict with which I had long been afflicted, although until then I had no clear conception of its why and wherefore. In a few days I myself knew that I should some day become an architect." [53]

Unquestionably, the whole episode was a bitter disappointment. It might reasonably have served as the impetus to make him change his life in order to triumph in the end. Hitler did indeed rise to the occasion, but not in the spirit of an Horatio Alger. He began immediately to employ his strongest weapons to dissolve the obstacle which stood in his way. His colossal ego provided the means of escape. A secondary school certificate was required to begin the preparatory courses for professional architect's training. Hitler did not have a secondary school certificate, and it is not certain he left the *Realschule* in good standing. If he had been genuinely devoted to an architect's career and believed he possessed sufficient talent to attain that goal, he would have freed himself from some of his wild pretensions and begun again at the bottom. It must be granted that not

[51] Heiden, *Der Fuehrer*, p. 52.
[52] *Mein Kampf*, p. 20.
[53] *Mein Kampf*, p. 20. Hitler's dramatic description may apply to his second rejection by the Academy. In his later years he stated that only educational deficiencies barred his admission to the Academy. Even when he rationalized his failure in this way, it still stung: "Every time he talked of this painful denial, he became sad and morose." *Zoller*, p. 54.

many young men in Hitler's position would have done this, but Adolf apparently did not even look into the matter. His personality and way of life prevented him from acknowledging his errors and accepting his rejection as a sign of the need for any change. His escapism was reinforced by his social affectations and his scorn for work which seemed dirty, degrading, or tiring. He was a confused and snobbish young man who had indulged himself for so long that he would neither work at an unpleasant task nor consider anyone except himself and the manner of life he enjoyed. His solution to rejection by the Academy was to go back to the Stumpergasse and settle down as if nothing had happened. In this sanctuary, he resumed what he grandly called his "studies," doodling and reading, with excursions around town or to the opera.

Hitler's disdain for reality had something grandiose about it. But as David Hume once pointed out, even though one can doubt the binding force of the external world, it has a nasty way of intruding on one's personal life. Hitler found this out, too, and in a direct way. In December 1907, word reached him in Vienna that his mother was dying. She had spent three horrible months fighting her illness and for the last month had been under constant medical care. She apparently withheld the gravity of her condition from her son throughout the struggle. It was only in the third week of December that a neighbor in the apartment house notified him that he should come quickly. From all indications, the news did not arrive in time; he reached Linz after his mother had died on December 21, 1907.[54]

Although doubts must arise about the devotion of a son who did not suspect the plight of his mother while she made her fight against cancer, Adolf, in his considerate moments, had been ex-

---

[54] Kubizek states that Hitler arrived before his mother passed away and gives a long and touching description of their relation during these weeks. *Kubizek*, pp. 120-26. Bloch also says he was there in time and even claims he drew a picture of her on her deathbed. *Bloch*, p. 39. Bloch is very unreliable on detail, and Jetzinger has clearly explained the holes in Kubizek's account. Jetzinger (G), pp. 175-79; Jetzinger (E), pp. 103-104, and 169-70. In his explanation, Jetzinger depends on statements traced to an unnamed postmaster's widow. The article "Adolf Hitler in Urfahr!" (*HA*, File 17, Reel 1) is clearly based on statements of the same woman, and though she discusses this period of Hitler's life, she does not mention Adolf as present at his mother's death. Since the article was tailored for a Nazi audience, this omission strengthens Jetzinger's conclusion that Adolf did not arrive in time.

tremely fond of Klara, and her death was a deep shock to him.[55] Viewed selfishly, as he was wont to do, her passing also deprived him of a sorely needed center of love and concern which might have helped him to work out the difficulties he faced.

On December 23rd, Klara was given a large and costly funeral. Her body was transported to Leonding and buried in the plot next to Alois. The orphans, Paula and Adolf, although torn loose from their routines and genuinely affected by the loss, were not left alone and helpless. Johanna Poelzl continued to run the house after the funeral, and there were the neighbors, the Kubizeks, and Angela's family as well. The key individual, however, was Johanna, for her presence provided the time and opportunity to work out the administrative problems following Klara's death. Unfortunately, we have no documentary evidence for one important step in this process – the division of the money. We do know that up through October 1907 the family had paid out approximately 250 kronen to meet the direct costs of Klara's illness. An additional 300 kronen was owed Dr. Bloch for his treatment during the last stages of the illness, and this amount was paid in cash on December 24th, the day after the funeral.[56] If one adds 200 or 300 kronen for incidental expenses associated with the illness, the total cost, including the funeral, could not have exceeded 1,200 kronen.[57] Since she had been in possession of a lump sum of 5,000 kronen some two years earlier, and her income had remained constant during the intervening years, it is difficult to see how the amount available at the time of her death was less than 2,500 to 3,000 kronen. The fact that there is no trace of a will paradoxically suggests that there was a sizeable sum of money and that she had divided it among the children prior to her end in order to avoid the death duty. Since the official death record states that "the funeral expenses have been borne by the children," it is clear that they did receive some money.[58]

All of this shows that, prior to any consideration of pension rights,

[55] *Kubizek*, pp. 126-28; *Bloch*, pp. 36 and 70. Bloch told both the *Hauptarchiv* investigator and the Collier's people that he kept the cards over the years because he wanted a memento of a boy so devoted to his mother. Bloch statement, *HA*, File 17, Reel 1.
[56] Dr. Bloch's Account Book, *HA*, File 65, Reel 13A.
[57] Record of funeral costs, *HA*, File 65, Reel 13A.
[58] *Jetzinger* (G), pp. 179-83; *Jetzinger* (E), pp. 104-105.

Paula and Adolf were not left penniless by their mother's death. Since Paula was not quite twelve, provisions had been made for Angela to raise her. The portion of the estate set aside for Paula was used to offset some of this expense. There is reason to believe that the available money was not divided evenly between Adolf and his sister and that the larger portion went for Paula's future support. It seems reasonable to conclude that Adolf's portion was between 500 and 1,000 kronen.[59]

Information concerning the children's pensions is much more precise. Paula and Adolf were eligible for a combined pension of 50 kronen a month until each reached the age of twenty-four. As soon as one of the children reached this age, the total amount of the pension dropped to 25 kronen. The children applied for the pension on February 10, 1908, but the application was prepared incorrectly and a second application had to be made through their guardian, Josef Mayerhofer, on February 25th. By this time, Adolf had already left Linz and was once again in Vienna. The reply that Mayerhofer received to the second application stated that the orphans would be granted the annual sum of 600 kronen and that Mayerhofer was authorized to divide the money between them as he saw fit. He allowed each child 25 kronen per month, treating little Paula, who was dependent on Angela's generosity, and Adolf as if they were equally deserving.[60] Mayerhofer undoubtedly had gained the impression from Adolf that he was studying in Vienna and needed the money for this purpose. Angela and her husband paid the price for Adolf's deception, for they had to make up the difference between the pension, Paula's legacy, and the costs of her maintainance.

The two months that Adolf remained in Linz following his mother's death, were spent taking care of details. In *Mein Kampf,* Hitler portrayed this period of his life as a time of great deprivation and uncertainty. In the spirit of Oliver Twist, he was faced with "stern reality" and the need to make a "quick decision." [61] Actually the main decision had already been made: he had gone to Vienna and failed. He could, of course, return to Vienna in the fall of 1908 and try the entrance examination at the Art Academy again. In the mean-

[59] "Adolf Hitler in Urfahr!" *HA*, File 17, Reel 1.
[60] *Jetzinger* (G), pp. 185-89; *Jetzinger* (E), pp. 109-13.
[61] *Mein Kampf,* p. 18.

THE EARLY YOUTH 113

time, there was the unpleasant possibility that he might have to go to work. Some of the members of the family, especially Angela's husband Leo, were rude enough to suggest this to him, and even old Mayerhofer tried to get him to forget Vienna and become an apprentice.[62] But Adolf scornfully rejected such mundane activities. He was a student, an artist, a painter, an architect, or whatever else was convenient at the moment, and he was not going to become a mere tradesman or worker. The family's urging and questioning continued, however, and gradually began to get on his nerves.

From all indications, he had not told the rest of the family that he had failed the entrance examination at the Academy. They were under the impression that he was actually participating in an organized program of study in Vienna. Kubizek did not discover that his friend had failed until months later,[63] and Mayerhofer's grant of an equal pension share to the boy suggests that he was also fooled. For his part, Adolf seems to have hoped for some kind of artistic employment and, barring that, a vacation in Vienna until the next round of examinations. On February 4, 1908, Magdalena Hanisch, a resident in the same apartment house as the Hitlers, wrote to a relative in Vienna to see if she would use her contacts in the art department of the Imperial Opera for Adolf's benefit. Whether or not this request originated directly with the boy, it embodied all of his dreams – the possibility of being occupied with painting and Wagner simultaneously. The woman to whom Frau Hanisch wrote, a Frau Motlach, worked very quickly. Two days later, on February 6th, Professor Roller, Painter and Director of Scenery at the Imperial Opera, replied that he would be happy to examine Adolf's painting and advise him on his future career. Both Frau Hanisch and Adolf wrote letters to Frau Motlach thanking her for her efforts on the boy's behalf.[64]

---

[62] *Kubizek*, pp. 133-34.
[63] *Kubizek*, pp. 157-58.
[64] Report by Geheime Staats Polizei in Vienna, December 30, 1941. *NA* material, Reichleader of the SS and Chief of the German Police, T-175, Roll 38, Folder 255. The original documents are not in this file, but the Gestapo, in its thorough way, included a description of them. It seems clear that the date of the Hitler letter was copied incorrectly and should read October 2, 1908, rather than October 2, 1909, especially as the envelope has the right date, 1908.

Professor Roller's offer to examine his work probably heightened Adolf's tendency to over-optimism and provided him also with a convenient pretext to return to Vienna. He could argue that he had plans to complete his studies and that, through Professor Roller, he had the prospect of employment in the near future. Adolf wound up his affairs in Linz within a week and tried to persuade Kubizek to accompany him to the capital. Kubizek had contracted a bronchial disorder in the course of his work in the upholstery shop, and this made his parents more receptive to plans for a different form of employment. His father was still reluctant to allow him to go to Vienna and study music, but at this point Adolf entered the discussion. He strengthened Kubizek's resolve by providing glowing descriptions of the capital and the way of life that awaited them there. Rather than stay in Urfahr and be heckled by his relatives, Hitler confided to Kubizek, he was going back to Vienna with the "little ready capital" he possessed, and hoped that Kubizek would go with him. Kubizek's parents, like other people in Linz concerned with the problem, seem to have been completely deceived by Hitler's story of his art studies and assumed that he was enrolled in the Art Academy. In the subsequent debate over their own boy's future it was his chance to reside with "art student" Hitler that helped tip the scales. They finally agreed to let August join his friend in Vienna.[65]

Although Kubizek was deceived by Adolf's stories of his studies, and was partly caught by his fascination for the older boy, he was serious about his plans to become a professional musician. Adolf, on the other hand, merely hoped that an appeal to Professor Roller would turn up something. He had no sympathy for Angela and her husband, and he was perfectly willing to walk out and leave his Aunt Johanna to go back to Spital.

Since Kubizek was more responsible than Adolf, he remained in Linz for a week or so to complete the arrangements which his family felt were necessary. Adolf, with no such reservations, left Linz for the last time somewhere between the 14th and 17th of February, 1908. By the 18th he was snugly back on the Stumpergasse, eagerly writing Kubizek to speed his departure: "Am anxiously expecting news of your arrival. Write soon so that I can prepare

---

[65] *Kubizek*, pp. 139-40.

everything for your festive welcome. The whole of Vienna is awaiting you; therefore, come soon. I will, of course, meet you." After a few comments about the weather and the prospects of renting a piano, he closed with best wishes to the Kubizek family and another bit of encouragement, "Beg you again, come soon." [66] This heartfelt appeal may have helped to do the trick. In the closing days of February, Kubizek boarded a train in Linz, loaded down with edible treasures provided by his mother. Adolf met him at the *Westbahnhof* and enthusiastically accompanied him to the Stumpergasse, where they devoured part of Kubizek's supply of food. Then, though it was already dark, Adolf dragged the tired and protesting Kubizek to the center of the city where he pointed out all the "magnificent buildings." But poor Kubizek could not rise to the occasion. "The night was shrouded in mist and I did not see much; in any case, I had enough to do with the impressions of my journey, and when we got home, on foot of course, at half past one in the morning, I was dog tired. Then Adolf started discussing our future plans and the program for the following day, but I was asleep before I heard much of what he said, much to my friend's annoyance." [67]

Despite his momentary chagrin, all the pieces of Adolf's world had fallen into place again. The life that the two boys had enjoyed together in Linz was to be repeated on a grander scale in Vienna.

---

[66] *Kubizek*, p. 141.
[67] *Jetzinger* (E), p. 116.

VI

THE FIRST YEARS IN VIENNA

In the days immediately following Kubizek's arrival, the boys worked hard to arrange his lodgings. They had originally thought it would be easy to find a room similar to Hitler's for about the same price, ten kronen a month, but after a series of trips through the dark and uninviting hovels available for that price, they were discouraged. Ultimately they came up with the idea of joining forces and sharing one large room. When they broached this scheme to Hitler's landlady, Frau Zakreys, she offered to move out of her moderately large room and let them occupy it, while she would take over the room in which Hitler was living. The deal was quickly closed and the rent of twenty kronen a month divided evenly by the boys.[1]

Once the housing arrangement was settled, Kubizek went off to attend to the details of his musical training. He rapidly completed the last phases of the Academy's admission procedure and received approval for his program of study. He succeeded in renting a large grand piano, which he needed for practicing, and had it moved into the room on the Stumpergasse. The piano took up most of the available space, and left Hitler only a narrow corridor for pacing. When the piano arrived, Hitler bemoaned his fate but gradually reconciled himself to the instrument. Even with the piano, the boys' living arrangements remained comparatively pleasant. There was enough room for two beds, a table, and narrow paths to maneuver around the furniture. The room was adequately heated and they even enjoyed a few rays of sunlight on the window during the late afternoon. Like nearly all subtenants in the capital, the boys were plagued by

[1] *Kubizek*, pp. 143-47.

an army of vermin, but their tormentors had selective tastes – they attacked Hitler but ignored Kubizek.[2]

Soon after Kubizek's arrival, he had to begin classes at the Music Academy. Every morning he arose early and ran off to school, while Hitler remained in bed. When Kubizek returned late in the afternoon, his work completed and anxious for an opportunity to practice, he would find Hitler lolling in the room. Sometimes he was drawing or reading. More than once, he had just returned from a tour of the city and, while Kubizek practiced, he discussed his impressions of the buildings he had seen and alterations he planned. Just as in the earlier days in Linz, he would seize a pencil or piece of charcoal and begin to sketch out a plan. Kubizek enjoyed these enthusiastic sessions, even though they interfered with his musical training. Slowly, however, he became a bit curious about the curriculum at the Art Academy which permitted Hitler to spend so much time at home. One day his curiosity got the better of him and he began to ask specific questions about Hitler's studies. Adolf, cornered, turned on him and in a violent outburst confessed that he was not attending the Academy because the "stupid" professors had failed to recognize his talent and had not admitted him. He railed on for hours denouncing the *Realschule*, the Academy, and all the people who had interfered with the realization of his dreams. When he finally calmed down he swore that he would yet triumph, for he was determined to become a self-taught architect. Kubizek was made to realize that his reading and drawing as well as his exploratory trips through the city were part of a program which he had established to prepare him for "his chosen profession." [3]

In the days that followed, Hitler's temper cooled, and Kubizek politely respected his plan for teaching himself. Adolf arose late every morning, a habit he retained all his life, and by the time he was fully awake, Kubizek had gone. After taking a few bites of whatever he could find, he began to read or draw. He loved to pore through architecture books, memorizing pictures of the most famous buildings; then, with names covered, he tried to identify them.[4] His reading was similarly playful and ranged over all subjects at random.

[2] *Kubizek*, pp. 259-60 and pp. 148-49.
[3] *Kubizek*, pp. 148, 153-54, 157-58.
[4] *Kubizek*, pp. 159-74.

He gathered tidbits of fact and opinion, seeking to confirm his biases rather than to build up any systematic knowledge of a subject.[5]

He was always busy, dashing from one interest to another because of an "architect's" need to understand every part of human life in order to build properly. Nearly every day he journeyed around the city, "learning architecture" by looking at it. He loved to stand and gaze by the hour at monumental buildings. When he returned home he would pore over guidebooks in order to master more detail. From time to time, following these walks, he would explain to Kubizek the need to improve the housing of the masses. His concern, however, was restricted to the outward appearance of the city's districts; he displayed no sympathy for the housing problems of the common man. He did not like the Viennese people, finding them far too easygoing and frivolous, and he studiously avoided close contact with them.[6] Although he suffered from Vienna's poor housing situation, he did not inquire into the actual living conditions of the people around him and felt no sense of comradeship with them.

After gathering his impressions, and buttressed by architecture books from the library, Hitler would sketch out the changes that had to be made in the city. He planned the demolition of whole streets and designed new housing developments for them. Then he would move on to what he enjoyed most – the laying out of great public buildings and monuments. There was nothing systematic about his work. Dozens of plans were begun, but none was ever completed. After roughing out his ideas on one project he would jump on to another. Designs for Vienna and Linz were mixed together without rhyme or reason. Eventually he hit upon the grandiose project of rebuilding the entire city of Vienna, district by district. Despite its staggering dimensions, this idea occupied him only temporarily, and he abandoned it in order to write a play. Soon afterward he decided to do an opera and to exploit Kubizek's talents for composing the music. Through several days and nights the Stumpergasse was the scene of continuous toil as the opera, "Wieland the Smith," began to take shape. After much ranting and

---

[5] *Kubizek*, pp. 175-84. Hitler later praised this kind of reading. *Mein Kampf*, pp. 35-37.
[6] *Kubizek*, p. 161.

raving because Kubizek could not translate his ideas directly into music, "Wieland the Smith" began to slow down and was shelved as a fragment like all previous projects.[7]

The plan to compose an opera was merely an extension of the one great interest that Hitler and Kubizek shared. The two boys spent every available evening attending the performances of the Imperial and the Civic (*Volks*) opera. For ordinary performances they were able to get a seat for two or three kronen by making use of the special arrangements for students. Nearly every evening, they would dash to one of the opera houses in order to be in line early. As soon as the doors were opened they scrambled to get good seats. After the performance, there was another race to reach the Stumpergasse before the curfew hour, to avoid paying a fine to the night porter. Kubizek enjoyed the works of all the composers, while Hitler was contemptuous of non-German music. Both boys considered Wagner performances at the Imperial Opera the height of bliss; they watched and listened as if they were participating in a religious service.[8]

It was a happy and comfortable existence, approximating the classic picture of young students immersed in the excitement of art and learning. For Kubizek the period of study in Vienna was the great adventure of his life. Hitler, despite his eagerness to play, was in a more ambivalent position. He had sufficient money to live comfortably by using his monthly pension and part of the money left by his parents. Aside from his costly passion for opera performances he was careful with money, ate frugally, and spent nothing on smoking or drinking.[9] His monthly expenditures amounted approximately to 80-90 kronen, which meant that his savings were declining by about 60 kronen per month. Even though his original fund was large and gave him a sense of security, the steadily falling bank

---

[7] *Kubizek*, pp. 193-202. Kubizek also told the *Hauptarchiv* investigators about the drama and the opera, but he asserted that it was a drama that was named "Wieland the Smith." Notizen fuer Kartei, August Kupizek [*sic*], *HA*, File 17, Reel 1.

[8] *Kubizek*, pp. 185-92. Gosset notes the near-religious attraction that Wagner had for Hitler in Vienna. Pierre and Renée Gosset, *Adolf Hitler*, Vol. I (Paris, 1961), p. 25. How he got in on a student ticket is not clear, but he could have obtained a regular seat for as little as two kronen. *Baedeker*, p. 13.

[9] Kubizek, p. 150. His frugality in Vienna was noted by a number of people. Honisch statement, *HA*, File 17, Reel 1; *Greiner*, p. 100.

balance undermined it again. The elaborate myth of justifying his existence by teaching himself architecture also failed to subdue completely his apprehension. He was moody, and often turned on Kubizek with bitter denunciations for no apparent reason. After a few minutes of ranting, however, he would calm down, and the incident would be allowed to pass.[10] He was still badly confused and disturbed about sex. Long, puritanic declarations about the need for self-control alternated with curiosity about the birth rate or the problem of prostitution. In order to facilitate "his studies," Kubizek once was dragged off for a stroll through the Siebenstrasse, the prostitutes' quarter. On this occasion, as in all moments of danger, Adolf heroically resisted every immoral advance.[11]

The ambivalence about his future, his moodiness, and his inability to resolve the difficulties of sexual maturation encouraged him to find some meaning for his life. His outer confidence remained unbroken for the most part, but he was obviously searching for the key to his dilemma. He found a partial solution in a renewed interest in politics. His architectural "studies" led him to the parliament building and, once inside, he was fascinated by the legislative process. The debates of the Austrian *Reichsrat* were colorful, sometimes preposterous spectacles with violent arguments, multi-language debates, and outright brawls. Adolf was enthralled by them. Dragging Kubizek with him, he sat in the gallery for hours and watched the scene below.

Hitler's interest in parliament does not appear to have been directly associated with a revived feeling of extreme nationalism. He had not been doing extensive reading in politics. Kubizek, at least, did not think that his national enthusiasm was at full flower.[12] He presumably was concerned with questions of social reform, but these merely echoed proposals advanced by the Christian Socialist mayor, Karl Lueger, then at the height of his power. Both in politics and in social questions, Hitler's interest remained theoretical, not practical.[13] A perfect social laboratory surrounded him. Vienna's sixth district,

[10] *Kubizek*, pp. 152-53.
[11] *Kubizek*, pp. 235-37.
[12] *Kubizek*, pp. 241-51. In *Mein Kampf* Hitler stated that he spent a year studying the parliament in Vienna. *Mein Kampf*, p. 78.
[13] *Kubizek*, pp. 160-62.

Mariahilf, was an area of small businesses and substandard housing occupied by proletarians and the lower strata of white collar workers. Numerous ethnic groups lived in the district, including the third highest percentage of Jews in the city. In the *Landtag* election of 1908, Mariahilf voted overwhelmingly for the Christian Social party and the Socialists.[14] If Hitler had wanted to learn about multi-national problems, social reform and the difficulties of the urban poor, he could survey them from his own doorstep. Since he did not, one may assume that an interest in political and social problems was not yet the dominant theme of his life.

Every indication points to a conclusion that Hitler would probably have been content to dabble along indefinitely if circumstances had permitted. However, in July 1908, Kubizek's first term at the Music Academy ended, and he had to return to his family in Linz. An arrangement was worked out whereby Adolf was to stay in the room during the summer. Both boys were to continue to divide the rent, even though Kubizek would not return until the late fall. Adolf was to carry on his personal "study" during the summer, and life would resume its usual course after Kubizek's return. During July and the first part of August Kubizek received cards from Hitler filled with personal chit-chat. Frau Zakreys had gone to visit relatives in Bohemia for a week or so and Hitler was looking after the place. The weather was bad in Vienna and the bugs in the room were still the plague of his life. He asked Kubizek to pick up some guides to Linz for him, for once again his building plans and turned toward the city he considered home.[15]

In early August, Adolf wrote that he was going to Spital for a short visit and confessed that he was afraid his sister would be there too, a prospect which he did not relish. Once again his strong dislike for both Paula and Angela was manifest. He went to Spital, in any case, and during this, his final visit to the old family home, he sent a short greeting to Kubizek. The card from Spital was the last word Kubizek received from Adolf; all contact was broken off until Hitler emerged as a political figure in Germany after the war.[16]

---

[14] *Statistisches Jahrbuch der Stadt Wien, 1908* (Vienna, 1910), p. 125.
[15] *Kubizek*, pp. 258-59.
[16] *Kubizek*, pp. 256, 260-62.

Hitler's most important movements in the fall of 1908 are clear although no first-hand account of his life is available. He returned to the Stumpergasse in September and settled down to his old routine. In October, he went again to the Art Academy and petitioned for admittance. Presumably, he had never told Kubizek that he intended to try to enter the Academy once more despite his low opinion of the professors who had rejected him. On the second occasion the results were even more crushing than before. The classification list merely recorded: "Adolf Hitler, Braunnau, a. I. Twentieth of April, 1889. German Catholic, Civil Servant [father], 4 [years] *Realschule*. Not admitted to the test." [17] The sample pictures he had submitted were presumably of such poor quality that the officials of the Academy saw no reason for reversing their earlier verdict. The "artist" Adolf Hitler was finished. His powerful ego had been dealt such a blow that he was unable to face the resumption of his artistic play with Kubizek.

In the middle of November, he informed Frau Zakreys that he was moving. He paid his share of the rent for the rest of the month and went in search of another residence. On the 18th of November he completed a police registration of his new lodging, room #16 in a building at Felberstrasse 22 in the 15th district.[18] The building was in the south-west portion of the city, adjacent to the *Westbahnhof*, a few blocks from the Stumpergasse. Two days after Hitler registered with the police, Kubizek returned to their old residence, but found neither his friend nor any trace of his whereabouts.

Hitler had run away in an effort to shake off his failure and to gain an opportunity to put his life into some kind of order. In his police registration for the Felberstrasse he listed his occupation as "student," not as "artist." [19] He had not gone to the Felberstrasse to play, and architectural toys would have to be temporarily shelved. Hitler needed answers, and he pared away the peripheral elements of his existence to get down to this task. Aside from the need to find a

---

[17] Heiden, *Der Fuehrer*, p. 53. Apparently nothing ever materialized out of the contact he had made with Prof. Roller of the Imperial Opera. But he later had great respect for Roller and regretted the death of his son in the Russian War. *Ziegler*, pp. 67, and 171-72; *Picker*, p. 182.

[18] Copy of Hitler's *Meldezettel*, August 20, 1909. *HA*, File 17, Reel 1.

[19] Copy of Hitler's *Meldezettel*, August 20, 1909. *HA*, File 17, Reel 1.

THE FIRST YEARS IN VIENNA

goal for his life, there was also the problem of money. He still had his 25 kronen pension, but even if he reduced expenditures, which was easier done alone than with Kubizek, this sum could not cover expenses. If he gave up opera visits and paid a lower rent, a sojourn on the Felberstrasse could still only last about a year. The eleven months spent on the Stumpergasse, from October 1907, to November 1908, had exhausted the money left by his father. Another year would dispose of his mother's bequest, assuming that it also amounted to 500 or 1,000 kronen.

Hitler stayed on the Felberstrasse just eight months, until August 1909. We know very little about his life during this time. One woman, who was slightly acquainted with him while he lived there, described him as polite and unusually reserved.[20] He was a solitary lodger, intent on resolving the crisis of his existence. Hitler claims that the catalyst which led him to new insights and a basis for his life appeared while he was attempting to work on a construction job.[21] Supposedly he was trying to learn the building trade and in the process discovered that he would have to join a trade union. After some ugly incidents with his fellow workers he was led to an awareness of the infamous Social Democrats, and thence to the unmasking of "the Jew" as the mastermind of the Marxist conspiracy. Hitler's explanation of the trend of his ideas is not totally impossible, but it seems unlikely. His attitude and outlook would have inhibited a recourse to degrading manual labor, such as construction work, unless he was bordering on starvation. He was not in this condition in 1909. Later, when he was really desperate, he resorted to charity rather than work as an unskilled laborer. In any event, Hitler was not very husky, and, after three years of idleness, he probably would have found it beyond his strength. Yet there is no point in totally rejecting Hitler's story. He may have looked in on a laborer's job while he was on the Felberstrasse and, in the process, could have been roughed up a bit by the workers.[22] Such a humiliation could have

[20] Statement by Marie Wohlrab and Marie Fellinger, *HA*, File 17, Reel 1.
[21] *Mein Kampf*, pp. 37-53.
[22] Hitler described his construction experience as being the origin of his anti-Marxism. *Mein Kampf*, pp. 37-53 and 80-81. Greiner uses a garbled version of the story (*Greiner*, pp. 42-45), while Jetzinger totally rejects the idea that Hitler ever did any kind of work. *Jetzinger* (G), pp. 192-96; *Jetzinger* (E), pp. 131-33.

motivated an all-out effort to get at the root of his difficulties.

In any event, while on the Felberstrasse, Hitler caught hold of an approach that seemed to offer a prospect of opening up the secrets of life and society. In a tobacco shop near his lodging he bought a magazine called *Ostara*. This publication was the product of the disturbed mind of one Lanz von Liebenfels, a mystical theorist whose attitudes and problems were quite similar to Hitler's own.[23] *Ostara* expounded a racial doctrine which contrasted blond, blue-eyed Aryan heroes with dark, hairy ape men. Human existence, according to Lanz, revolved around the racial struggle between these two groups. He called upon the public and the state to take all means to strengthen the Aryan cause. Since race and blood were the points at issue, the protection of the Aryan female was essential. *Ostara* was filled with lurid tales and illustrations describing the perils which awaited blond heroic women who fell into the clutches of ape-like men. Lanz also was tormented by visions of the sexual impotence of Aryan males and the all-powerful female sexuality which drew Aryan women towards the allegedly potent ape-like men.[24] The sexual arguments, as well as other aspects of the doctrine, were supported by a rich admixture of occult features including old Germanic spells and number mysticism.

Ostara is the kind of publication that naturally appears in what has been called "subterranean intellectual life."[25] A mixture of the occult and the erotic that sprang from the needs of one lost soul, it found its market among the host of homeless individuals who inhabited the cheap lodging houses of a great city. In the March 1908 issue of *Ostara*, there was only one advertisement in addition to those for Lanz and his friends. This was a full-page promotion for a book to aid young people in selecting a career, entitled, "What shall I become?" (*Was soll ich werden?*).[26] The advertiser had gauged *Ostara*'s readership exactly. Whether in the environs of a Salvation Army shelter in America or on Vienna's Felberstrasse, the young solitary clutching his self-respect and in desperate need of support

---

[23] *Daim*, passim. A tie between Hitler and the occult is also made by *Greiner*, pp. 86-93.
[24] *HA*, File 1229, Reel 52.
[25] Daim takes over the phrase from Friedrich Herr. *Daim*, p. 17.
[26] *HA*, File 1229, Reel 52.

remains the chief consumer of such publications. The answers they provide promise to guide lost men to an understanding of their condition and to new strength through the discovery of some secret explanation for the world's problems. *Ostara* provided a cosmic system that could explain life, death, and all the phenomena that had so baffled its readers before their enlightenment. It even furnished a scale (*Rassenwertigkeitsindex*), by which the individual could find out what kind of man he was. So many points were given for color of hair, skin, etc. After adding up the points, the reader consulted the index to determine his racial group. Anyone who found *Ostara*'s doctrines remotely congenial could emerge at least as a "mixed type" (Hitler would have been a "mixed type"), and thereby qualify to participate in the great struggle against the lower races.

The racial message of *Ostara* – and one may assume the erotic element as well – exerted some influence on Hitler while he was living on the Felberstrasse. He bought *Ostara* regularly, and even sought out Lanz in 1909 in order to obtain back issues of the publication. Much to his joy, Lanz provided these without charge. Fifteen months later, after at least three changes of address, Hitler was still carrying his collection of *Ostara* with him.[27] However, *Ostara* was too fantastic and too detached from day-to-day concerns to provide a completely satisfying philosophy for the young Hitler. Lanz was an oracle, not a political leader. He did not have a detailed political or social program, he equivocated with respect to the Jews, and he failed to come to grips with the issue of German nationalism. He probably gave Hitler some ideas, but his real significance lies in the fact that he pointed out directions in which Hitler could find more compelling answers. For Lanz showed the way to such Germanic theorists and mystics as Guido von List – men who were creating justifications for German supremacy out of ideas and events of the distant past. He also suggested a need for an aroused Germandom based on racial anti-Semitism. Though *Ostara* played down "the Jewish Question," it also eulogized Schoenerer and looked favorably on the *Alldeutsche*.[28]

Hitler may very well have followed up both of these lines of thought. The specifics of what he read are again a mystery, but it is

[27] Daim, pp. 20-21, 243-44, note 8, and 248, note 38.
[28] Pichl, Vol. VI, pp. 531-32.

unlikely that he struggled through such weighty tomes as Chamberlain's *Foundations of the 19th Century*. More likely, as he hints in *Mein Kampf*,[29] he depended primarily on pamphlet literature for the raw material from which he pieced together a racial doctrine that was in a sense simultaneously historical, social, and political. It was a slow and uneven process, and he did not make much headway in 1909. Yet from this point on he was committed to the task of constructing a personal philosophy, out of heterogeneous trends and currents, which finally jelled as the *voelkisch* ideology shortly before World War I. As such, it was a major turning point in his development.

In the fall of 1909, Hitler's "studies" were temporarily cut short. He had to leave the Felberstrasse. On August 22, 1909, he registered his new address with the police as Sechshauserstrasse 58, room #21.[30] This building lay in the 14th district, only a few blocks south of the Felberstrasse. Hitler did not sneak out of the Felberstrasse residence; he filled out the moving slip properly, complete with his forwarding address. He listed his occupation as "writer," rather than "student" as on his previous police registration form. Presumably the rent was paid, and he could still maintain the gloss of respectability. However, he was in serious trouble. His money was nearly gone. Even with his 25-kronen monthly pension, his prospects were grim with winter approaching.

It was time-consuming, the business of getting poor.[31] Every penny had to be stretched to the limit, while surplus belongings were turned into cash. At the same time appearances had to be preserved, for the landlord must not suspect that the rent payment was in danger. Constant vigilance had to be combined with studied deprivation. The road to poverty operates against the search for work in the most determined of men. The individual is too busy, too racked by worry and uncertainty to plan accurately. Somewhere en route the garments which certify respectability are turned over to the pawn shop or the old clothes dealer. To seek work clad in tattered clothes is for most men a confession of failure and shame. Hitler, never anxious for

---

[29] *Mein Kampf*, p. 56.
[30] Copy of Hitler's *Meldezettel*, August 22, 1909. *HA*, File 17, Reel 1.
[31] A work which gives a revealing glimpse into this process is George Orwell, *Down and Out in Paris and London* (New York, 1959).

employment under the best of circumstances, made no effort to find a job.

After holding on for about three weeks, he slipped out of his lodging on the Sechshauserstrasse. The police form which registered his move was not filled out by him, and the space for a future address was left blank. In reply to the question "when did he move out?" there was written "unknown." [32] The registration slip was dated September 16, 1909. Presumably Hitler had exhausted his money and skipped out of his lodging without paying the rent. For three months there is no record of him in the official registers of the police. No account of anyone who knew him in this period has survived. There are hints that in October or November he slept in a cheap coffee shop on the Kaiserstrasse, and for a while on the Simondenkgasse.[33] If he did, no registration was made with the police. He later claimed that one of his landlords during this period took advantage of him and seized his small bundle of possessions.[34]

Hitler was on the run, and total poverty pressed him hard. In desperation he took to the streets, slept on benches and what the tramps call the "green blanket," i.e., the park lawns. October and November were bad months for sleeping on benches in Vienna; the weather was cold, with flurries of snow and abundant rain.[35] Hitler was an inexperienced and helpless tramp, too squeamish to endure the havens used by professional tramps in bad weather. If he had been tough enough, he could have covered the cost of a cheap flophouse with his 25 kronen a month. For the really hardened, sewers, adjacent to the main canals, were used as nightly shelter during the

---

[32] Copy of Hitler's *Meldezettel*, August 22, 1909. *HA*, File 17, Reel 1.
[33] The stay on the Kaiserstrasse is mentioned by *Hanisch*, April 5, 1939, p. 239. The room on the Simon Denkgasse originates in Heiden, but it is questionable, since all Hitler's other addresses lay in the southern part of the city while this is far to the north. Heiden, *Der Fuehrer*, p. 55. The use of bars for tramp lodging was not an uncommon phenomenon at the turn of the century. In America it occurred so frequently the tramps had a special name for a bar in which they could sleep; it was called a "two-cent dosser." Josiah Flynt, *Tramping with Tramps* (New York, 1907), p. 119.
[34] *Hanisch*, p. 239.
[35] Snow and rain were especially bad during the last week of November and the first week of December. *Jahrbuch der KK Zentral-Anstalt Fuer Meteorologie, etc. Jahrgang 1909*, pp. A 108 and A 118.

winter.³⁶ But Hitler probably did not join the miserable wretches in the sewers. Instead, he dodged in and out of cheap lodging houses, resorting to the park when all else failed. Since he was thinly clad, he must have taken a good deal of punishment in a short period of time.

By the middle of December 1909, he was desperate enough to take his place openly in the ranks of the tramps. He drifted to Meidling, a district of Vienna south of his familiar territory between the Stumpergasse and the Felberstrasse. There, directly behind the south station, was the *Obdachlosenheim*, a shelter maintained by a Viennese philanthropic society for the benefit of the homeless. The Meidling shelter was a huge establishment barely a year old, able to provide lodging for a quarter of a million destitutes during 1909.³⁷ It was designed to care for that desperate segment of the population that had failed completely in the city. Hitler's entry into the *Obdachlosenheim* was a declaration of utter defeat.

Shortly before Christmas (the exact date is unknown), he took his place in the long line of beaten men and women which formed in front of the shelter every evening. The people stood quietly, broken and dejected, until the gates were thrown open. They were segregated by sex, children going with the mothers, and led into long halls where benches were provided. If the crowd was too large for the regular facilities and the weather was severe, other large barn-like buildings also were used on a temporary basis. When Hitler arrived at the shelter he was fortunate enough to be accommodated in the main building, and upon taking his place in the hall received a card entitling him to a week's lodging. Showers were provided for all, and vermin-infested garments, such as Hitler's, were disinfected. The method used to disinfect was clumsy and often seriously streaked, spotted and otherwise damaged the clothing. After their showers, the new arrivals returned to the main hall, which was fitted out with tables at one end where they were served a portion of bread and soup before retiring to assigned dormitories.³⁸

In the dorms, the professional tramps were in control because of their large numbers and their experience and skill in prospering

---

[36] William Alexander Jenks, *Vienna and the Young Hitler* (New York, 1960), pp. 33-36.
[37] *Statistisches Jahrbuch etc., 1909*, pp. 836 and 838.
[38] Hanisch, p. 239.

under such conditions. Each man had a wire-spring cot with two brownish sheets and his clothes for a pillow. Great care was taken by the professionals to make certain their clothing and shoes were kept in the best possible condition. Conversations began, experiences were swapped, and new plans were made for future travels. For Hitler, that first taste of camaraderie with tramps must have been the most galling experience imaginable; he sat on his cot dejected and silent. His neighbors took note of him and tried to be helpful. When they discovered he was hungry, bread was found, and an old beggar volunteered the suggestion that Hitler should go the next day to the convent on the Gumpendorferstrasse, where soup was given to the poor between nine and ten. This form of begging was known among the tramps as "calling on Kathie," presumably because that was the name of the Mother Superior or of the convent itself (St. Katharina). The next morning Hitler and some of his companions went the five or six clocks to "call on Kathie." Ironically, the convent was situated only a few doors from the Stumpergasse, where Hitler had resided as the young gentleman two years before.

In the ensuing days, Hitler passed under the protection of the tramps because he was completely helpless. A drifting servant named Reinhold Hanisch, who had a cot near Hitler's and was also "calling on Kathie," tried to help him and succeeded in "raising his spirits" somewhat. Hitler also received help from a number of other people. When he did not go to the Gumpendorferstrasse, he followed the advice of another inhabitant of the shelter and took advantage of the soup distribution made by a neighboring hospital. He was still very tired, his feet had given out, and his clothes were badly tattered and streaked from the disinfection procedure used by the shelter. During the first five days' stay he learned enough, and was helped sufficiently, to master the system. There was a brisk traffic in the cards issued by the shelter. Veterans who had used up their cards bought up the unused portions of those who were moving on. By using this method Hitler was able to remain for the better part of two months.[39]

---

[39] *Hanisch*, p. 240; Hanisch statement, *HA*, File 64, Reel 3. During the investigation of Hanisch's case in 1936, the police confronted him with a long list of police registrations by Hitler and himself which seemed to indicate that he did not meet Hitler in the Meidling shelter in December 1909. *HA*,

During this time he drew closer to Hanisch, who was helpful and experienced in the ways of tramping. Hanisch had spent a number of years in Berlin, was strongly nationalistic in outlook and had at one time been interested in a painter's career. Hitler was enthusiastic about Germany and constantly begged Hanisch to tell him about conditions in the Reich. For his part, Hanisch was impressed by the fact that Hitler had enjoyed some education, had read widely, and claimed to be a painter. The two joined forces. Under Hanisch's direction Hitler began to get hold of himself again after the fearful plunge to the bottom of the pit.

Hanisch taught Hitler how to master the worst problems growing out of the cold and how to acquire a bit of money. Their most serious difficulties were occasioned by the fact that they could not stay in the shelter during the day. It was essential for them to find some kind of protection in the bad weather. On the coldest days would make a wide circuit which began at the shelter, with the first stop at the Gumpendorferstrasse for food, from there to the warming room in Erdberg, and back to the shelter in time for the opening of the gates. The trip involved about two and a half hours' walk in each direction and was hard on Hitler because of his weak condition and thin, tattered clothes which gave him little protection.[40] It was the best, however, that the life of the tramp had to offer; the alternative was to stand or crouch in a doorway and risk frostbite or the arrival of the police. Hitler and Hanisch made the daily trip through town during the heart of the winter of 1909-1910. Occasionally, especially desperate or in a moment of exhilaration, they looked for temporary work. Sometimes Hitler went to the Westbahnhof hoping to find a traveler who needed help with his luggage, but he was

---

File 1741, Reel 86. Faced with the list, Hanisch changed his story, but he seems to have been right the first time. The police list was replete with errors, as Hitler's *Meldezettel* clearly indicates. Furthermore, Hanisch stated before a Viennese court in August 1910 that he had met Hitler in December 1909 in the shelter. This statement was not challenged by Hitler or the court. Heiden, *Der Fuehrer*, p. 71. For an estimate of the major sources relating to Hitler between late 1909 and 1913 see Appendix II.

[40] *Hanisch*, p. 239; Hanisch statement, *HA*, File 64, Reel 3. Greiner's first description of Hitler tallies fairly well with the picture presented by Hanisch, but it is impossible to determine what period Greiner is describing. *Greiner*, pp. 14 and 16-18.

weak and his appearance was so disreputable that he seldom succeeded. When heavy snow fell, Hanisch and some others took Hitler along to shovel snow, but his bad feet and flimsy attire made him suffer terribly, and he almost turned blue with the cold.[41] On one occasion he considered answering a request for ditchdiggers, but Hanisch dissuaded him. He was certain that Hitler was too weak for the work, but the argument he used against the job was that once a person started such hard manual labor, "it is very difficult to climb up." [42] In the end Hitler did not answer the ditchdigger call; instead he made the rounds, "called on Kathie" and trudged to the warming rooms.

As the bad weather continued, Hitler slowly sank back into a state of depression. Hanisch began to worry about his health. His concern and sense of devotion increased when Hitler happened to mention that his family has some money and if he could acquire some it might be possible to paint a few pictures. Hanisch immediately suggested that Hitler send for the money to get himself an overcoat and also to acquire the materials to paint. He added that he would be happy to sell any pictures Hitler produced.[43] Hitler procrastinated for understandable reasons. The prospect of writing to Angela for money was not pleasant. Finally Hanisch's urgings prevailed. Hitler promised to try provided he could obtain some writing materials. Hanisch and a salesman from Silesia, who also had caught the whiff of money, took him to the Cafe Arthaber by the Meidling station, and there Hitler wrote for help.[44] Perhaps he finally mustered enough courage to write to Angela, but it seems more likely he wrote to his Aunt Johanna and told her he needed extra money to complete his studies. From whomever the addressee came a quick reply containing approximately 50 kronen.[45] Hanisch suggested that Hitler go

---
[41] *Hanisch*, p. 240; Hanisch statement, *HA*, File 64, Reel 3. The story that Hitler sought work at the *Westbahnhof* is plausible. During the previous two years his life had rotated around this central point; when in trouble, he seems to have returned to familiar territory to get help.
[42] *Hanisch*, p. 240.
[43] *Hanisch*, pp. 240-41 and Hanisch statement, *HA*, File 64, Reel 3. Hanisch was more honest about his own motives in the earlier unpublished note than in his *New Republic* article.
[44] *Hanisch*, p. 240; Hanisch statement, *HA*, File 64, Reel 3. A badly garbled version of this series of events appears in *Greiner*, pp. 18-19.
[45] *Hanisch*, p. 240. Hanisch was badly confused concerning the details of

to the Jewish quarter and buy an overcoat, but Hitler refused because he was afraid he would be cheated. Finally, Hanisch took him to the government pawn shop, the *Dorotheum,* where he acquired a dark winter overcoat for 12 kronen.[46]

Having solved the most pressing problem of the cold, Hitler took a few days' rest to recover from the worst hardships of the winter. Then, following Hanisch's advice, he took steps to begin painting pictures to be sold as postcards. To carry out this project he had to find lodgings where he could work during the day. After some consideration, he decided to move all the way across Vienna to the Men's Hostel or *Maennerheim* in the north-east corner of the city. There he would be able to paint and enjoy more agreeable quarters than he had in the Meidling shelter. On the 9th of February, 1910, after two years in the south-west part of Vienna, Hitler moved into the Men's Hostel in the 20th district.[47] Two days later, Hanisch left Meidling and took a temporary job as a servant. After four days on the job he followed Hitler to the Men's Hostel in Brittgenau. There they worked out their plan for painting and selling picture postcards.[48]

Hitler's family, especially in his belief that there was only one sister. Greiner was similarly confused. *Greiner,* pp. 14-15. Jetzinger speculates that it was Johanna to whom Hitler appealed for money. His argument is plausible. *Jetzinger* (G), p. 223; *Jetzinger* (E), pp. 134-35.

[46] *Hanisch,* p. 240; Hanisch statement, *HA,* File 64, Reel 3.
[47] Copy of Hitler's *Meldezettel,* February 9, 1910. *HA,* File 17, Reel 1.
[48] Investigation of Hanisch, *HA,* File 1741, Reel 86; *Hanisch,* pp. 240-41.

VII

THE LATER VIENNA PERIOD, FEBRUARY 1910 TO JUNE 1913

The haven in which Hitler and Hanisch carried out their work was the hostel for men, or *Maennerheim*, at 22 Meldemannstrasse in the Brittgenau, a district next to the Jewish quarter of Leopoldstadt on the banks of the Danube. The Brittgenau was an industrial suburb, a laboratory sample of the social problems associated with such an area in a rapidly developing economy. Far greater ethnic variety prevailed there than in most areas of the city. There were a sizeable Czech-speaking minority, a noticeable sprinkling of Poles, and more Jews than in any district of the city except Leopoldstadt. This population was not merely diverse; it was also mobile. A high percentage of the residents planned to remain only temporarily.[1]

In 1900, Brittgenau had been taken into the city and designated the "20th district." Shortly afterward, the "Emperor Franz Joseph I Jubilee Foundation for Citizens' Housing and Welfare Institutions" built its hostel for men in the northern corner of the district, approximately three blocks from the northwest railroad station and seven or eight blocks from the Danube.[2] The *Maennerheim* was a large building designed to house approximately 500 men. The offices and principal eating room occupied the main floor, while the upper levels contained endless rows of small sleeping cubicles. Cubicles were an innovation for the period. They provided the lodgers with much more security and privacy than the customary open dormitories. The cubicles each contained a simple bed, a little table, clothes rack and

---

[1] 1910 census insert (no pagination) in *Statistische Jahrbuch, 1910*. The election results are in *Statistische Jahrbuch, 1911*, pp. 126-27.
[2] Kuppe, p. 417; Jenks, *Vienna and the Young Hitler*, p. 26.

mirror. They were well maintained and featured a genuine luxury for migrant men – clean white sheets.

In various corners of the building, especially in the basement, services catered to the inhabitants' needs. A canteen offered food and beverages at low prices, although no alcoholic drinks were permitted. If lodgers preferred to cook their own meals, a large communal kitchen was at their disposal. Concessionaires, such as tailors and cleaners, were available, but there were also rooms where the lodgers could do their own laundry. Basement lockers could be rented by those who did not want to carry their valuables with them. On the upper level, various lounges were available for use during the day, including a very popular reading room.[3]

Operating procedures were simple. An individual could rent a room for 50 heller (half a krone) a night; this guaranteed him a clean cubicle and the use of the home's facilities. Lower weekly rates were also available, and long-term residents were allowed to occupy the same cubicle indefinitely. However, one condition held for both transient and permanent lodgers: the cubicles had to be vacated during the day. It was this rule that made the reading and lounging rooms important.[4]

The home, which provided excellent facilities at moderate rates in the middle of one of the most expensive cities in Europe, never lacked clientele. The great majority were the transient poor, men either seeking work or employed at temporary unskilled or semi-skilled jobs. There was, in addition, a heterogeneous group of permanent inhabitants who lacked family and friends in the city. Some were low-level white collar workers; others were craftsmen and semi-skilled laborers. There was also a sprinkling of lost academicians and lonely retired men without a home.[5] Except for the absence of women and children, the *Maennerheim* was a microcosm of the 20th district. The ethnically mixed residents depended on low-level in-

---

[3] Jenks, *Vienna and the Young Hitler*, pp. 26 ff.; statement by Karl Honisch, *HA*, File 17, Reel 1; *Greiner*, pp. 10-11.
[4] Statement by Karl Honisch, *HA*, File 17, Reel 1; Jenks, *Vienna and the Young Hitler*, p. 28.
[5] *Hanisch*, pp. 241 and 297. Statement by Karl Honisch, *HA*, File 17, Reel 1. Konrad Heiden, *Hitler, A Biography* (London, 1936), p. 16. For the high cost of living in Vienna see *Baedeker*, p. xii.

dustrial employment and possessed few ties to the area in which they lived.

When Hitler and Hanisch entered the *Maennerheim* in the winter of 1910, their new quarters must have seemed little short of paradise after Meidling. They quickly appropriated part of the reading room as the perfect location for their painting business. The reading room was open during the day and was usually occupied by people trying to make money at odd jobs, such as addressing envelopes or preparing advertisements.[6] The two men procured the material necessary for water color painting, and Adolf started preparing pictures, first in postal card size. He worked slowly, copying photographs or paintings of Vienna scenes. With rare exceptions, he avoided portraying the human form, but worked on the spacing and detail of his water colors as if he were producing architectural plans. Hanisch soon became impatient and urged him to throw anything on paper so they could get started. As quickly as Hitler could turn out small stocks of completed cards, Hanisch took them out to sell. Most of them were hawked in the taverns of the Prater on weekends.[7]

Within a short time both men realized that there were more profitable ways to market water colors than by peddling postal cards. Frame makers conducted a substantial business in Vienna, especially in the first and fourth districts. They customarily marketed their product complete with pictures, thus creating a steady demand for cheap illustrations. Another market was provided by the then fashionable couches with picture frames on the back. In response to the urgings of Hanisch, Hitler went to work on larger works, some in oil, for frame workers and furniture manufacturers.[8] Again, he painted only scenes of Vienna, sometimes touching them up to represent the city a century earlier. In this period Hitler never attempted an original painting, but always copied an existing picture. When he found a successful motif, he would repeat it a number of times, continuing until the market was exhausted. Most of his pictures were about twelve by eighteen inches, although during his stay in Vienna

---

[6] A striking similarity between two separate descriptions of the reading room group appears in *Hanisch*, p. 241, and the statement by Karl Honisch, *HA*, File 17, Reel 1.
[7] *Hanisch*, pp. 240-41; Hanisch statement, *HA*, File 64, Reel 3.
[8] *Hanisch*, p. 240.

he did some nearly twice as large. Once he had systematized this kind of painting, he could turn out a steady stream of work. When he wanted to paint diligently, he was able to produce one picture a day of fair quality, which earned about five kronen from the dealers. On rare occasions, a Hitler original sold for as much as 10 kronen, but even then he received only half the amount because he had agreed to split all proceeds with Hanisch.[9]

The Hanisch-Hitler partnership was quite successful at the beginning and soon elevated them above the worst deprivations of tramp life. New prosperity gave them a chance to catch their breath and take stock. In the early spring of 1910, Hitler's appearance was nearly as pathetic as it had been four months before in Meidling. To be sure, he was no longer suffering from cold and had enough to eat, but his streaked and tattered clothing looked disreputable. Only the overcoat acquired in the *Dorotheum* helped save appearances. He had let his hair grow long and even developed a crop of whiskers which earned him the name of "Paul Krueger," because he looked so much like the South African statesman.[10] It was an ironic echo of the Boer war battles he had fought as a child in Leonding!

With the return of better days, Hitler could not resist the temptation to indulge in some of his old pastimes. Sometimes he scraped together a few extra kronen and headed for the opera. When he lacked the price of a ticket, he went to free performances, ranging from the organ at the scenic railroad to a free band concert. On such occasions he lectured his companions on music and composers, invariably pointing out the pre-eminence of Wagner, who in his opinion completely overshadowed all other musicians.[11] The need to find inspiration for new paintings often led Hitler and Hanisch to the galleries. Here again Hitler seized every opportunity to expound his views on the arts. He was particularly enthusiastic about the work

[9] Hanisch, p. 241; Hanisch statement, *HA*, File 64, Reel 3. There is a great deal of incidental material on Hitler's painting in the *Hauptarchiv*, especially Files 25, 29 and 37. A garbled explanation of the painting system appears in *Greiner*, p. 12.
[10] Hanisch, p. 242; Heiden, *Hitler, A Biography*, p. 15; *Greiner*, pp. 20-21.
[11] Hanisch, p. 271. Describing Hitler in 1913, Honisch also emphasized the importance of his occasional opera visits. Statement by Karl Honisch *HA*, File 17, Reel 1. One wonders if he visited the small Wagner Museum then operating in Vienna. *The Newest Guide through Vienna and Environs* (Vienna, 1912), pp. 147-48.

of the architect Gottfried Semper, who had designed many of Vienna's monumental buildings. Often in the *Kunsthistorisches Museum* he would completely forget about paintings in his enthusiasm for the building and it was only with difficulty that Hanisch could bring his attention back to the business at hand. Whenever Hanisch pointed out paintings which might be used as models for improving his work, Hitler became bitter and morose.[12]

Hitler was happiest in the *Maennerheim*, among comrades whose principal subjects for discussion were schemes for making easy money. He found enthusiastic companions in Josef Greiner, once a lamplighter, and an ex-priest named Grill. Together they dreamed up techniques for separating the public from its money, ranging from a hair restorer to a cream supposed to keep windows from breaking. The three young men spent their time continuously debating and arguing. Their attention wandered to other subjects – from politics and economics to astrology and the occult. Hitler always had a strong opinion and found ample opportunity for partisan debate.[13]

The only man who resented these activities, aside from the somewhat apprehensive administrator of the hostel, was Hanisch, who found it increasingly difficult to get Hitler to paint. Adolf was lazy. As soon as he had a little money in his pocket, he lapsed into his old habit of dawdling and arguing with his neighbors. Hanisch urged and pleaded with him, pointing out that if he worked systematically they might actually earn a comfortable living and not exist just as aristocrats among the vagrants.[14] Hitler always promised to try harder, but the lure of discussion or the opera invariably proved too strong. In late May and early June 1910, Hanisch managed to hold him at work long enough to produce a number of paintings. After selling these pictures, Hanisch hoped to plow back the profits and expand the scale of their operation, but he failed to reckon with Hitler's laziness. Hitler had become quite friendly with a Jewish part-time art dealer named Neumann, who often came to the *Maennerheim* to buy paintings and other art goods produced by the resi-

---

[12] *Hanisch*, p. 298. The attempt to use trips to the *Kunsthistorisches Museum* as an incentive was highly speculative. It cost one krone to enter. *Baedeker*, p. 17.
[13] *Hanisch*, p. 241; *Greiner*, pp. 35-42, 102-105; *Daim*, pp. 31-32.
[14] Hanisch statement, *HA*, File 64. Reel 3; *Hanisch*, p. 241.

dents. Hitler and Neumann had a number of long discussions in which they even considered the possibility of immigrating to Germany together. Finally, on June 21st, Hitler left the *Maennerheim* in the company of Neumann and rented a hotel room. When Hanisch finally caught up with him, Hitler was by himself. He told his partner that he required a rest from his arduous toil and therefore planned to enjoy himself for a while. He added that, when his vacation ended, their business operations could resume. Apparently, the schemes he had concocted with Neumann had already been abandoned. Five days later, on June 26th, his adventure ended and, most of his money gone, he returned to the *Maennerheim*, forced to labor once more.[15]

During the rest of the summer, he followed a similar schedule. He worked diligently for a few days until he got some money, then played until he had to work again. On one occasion when he had some money, he went to a short silent film entitled *The Tunnel*, which vividly portrayed a successful demagogue. Hitler was fascinated. The film illustrated the power that could be achieved over the masses. For days, his companions in the home were harangued on the power of haranguing.[16] His interest in political questions, especially in political leaders, revived during the early months in Brittgenau. The biggest political questions of the day concerned the leadership and policies of the Christian Socialist Party. Their great leader, Karl Lueger, had died in March 1910. His lieutenants, of lesser stature, were squabbling over his political inheritance. Hitler had been fascinated by Lueger, despite the latter's identification with clerical politics, because he advocated social reform and possessed a sure touch in controlling a party which appealed to the masses.

In *Mein Kampf*, Hitler related the emotion which overcame him on March 10, 1910 as he watched the funeral procession bearing Lueger to his grave.[17] With Lueger gone, Hitler's attitude toward the Christian Socialist Party gradually cooled. He felt the party was too

---

[15] *Hanisch*, p. 241. Hanisch's story is fully supported by the police registration material in the *Hauptarchiv*. *HA*, File 1741, Reel 86 and File 65, Reel 13A.

[16] Hanisch statement, *HA*, File 64, Reel 3; *Hanisch*, p. 242.

[17] *Mein Kampf*, p. 121; Heinrich Schnee, *Karl Lueger: Leben und Wirken eines grossen Social- und Kommunal Politikers* (Berlin, 1960), pp. 108-109; *Greiner*, pp. 80 and 97; *Hanisch*, pp. 241-42.

sympathetic to the subject nationalities of the Empire and was, therefore, anti-German. At this period, he seems to have inclined toward Lutheranism rather than Catholicism, and the Christian Socialists were condemned for their clericalism. Later, he was to attack the party, and Lueger as well, for their "indulgent" variety of anti-Semitism.[18]

Hitler's attitude toward the Social Democratic Party did not suffer from any ambivalence; he was totally opposed to everything it stood for. Throughout his Vienna years, there is a steady and consistent record of his violent denunciations of the Socialists, which often led to embarrassing incidents.[19] He disliked their atheism, their attacks upon the state, and their efforts to gain total power. On only one point did he give them credit: like the Christian Socialists and the actor in *The Tunnel*, they knew how to put on a political show and could control the masses.

In the course of long political discussions, Hitler invoked a special authority symbol whenever he was seriously challenged. The prestige of his "respected father, Royal Customs Official Alois Hitler" was used to silence opposition and gain credence for ideas which usually had no relation to those of his late father. After all the conflicts during childhood over the importance and appeal of bureaucratic life, it seems ironic that Adolf would use his father and his father's status to prop up his own position among people whom old Alois would certainly have scorned! [20]

Not all of Hitler's reading room companions were impressed by his arguments or his authorities. He often had to endure insults and was once called a "reactionary swine," [21] but the appeal of arguing never wore off. He was always ready to put down his brush and go back to the attack. His total lack of resistance to the distracting influences of reading room discussions finally made his partner throw up his hands in despair.[22]

---

[18] *Hanisch*, p. 271; *Greiner*, p. 95; statement by Jacob Altenburg, *HA*, File 1741, Reel 86.
[19] *Hanisch*, pp. 241-242, 297; statement by Jacob Altenberg, *HA*, File 1741, Reel 86; *Greiner*, pp. 22-23, and 30; statement by Karl Honisch, *HA*, File 17, Reel 1.
[20] *Greiner*, pp. 14-15; also *Hanisch*, p. 240.
[21] *Greiner*, pp. 22-23.
[22] Hanisch gave a number of descriptions of these developments. *Hanisch*,

Hanisch arranged for a large painting order in July, but Hitler failed to meet delivery schedules. Thereupon, Hanisch tried to paint some of the pictures himself and discovered that he could do it satisfactorily. Before long, Hitler became suspicious. He tried to produce more of his own paintings and urged Hanisch to market them. Their relations quickly deteriorated. Finally, in July, in what may have been an attempt to heal the breach, Hitler painted a fairly large picture of the parliament building and Hanisch agreed to try to sell it. According to Hanisch, he did sell the picture and split the 10 kronen he received with Hitler. But according to the latter, Hanisch stole the picture, sold it, and pocketed the money. In any case, Hitler summoned the police, and Hanisch was arrested in early August. In his complaint, Hitler asserted that the picture was worth 50 kronen, and that he had not received any money from its sale. The picture in question, or a variation of the same motif, was available in the 1930's and Greiner, who saw it then, concluded that its value was far closer to 10 kronen than to 50 kronen.[23] The court failed to concern itself with the value of the picture or even who had done what to whom. In a grand anti-climax, it was discovered that Hanisch was living under an assumed name, calling himself Fritz Walter. The end result was that on August 11, 1910, Hanisch was sentenced to a few days in jail. Nothing was done about the painting or the alleged fraud. Hitler returned to the *Maennerheim* nursing the conviction that he had been ill-used.

Once again he was at loose ends, and, as on earlier occasions, apparently returned to the fixed idea of entering the Art Academy. He went to the *Hofmuseum* and contacted Professor Ritschel, who was in charge of the care and restoration of pictures. He asked the professor to recommend him for admission to the Academy.[24] One of Ritschel's assistants remembered that Hitler brought along a large portfolio of his paintings, produced with great architectural precision, which he displayed in support of his request. Either the professor was not sufficiently impressed or Hitler ultimately decided

---

pp. 299-300; Hanisch statement, *HA*. File 64, Reel 3; Hanisch's police disposition and amendments, *HA*, File 1741, Reel 86. Heiden has an extended treatment (Heiden, *Der Fuehrer*, pp. 69-71); *Greiner*, pp. 12-13 and 109.

[23] *Greiner*, p. 110. A later statement by Hanisch on a Parliament painting appears in *HA*, File 40, Reel 3. Heiden, *Der Fuehrer*, pp. 70-71.

[24] Statement by Prof. Leidenroth, *HA*, File 1741, Reel 86.

not to renew his application, for there is no record of a formal petition to the Academy in 1910.

Hitler decided instead to carry on his life at the *Maennerheim* and to take over the sale of his pictures himself. He preempted a corner of the reading room and sat there every day painting water colors. During the early part of the morning, he sketched out the picture, completing the detailed work and the coloring in the afternoon. When he had a sufficiently large supply, he made the rounds of the frame and picture dealers. The bulk of his paintings were sold to Jewish dealers, such as Altenberg and Landesberger. Relationships were polite and not marked by incidents. The highest price that Hitler received for a picture was about twelve kronen, but he often got no more than three or four. Thirty-four years later, at the height of his power, he could still describe these sales without expressing bitterness over the low prices. He frankly acknowledged that the pictures were trifles, painted solely to earn him a living. At the time, he was hampered by his poor salesmanship. He always returned to the same dealers to sell his wares and could not overcome his embarrassment and humiliation because he was forced to sell his work in this way.[25]

From 1911 to 1913, he continued to practice his trade as a painter. There was a steady demand for his work, and he settled down to systematic production without much interruption for play. With Hanisch gone, Hitler was able to approximately double his income by pocketing the full proceeds of the sales. This stabilization of his manner of life was accompanied by a marked improvement in his appearance. He took greater care to keep his hair cut and his face cleanly shaven. His clothes, though old and worn, were always kept clean and neat.[26] Hitler had become a petty businessman on the fringes of the art and decorating trade and as such was required to fit his habits and appearance to the dictates of the commercial

---

[25] The description of his technique is partly based on Honisch's account of his work in 1913. Statement of Karl Honisch, *HA*, File 17, Reel 1. Altenberg provided a description of his work and salesmanship. *HA*, File 1741, Reel 86. A most interesting account of Hitler the painter is contained in a fragment of a *Table Talk* entry made by Hitler in March 1944. This item, not included in the published portions of *Table Talk*, is in *HA*, File 36, Reel 2.

[26] Statement by Jacob Altenberg, *HA*, File 1741, Reel 86.

world. His other expenses were low; he was economical in his habits and his lodgings were cheap.

From all indications, he remained completely aloof from women, in part because of the continuation of his adolescent reserve. The shame he felt about his degraded status and shabby appearance reinforced this attitude. He not only abstained from any contact with women but also habitually attributed countless social evils to their immorality.[27] In another environment, such a contrived defense might well have been chipped away by social contacts with girls, but in the womanless *Maennerheim* he was able to maintain the stance of puritanic abstinence. He also did not drink; the ban on alcohol in the home reinforced this. His smoking was restricted to an occasional cigarette.[28]

The rent in the hostel was only three kronen a week. He usually cooked his own meals as a member of a cooking cooperative using the kitchens provided by the home. This substantially reduced his expenses. When he bought a meal in the dining room, the cost was low and the quantity and quality were both surprisingly good. As he discovered from his fellow lodgers, there were numerous places where he could pick up acceptable, clean clothing at moderate prices. His only extravagances were visits to the opera or an art gallery from time to time, but these were now well within his means. All together, his monthly living expenditures probably came to about 35 or 40 kronen, allowing 13 kronen for rent and 20 to 25 kronen for food and incidental expenses.[29] His income probably averaged over twice this amount. He received his 25 kronen orphan's pension until mid-1911 and had a gross income from his painting of 80 to 100 kronen a month when he worked regularly. The latter was not clear profit, since he had to pay for art supplies and carry himself over periods when business was slow or when he was distracted. Nevertheless, his painting must have netted an average of 50 to 75

---

[27] *Hanisch*, pp. 297-98; Greiner tends to the same conclusion but his exaggerations are particularly noticeable on this point. *Greiner*, pp. 29, 54-67, 98-99.

[28] Statement by Karl Honisch, *HA*, File 17, Reel 1; *Greiner*, p. 100.

[29] These estimates are based on the material provided in the following sources: *Hanisch*; statement by Karl Honisch, *HA*, File 17, Reel 1; Hitler's *Table Talk* comment, *HA*, File 36, Reel 2. In *Mein Kampf*, Hitler indicated that he was better off in approximately this period. *Mein Kampf*, p. 34.

kronen a month, a sum which greatly exceeded his living expenses, even without the orphan's pension.

This does not cover all of Hitler's income in 1910 and 1911. He apparently also benefited from a substantial inheritance. In December 1910, his Aunt Johanna Poelzl withdrew her life savings of 3,800 kronen from the bank without having made any public or legal disposition of the money.[30] In March 1911 she died without leaving a will. A survey of bank records made forty years later suggests that none of her logical heirs received sizeable sums between December 1910 and March 1911. In April 1911, Adolf's half-sister Angela began an action to claim Adolf's share of the orphans' pension which he and Paula had received since Klara's death. Angela insisted Adolf had no right to the money and that it should be used to help defray the cost of raising Paula. In a ruling by the Linz court on May 4, 1911, it was stated that Adolf had agreed that his share go to Paula because he was then "able to maintain himself." In addition, the judgment concluded on the basis of "inquiries" that Adolf had received "considerable sums of money for the purpose of his training as an artist from his Aunt Johanna Poelzl." [31]

The court ordered the guardian, Mayerhofer, thenceforth to apply Adolf's share of the pension to Paula. It is logical to assume that the "considerable sums of money" referred to part or all of the cash that Johanna disposed of between December 1910 and March 1911. Angela probably learned of this gift at the time of Johanna's death. She was in financial difficulties herself as a result of her husband's death in 1910. She traced Adolf and made him "agree" to renounce his portion after "inquiries" had produced the facts.

The transactions involving the probable disposition of much of Johanna's money and Angela's court action underscore the level of financial security that Hitler had achieved by 1911. He had sufficient money to allow him confidence and some leisure. Even more, he had acquired skill in a moderately profitable trade. He was in a position of real independence for the first time in his life. And, to some extent, Hitler had learned his lesson. He had become sufficiently experienced to plan ahead and save some of his income.

[30] *Jetzinger* (G), p. 230-31; *Jetzinger* (E), pp. 140-42.
[31] *Jetzinger* (G), p. 226; *Jetzinger* (E), pp. 137-40. A garbled version is in *Greiner*, p. 15.

By remaining in the *Maennerheim*, he could save money and still have fairly pleasant accommodations, but his attachment to the home went deeper. It was a haven for those who had no place in society; in terms of education, skills, and ability to cope with his world, Hitler was still a marginal man.[32]

In the reading room he associated with rootless men clustered together in search of strength from their collective weakness. To an outside viewer, they were scarcely more than a pathetic collection of individuals struggling to preserve the tatters of their self respect. In their own eyes, and also in comparison to the great mass of transient lodgers who took temporary refuge in the *Maennerheim*, they enjoyed substantial prestige. They were, after all, better than the common horde so much in evidence. They referred to themselves as the "intellectuals" [33] and took great pains to stress every aspect of their education or experience which tended to distinguish them from common vagabonds. Their insistence on the importance of permanent residence in the home was carried to absurd lengths. They maintained a careful distinction between their manner of speech and that of the transients and developed minor traditions, such as reserving certain chairs for the oldtimers in their group.[34]

Hitler could not remain unaffected by the social outlook of the reading room crowd because it came so close to his own concepts of middle-class superiority. Furthermore, when he looked down from his sanctuary upon the miserable lower orders, he must have seen them as members of the group from which he had so recently escaped. Hitler, who saw social relationships in a distorted mirror, readily accepted the transients of the lodging house as his stereotype of the working class. The distortion was increased by the fact that the humiliations and degradation which he had suffered as a helpless vagabond were still very much alive.

---

[32] Statement by Karl Honisch, *HA*, File 17, Reel 1. Hitler managed thenceforth to hold on to some savings. Though he complains of his poverty during the early *Kampfzeit*, he also speaks of his "small savings." *Mein Kampf*, p. 591.
[33] The term is used by Honisch. *HA*, File 17, Reel 1.
[34] Examples of this are sprinkled through Hanisch, and are even more obvious in Honisch. *HA*, File 17, Reel 1. Both *Greiner* and *Goerlitz und Quint* maintain that Hitler also lived in a hostel on the Wurlitzergasse at this time, but the police registrations indicate this is inaccurate.

For nearly three years following the break with Hanisch, he remained in the reading room circle. His routine virtually never varied. No significant changes were discernible in his appearance or his system of painting at his chosen spot by the window. He was generally respected by his companions because he was a veteran in the home and had some of the mystique of an artist. He was polite to everyone, but his politeness never gave way to familiarity. He was reserved, and he was also remote, letting no one come too close. When spoken to, he replied courteously; when someone was in trouble, he responded, but in general he was content to paint and mind his own business.[35]

His calm facade remained unruffled until a discussion of political or social questions began. Even then, he usually kept on working for a time, listening and contributing an occasional remark. Inevitably though, some statement would be made that irritated him. Then, according to Karl Honisch, who was a member of the reading room group in 1913, he would be completely transformed. Jumping up from his place at the table, he would throw down his brush or pencil and start a long and violent harangue. As he spoke, his face became animated. He would punctuate important points by throwing his head back and forth to add extra emphasis. Throughout, the characteristic dangling forelock tumbled down over his face. After raging and gesturing wildly for a few minutes, he would slow down and search the faces of the group for a sign of sympathetic understanding. Unable to discover anything but the stolid visages of his *Maennerheim* companions, he would abruptly stop speaking and, with a resigned wave of the hand, sit down and resume his painting.[36]

The ideas put forth in these tirades were partly obscured by his own enthusiasm and anger. That he attacked the "reds" and "Jesuits" (the Christian Socialists) is certain. He also seems to have expounded some of his old Pan-Germanic enthusiasms. However, the spasmodic outbursts in the reading room did not accurately reflect the degree to which Hitler's political ideas had ripened by 1912-1913. He had by this time read extensively in the polemical literature of the period.

[35] Statement by Karl Honisch, *HA*, File 17, Reel 1.
[36] Statement by Karl Honisch, *HA*, File 17, Reel 1.

His enthusiasm for Schoenerer's cause cooled considerably as he became more skeptical about the organizational ability and the political judgments of the old warrior. Schoenerer's failure to build up a mass movement was particularly distressing to the political tactician in Hitler.[37] By 1912, Schoenerer had faded into obscurity; what was left of his organization was difficult to take seriously. The independent Pan-Germans under Wolf still survived as a secondary political force, advocating the old program of more political power for the Germans and making strenuous, even wild, demands that all Germans be united in a single empire. Hitler never seems to have warmed to Wolf's group, however, though he was in sympathy with its political aims.[38] The absence of an effective appeal to the masses alienated him. Wolf never achieved Schoenerer's personal ascendency among his followers; neither man had the magnetic appeal necessary to attract and hold a sizable following.

For these reasons, the established Pan-German organizations could not appeal to Hitler, and the nationalistic movement in Bohemia was also of little interest.[39] The nationalist labor movement in Bohemia began its expansion in 1904. By 1913, it had evolved into a moderately cohesive group of organizations describing themselves as "National Socialist." The similarity of their objectives to those of the later Nazis, and their use of the same name, might tempt one to conclude that Hitler quietly absorbed their doctrines while he was in Vienna and merely carried them across the border into Germany. The Bohemian program of that era, which emphasized the national and ethnic bases of society and the need for action to protect German workers and German interests from Czech encroachment, tends to bolster this assumption. On the other hand, the differences were of greater significance. The Bohemians were primarily nationalists, not racists; their anti-Semitism was peripheral and never gained complete acceptance within the movement. More important, the movement was a Bohemian phenomenon, an outgrowth of regional conflicts between Czechs and Germans. Its failure to expand beyond

---

[37] *Mein Kampf*, pp. 98-100.
[38] The only source that presents Hitler as sympathetic to Wolf is the *Hauptarchiv* statement by Hanisch. *HA*, File 64, Reel 3.
[39] The most recent treatment of the Bohemian groups is Andrew Whiteside, *Austrian National Socialism Before 1918* (The Hague, 1962).

Bohemia served as an additional obstacle to Hitler's acceptance. In his later public or semi-public explanations of his political development, he never included Bohemian National Socialism among factors which had influenced him. This silence was not an effort to disguise ideological theft. The sharp divergence between Hitler's social outlook and that of the Bohemians precluded close connections. The early National Socialists were led by journeymen who felt threatened by the increase in Czech industrial workers in Bohemia. Their political organization was designed to provide a nationalistic defense of the special interests of working groups. The working class, even the proletarian character of Bohemian National Socialism, was alien to Hitler's rigid middle-class sense of superiority. He wanted nationalism, particularly Pan-Germanism, with a mass appeal, but not of a variety having lower-class origins and subordinated to lower-class interests.[40]

None of the social philosophies of the pre-World War I period had the combination of doctrines necessary to grip Hitler and sweep him into an established party. He had to pick and poke at the whole spectrum of political thought to assemble an ideology he found congenial. Since he turned a blind eye to actual social conditions, it was only through reading periodicals and pamphlets that he could ferret out the points he wished to use. His reading was spotty, yet purposeful. He carefully selected arguments and facts he found agreeable, and then ostentatiously displayed them in the reading room arguments.[41] In the course of what was evidently a drawn-out process, he ultimately hit upon the basic concept which suited him best: racism, and particularly anti-Semitism.

In arriving at this concept, Hitler resumed a train of thought begun on the Felberstrasse and interrupted by the grim poverty of Meidling. Credit for a portion of his racist theories can be given to *Ostara* and Lanz von Liebenfels; additional confirming and sup-

---

[40] It is peculiar that Professor Whiteside speculates on a possible relationship between the Bohemian movement and the later German Nazis but does not consider a possible influence of the Bohemians on Hitler while he was in Vienna.
[41] Hitler later gloried in the amount he had read in Vienna and his claims have been accepted by many. *Zoller*, p. 36; *Gosset*, pp. 50-51; *Greiner*, p. 83. One should be somewhat skeptical about the breadth of Hitler's reading, but there is little doubt that he did pore over partisan political literature.

porting ideas came from the organized Pan-Germans and other groups. However the extension and refinement of these doctrines were of greater significance.

According to the racial anti-Semites, Jews were an alien and subversive element in society, separated from their neighbors not merely by religion, but also by the taint of inferior blood. Furthermore, this allegedly inferior group was able to control society and corrupt everything in order to place all power in its own hands. Superimposed on these basic concepts were the fables, old and new: ritual murders, the Fagin imagery, and every anti-Jewish anecdote that could be uncovered. These, although colorful and important in gaining supporters among the rank and file, were secondary to the paradoxical axioms of the anti-Semites: the Jews, a tainted and inferior race, also ruled the world.[42]

In *Mein Kampf* and elsewhere, Hitler stated his conversion to racial anti-Semitism came while he was living in Vienna. In addition to his avowed youthful sympathies for Schoenerer, he claimed that he was led to this belief by an encounter with an eastern Jew and by the "study" of anti-Semitic literature. Precisely when his conversion took place is not clear. He wrote that he became a confirmed racial anti-Semite "within a year" after his arrival in the capital. This appears unlikely; during that period he was still dreaming dreams with Kubizek on the Stumpergasse. More probably it was during the year of his flight from the Stumpergasse and his discovery of sanctuary at the *Maennerheim* that the basis was laid for his beliefs.[43]

Several important considerations concerning the young Hitler revolve around his acceptance of racial anti-Semitism. As previously noted, it was not difficult to become an anti-Semite in prewar Vienna. Organized groups were working assiduously to spread anti-Semitic propaganda, and centuries of religious and economic prejudice had etched anti-Semitic attitudes deeply into the minds of many Austrian Germans. Their environment was saturated with anti-Semitic catch phrases and stereotypes. The necessary guidelines for making an

---

[42] An excellent, intuitive discussion of the question is given by Jean-Paul Sartre, *Portrait of the Anti-Semite* (New York, 1946).
[43] *Mein Kampf*, pp. 55-60; *Adolf Hitlers Reden*, p. 96; Hitler's autobiographical statement, *HA*, File 17, Reel 1.

alleged Jewish conspiracy the central core of a *Weltanschauung* had been worked out in detail by *voelkisch* thinkers.

Racial anti-Semitism had many attractions for a bitter but ambitious young man. Above all, the doctrine supplied a simple, effective and ego-satisfying explanation of self and society. One could transfer all weakness and inadequacy to the Jewish stereotype; every failure could be explained as the work of the same malevolent chameleon. To the young Hitler, desperately needing self-justification, the discovery of a hidden Jewish conspiracy, working its influence on all economic, political and religious affairs, was a godsend. The path to the self-confidence and security which had eluded him so long clearly lay in the direction of racial anti-Semitism.

Reading and study of anti-Semitic literature was the most important factor in Hitler's adoption of Jew-hatred as an ideology. His vivid account of one personal incident which allegedly involved an eastern Jew should not outweigh his own admission that "study" provided the key.[44] The theoretical and abstract plane on which his anti-Semitism developed was reflected in his relations with other people. Through his adolescence and early manhood, he had close personal contacts with a number of people whom the racists considered inferior. During his last year in Linz, he had a Polish piano instructor and a Jewish doctor. His landlady on the Stumpergasse was Polish, and Kubizek was apparently of Czech origin. In the *Maennerheim* he was very friendly with Neumann, a Jewish art dealer, and in 1912-1913 he had a pleasant personal and business relationship with Jacob Altenberg, another Jewish art dealer. As late as 1936, Hanisch insisted Hitler had not been anti-Semitic when he lived in Vienna; he presented a long account of Hitler's cordial relations with Jews in order to prove it.[45]

The apparent contradiction between Hitler the racist and Hitler the companion of "racial inferiors" may be resolved by underscoring the theoretical character of his racism. He seems to have been able to compartmentalize his ideology, not letting it intrude on his daily business and social life. This helps explain the apparent absence of conflicts with Jews during his years in the hostel, and the rather

---

[44] *Mein Kampf*, pp. 55-60; *Adolf Hitlers Reden*, p. 96; Hitlers's autobiographical statement, *HA*, File 17, Reel 1.
[45] *Hanisch*, pp. 271-72.

surprising fact that the only two witnesses to his political discussions during 1912-1913 make no mention of anti-Semitic remarks.[46] As long as he kept his ideology in the background it was possible to go on living in an uncongenial environment. In the process, a large gap opened between his ideas and the life around him. The Jewish stereotype, vague and yet many-sided, became even more amorphous and flexible. The compartmentalization, once established, discouraged any effort on his part to measure the stereotypes of his ideology against the individuals with whom he associated. How long he could have maintained this precarious balance it is difficult to say. In the spring of 1913, he left the *Maennerheim*.

In the early months of 1913, Hitler told his companions in the reading room that his sojourn in Vienna was about to end. He often spoke of his great plans for the future. Munich was his destination. Once there he would apply for admission to the Art Academy. The revival of his artistic dreams in the face of the rebuffs and disappointments suffered in Vienna is surprising, yet it seems to have been genuine.[47]

There was an additional reason for his departure, about which he was much more reticent. Under Austrian law, he should have registered for military service in 1909 but had failed to do so. He had also ignored the requirement to report in the three following years.[48] By 1913 he apparently had reached the conclusion that the law requiring him to appear for possible induction had been satisfied because he had survived three years without being caught. It never seems to have occurred to him that because he had not appeared before the authorities he was still subject to induction and also to prosecution as a draft dodger. He optimistically concluded that after his twenty-fourth birthday (April 1913) he would be able to leave Austria without danger of pursuit by the Austrian authorities. He was wrong,

---

[46] Statement by Jacob Altenberg, *HA*, File 1741, Reel 86; statement by Karl Honisch, *HA*, File 17, Reel 1. Many aspects of theory and "encounters" in the development of anti-Semitism have been treated in the psychological literature. See T. W. Adorno, Else Frenkel-Brunswik, et. al., *The Authoritarian Personality* (New York, 1950); and *Ackermann*. The whole trend of anti-Semitic thought in the decade before the war was more abstract and theoretical. *Mosse*, pp. 190-237; and *Pulzer*, pp. 236-58.
[47] Statement by Karl Honisch, *HA*, File 17, Reel 1.
[48] *Jetzinger* (G), pp. 253-72; *Jetzinger* (E), pp. 144-59.

THE LATER VIENNA PERIOD, 1910–1913 151

and in 1914 he had great difficulty disentangling himself from the ensuing maze of legal complications.

When he left the *Maennerheim* and Austria such concerns were remote; his departure took place in an easy and carefree atmosphere. After packing his scanty belongings in a single piece of hand luggage, he found another resident of the home who planned to go to Germany. On June 24th, 1913, the two men started on their way, accompanied a short distance by their friends from the home. They apparently set out on foot, but soon switched to public transportation. On the 26th of June, Hitler crossed the border into Germany. He quickly went on to Munich, registered with the Munich police as a "painter and writer," and gave his address as Schleissheimerstrasse 34.[49] The Austrian phase of his development was over. The fateful German phase was about to begin.

---

[49] Copy of Hitler's *Meldezettel* and statement of entrance to Germany, *HA*, File 17, Reel 1. The word "Schriftsteller" may have been added to the police records at a later date.

VIII

THE YOUTH AND THE MAN

Hitler's departure from Austria in the early summer of 1913 is the terminal point of this study. Except to conduct a few border discussions with Austrian National Socialists in the early 1920's, he did not return to his homeland again until the *Anschluss*. The formative years spent in Austria as a child and young man obviously continued to exert great influence, but the key question is in what ways did this early period put a distinctive stamp on the later man? How many of the characteristics which helped to make Hitler the spellbinding speaker, *voelkisch* leader and successful dictator had already developed by 1913?

Such questions invite logical pitfalls. When the end result is known, it is a simple matter to find early signs and foreshadowings which point to the final conclusion. Conversely, it is easy to ignore the important fact that youth is not adulthood. Prudence requires that significant features of his life and activities which had not developed in 1913 be outlined first, even though they are widely known.

Hitler was a young man in 1913, barely twenty-four years old. He had no important friends or acquaintances in the political or economic life of Germany or Austria. His opinions on German conditions were based solely on second-hand information. He had no political experience, had never been a member of any political group, and had not had the opportunity to examine the inner workings of a political or propaganda organization. He had difficulty meeting people, was somewhat diffident when facing important men, and had no experience in public speaking, except for his outbursts in the reading room of the *Maennerheim*.[1] His ideological position, though sketched out in broad strokes, still lacked the clarity and cohesion that would be provided by direct contact with men like Dietrich Eckhart and Alfred Rosenberg.[2]

Despite the harshness of his life in Vienna, he did not manifest then those qualities of toughness and brutal ruthlessness that characterized his later years. As a young man, he had shown streaks of selfishness and petty meanness but not the cold determination that disregarded all human feeling. His own opinion – that he acquired a hard cutting edge from his experiences in the war – well may be correct.[3] The war also supplied a resolution of his uncertainties about a career. He went to Munich in 1913 still chasing the will-o'-the-wisp of an artist's life. His dream of admission to the art academy in Munich failed to materialize, and he was forced to live by selling paintings as he had done in Vienna. However, in Munich he did not find a large commercial art market, and he was forced to hawk his pictures in beer halls and from door to door.[4] Financially, the move to Munich was a failure and probably heightened his confusion about what he wanted to do with his life. It is not surprising, therefore, that he fell on his knees and thanked heaven when war came. The war provided him with an opportunity to realize his ideological dreams; more immediately, it also provided an escape from an increasingly serious economic dilemma. The Hitler who emerged from the conflict was a tougher, more resolute man, who could move from his assignment as an army political instructor into the rough-and-tumble of small party politics.[5] Gone were the frustrating career

[1] *Picker*, p. 323; statement of Karl Honisch, *HA*, File 17, Reel 1.
[2] The ideological role of Eckhart is emphasized by *Mosse*, pp. 296-97. Eckhart's position is described and analyzed in Ernst Nolte, "Eine fruehe Quelle zu Hitlers Antisemitismus," *Historische Zeitschrift*, Vol. 192, No. 3, pp. 584-606.
[3] "It was with feelings of pure idealism that I set out for the front in 1914. Then I saw men falling around me in thousands. Thus I learned that life is a cruel struggle and has no other object but the preservation of the species. The individual can disappear, provided there are other men to replace him." *Table Talk*, p. 44. Prof. Mosse states that the Nazis were ideologically opposed to Social Darwinism. Many of them were, but Hitler himself was very receptive to it and frequently expressed himself in Social Darwinist language. *Table Talk*, pp. 44, 134, 141.
[4] Examples of this are in *HA*, Files 30, 31, and 36, Reel 2.
[5] Ernst Deuerlein, "Hitlers Eintritt in die Politik und die Reichswehr,"

conflicts of prewar years. For the first time he could harmonize his ideology and ambitions. The war also created the arena in which he could display what proved to be his talents. The confusion of postwar Germany provided the ideal environment for an ambitious young man – an outsider in the old order – to succeed as a radical politician.

Since so many of the distinctive features of the Hitler history knows appeared in the years immediately following 1913, the carryovers from childhood and youth appear less striking and dramatic. Yet he surely acquired certain characteristics and predispositions from his Austrian experience which greatly accelerated his evolution and contributed to his success. His ideology was tailored to fit thinking both in wartime Germany and in the period of conservative reaction following the revolution in Bavaria. It needed additional polishing, but the major tenets had been grasped. More important, they had penetrated deeply. Racial anti-Semitism had long been Hitler's answer to the problems of identity and purpose which had troubled him as a youth. The circumstances of his childhood, his alienation from his father and the period of adolescent withdrawal all exerted pressures upon him. He had not broken under these pressures, nor had he followed the customary road of reluctant adjustment to middle-class society. He had fought for his identity as a deliberate outsider in both Linz and Vienna. The concepts Hitler used to find himself were less dispensable than the personal props employed by the average man, for they were worked out with a minimum of social empathy. They were his; he stood or fell with them.

In the course of his youthful development, Hitler also acquired certain characteristics which later helped him in politics. He learned to place emphasis on self-reliance and developed an unusual degree of lonely reserve. At Linz, in and out of school, he was a "loner"; in Vienna he learned to exist within a group but to erect walls which isolated him from other people. In the *Maennerheim*, the only way he could escape the unpleasant features of his environment was to remain above it, polite and outwardly agreeable, but always suggest-

---

Vierteljahrshefte für Zeitgeschichte, VII (April 1959), pp. 179-85, 191-205; Reginald H. Phelps, "Hitler and the Deutsche Arbeiterpartei," *American Historical Review*, LXVIII, No. 4 (July 1963), pp. 974-86.

ing personal undercurrents which would not be exposed to the multitude.[6] In this way he let the vagrants' world influence him and still retained enough personal strength to pull free. This reserve was an essential precondition for his later performance as Fuehrer. The role of leader demanded that he be within and yet stand apart — the very talent he had acquired in the hostel.

The *Maennerheim* also seems to have made an important contribution to the development of his social thinking. His short experience as an actual tramp has received heavy emphasis from biographers, but it was during the three years of settled existence in the *Maennerheim* that he had the best opportunity to study social groups. His low opinion of the masses because of the ease with which they could be manipulated probably owed much to this experience. More specifically, his stereotype of the worker, well-intentioned but confused and elemental, undoubtedly derived from the discussions of the "intellectuals" in the reading room.

Another characteristic of the later Hitler already discernible in childhood and youth was his difficulty in making long-range decisions. As a boy he was unable to accept the fact that a series of small decisions, made or postponed, ultimately amounted to a major decision. He seldom looked far enough to see a series form a trend. Only at the last moment would he awaken to the situation; by then, it was often too late to do anything but follow the logic of events. In his struggles over the *Realschule*, his artistic dreams in Vienna and his refusal to face financial problems, he displayed both shortsightedness and inability to deal with an accumulation of minutia. Some biographers have pointed to similar failures in his adult life, such as the long deferred decision concerning Roehm in 1934 or his apparent hesitancy on the eve of the *Anschluss*.[7] Yet the implications of this apparent character defect go deeper. What had been a debilitating liability as a child may have been a significant asset as a politician. In the 1930's and 1940's, the adult Hitler still delayed difficult decisions, apparently hoping that a way out would present itself and solve the problem for him. After the alternatives had been narrowed, he could then place himself at the head of the trend and

---

[6] *Table Talk*, p. 360; statement by Karl Honisch, *HA*, File 17, Reel 1.
[7] Such incidents are especially prominent in *Bullock*.

became an "instrument of history." In the process, most routes of escape were closed to his opponents, and he more than once was able to apply one of his ostentatious displays of power directly upon them. He discovered few people could stand against this pressure once the issues had been defined and little maneuvering room remained. One of his most effective political weapons was an outgrowth of personal weakness.

Finally, one must consider the unusual breadth and depth of Hitler's experiences in Austria. Allowing for his later exaggerations, the fact remains that he had seen and done a great many things in his first twenty-four years. Aside from his middle-class upbringing, he had received some insights into peasant life from his parents. He had lived in small towns and major cities. In Vienna, he lived with tramps and migrant workers and even had experience as a day laborer. He had a brief and rather unsuccessful encounter with the secondary school system, but he had also worked independently as a small artist-businessman. No other middle-class *voelkisch* leader could point to a similar range of first-hand knowledge.

Yet, on balance, more was probably lacking than present in 1913. Hitler was to prosper as a revolutionary leader in a society revolutionized by defeat, inflation, and depression. When he arrived in Germany, he was a lost man in a society that seemed stable and self-assured. In the next few years, German society lost its self-assurance and equilibrium. In chaos, the young refugee from the *Maennerheim* at last found his home.

APPENDIX I

THE ALTERATION OF THE NAME AND THE JEWISH GRANDFATHER STORY

Among the numerous explanations for the change of name by Adolf Hitler's father from Schickelgruber to Hitler, the most sensational has been advanced by Franz Jetzinger. In the German edition of his book, *Hitlers Jugend* (pp. 28-35), and especially in the later English abridgment, *Hitler's Youth* (pp. 19-30), Jetzinger argues, with increasing enthusiasm, that Alois Hitler's father was really a Jew from Graz by the name of Frankenberger. Furthermore, he asserts that Alois and Johann Nepomuk were influenced by this alleged fact when they changed Alois' name.

Jetzinger's only source for these surprising contentions is *Im Angesicht des Galgens (In the Face of the Gallows)*, written by Hans Frank, former Nazi lawyer and Governor General of Poland, while awaiting execution at Nuremberg. In a narrative studded with demonstrable errors – in part exposed by Jetzinger's research – Frank states that toward the end of 1930 he went to Austria on Hitler's orders to investigate a threat of exposure of an alleged Jewish ancestor of the Fuehrer. In Graz, Frank claims that he learned Alois' mother had been employed by the Jewish family Frankenberger, that she had become pregnant while in their employ, and that the family paid her support money in later years on the assumption that the child's father was young Frankenberger. When he returned to Germany, Frank said he reported his findings to Hitler, who confirmed the payments, but asserted that both he and his father knew that Alois' father was not a Jew. Frank's narrative is vague and lacks confirming evidence. He claims letters were extant to support his story, but neither he nor anyone else has been able to produce them. One has to accept or reject the story on Frank's word alone.

APPENDIX I

A number of considerations argue against its acceptance. At the time the book was written, Frank was passing through a psychological crisis, as the book and the comments of the attending psychologists clearly show.[1] The book is replete with errors of fact. He meanders through long, often pointless, reminiscences, filled with expressions of self-pity and self-justification. Perhaps to his disturbed mind, still cluttered with racist notions about the power of "Jewish blood," the Jewish grandfather story offered comfort by suggesting that the ultimate cause of all his trouble lay in the poisonous influence of Hitler's Jewish ancestry rather than in the actions of his lieutenants. No conclusion on this score can be final; Frank never explained what he was trying to prove or whether or not he believed the story himself.

Further doubts arise from Frank's description of the circumstances which caused his alleged investigation in 1930. Frank states, and Jetzinger agrees, that a letter from William Patrick Hitler was the original source of the allegation of Jewish blood in the Hitler family. William Patrick Hitler was the son of Alois Hitler, Jr., the Fuehrer's half-brother. Alois Jr. had passed through Ireland in 1909, stopping long enough to marry and produce a baby who received the name of William Patrick. In 1933, Alois Jr. and William Patrick headed for Germany in order to exploit their relative's success. William Patrick made a number of attempts to gain favors from the Fuehrer during a stay lasting five years, but he was never satisfied with his treatment.[2] In 1938, he went to the United States on an anti-Hitler speaking tour and later wrote an article entitled "Mon Oncle Adolphe," which appeared in *Paris Soir* in August 1939. The article is not currently available, but it is said to have contained veiled hints about secrets in the Fuehrer's ancestry, although without any details or evidence. If the publication of this article led to the investigation, then Frank has confused a letter with an article, and 1930 with 1939, points which should erode confidence in his reliability. On the other hand, if it was an earlier statement by William

[1] Douglas M. Kelley, *Twenty-Two Cells in Nuremberg* (New York, 1961); and G. M. Glibert, *Nuremberg Diary* (New York, 1947). While he questions Frank's grip on reality, Gilbert still accepts his account of the Jewish grandfather story as providing background on Hitler. G. M. Gilbert, *The Psychology of Dictatorship* (New York, 1950), p. 17.

[2] "Hitler vs. Hitler," *Time*, Vol. XXXIII, No. 15 (April 10, 1939), p. 20.

Patrick which so concerned Hitler, why didn't he settle the issue when Patrick was in Germany between 1933 and 1938? The story is not strengthened by Jetzinger's partial dependence on it to explain the change in Alois' name. Jetzinger seems to think a serious stigma was attached to being part Jewish in the liberal bureaucracy and that Alois changed his name to pass as a gentile. Indications from more reliable sources are that if one was afraid of anti-Semitism in the Austria of the mid-1870's, the bureaucracy was probably the best place to hide; keeping quiet would have been a better defense than drawing attention by a name change. Once again Jetzinger's stand is unconvincing.

The final point in Jetzinger's case is the publication of a picture he claims is that of Alois Hitler. In the caption, Jetzinger calls attention to the "Jewish" features of the man in the photograph. However, a comparison of this picture and three authentic pictures of Alois (Plates 2-5), indicates that Jetzinger's comments, valid or not, refer to a picture of another man.

After the appearance of the German edition of Jetzinger's book in 1956, *Der Spiegel* published a rejoinder by an investigator at the University of Graz.[3] This author made some of the points above and also reported that local records showed no trace of the Frankenbergers in Graz at the time Frank indicated. In addition, he cited substantial evidence supporting a conclusion that there were no Jews in early nineteenth-century Graz. In the English abridgement of his work, Jetzinger dismissed the *Spiegel* story, not by presenting new evidence, but by restating with increased emphasis that he believed Adolf's paternal grandfather was Jewish.

There the problem rests. A more satisfactory and less sensational explanation of the name change has already been presented. Still, the identity of Alois' father remains a mystery, with little prospect that conclusive evidence will ever appear. The family tradition was that Alois' father was Johann Georg Hiedler; all investigators who have dealt with the problem agree that Adolf Hitler believed this. Even Frank stated that, after his investigation, Hitler still did not believe he was part Jewish. Since the question was not raised until the 1930's, it is safe to conclude that the Jewish grandfather story,

[3] "Hitler-Kein Ariernachweis," *Der Spiegel*, 11th year, No. 24 (June 12, 1957), pp. 54-59.

real or imagined, played no part in the development of Hitler's anti-Semitism. It assumed importance for Frank, who was seeking a way to escape from his feelings of guilt and it has, of course, been seized upon by anti-Nazis as the final irony in Hitler's career. It may even provide some small comfort to his surviving victims. Unfortunately, it also appears most unlikely and, without substantiating evidence, must be considered inadmissable to the Hitlerian canon.

APPENDIX II

HITLER IN VIENNA: THE DESCRIPTION IN *MEIN KAMPF*, AND THE WRITINGS OF HANISCH, HONISCH AND GREINER

Among first-hand accounts of Hitler's life in Vienna, the leading place is obviously held by *Mein Kampf*. Hitler's own description of his childhood and youth is often used as the basis for explaining his later career and ideology. This is exactly what Hitler intended. He described his life in Austria as a school in which he studied and mastered the political and social issues of our time. As an historical record of his early life however, *Mein Kampf* has serious limitations. Few, if any, of the facts Hitler advanced are blatantly false, but he thrived on omission and special emphasis. For example, he does not say when he went to Vienna or where and how he lived. Instead, he casually mentions that he went "for the third time" after the death of his mother – without providing a date – and then describes his life in the capital in terms of "the harshness of fate" and the hunger which was his "faithful companion." The account does not follow a chronological sequence; individual episodes in his life are broken up and used wherever they best serve his argument. Four or five broad trends dominate the content and structure of the first chapters.

The first theme is the image of Hitler as the self-possessed, dominant personality. He is never a real child – never the anvil instead of the hammer. Failure is always the beginning of a new struggle and a final achievement. Repeated use of such terms as "indomitable will," "defiance," and "my will to resist," underscore his political purposes. In addition, they reflect another theme which Hitler emphasized: his success as a self-made man. He was at great pains to point out that he came from a solid middle-class background. Even when he attacked features of bourgeois mentality, it was to be understood that he was not a creature of plebeian origins. However, due to a series of accidents – his failure in *Realschule,* the death of his father, etc. – he had been forced to fight to realize his dream of an artist's career. This approach enunciated two middle-class articles of faith: respect for individual achievement and the value of good upbringing. Furthermore, since he had sunk to the bottom and risen again, he possessed first-hand knowledge of two unpredictable elements that troubled the nervous middle class: the worker and the masses. He understood and sympathized with everyone ranked below the discredited aristocracy. The fact that he had lived at a wide range of social levels was a telling campaign argument.

Hitler continually stressed the unusual breadth of his experience and implied that it provided him with a unique claim to leadership. He gave credit to reading – selective purposeful reading – but almost invariably omitted the names of the books he had read and never acknowledged a specific obligation to other political theoreticians. This may have reflected his awareness of *voelkisch* suspicions of abstract reasons as much as his eagerness to glorify himself.

He wrote endlessly about his ideological discoveries in Vienna. His objective in part was to justify his work as Fuehrer of the NSDAP up through the time of the *Putsch,* but he also wished to familiarize the German public with his aims. Even more, he was lecturing the *voelkisch* leaders on the facts of political life. The experience of Vienna had shown that the *voelkisch* ideology had to be united with a mass movement under the determined leadership of a man who from experience knew the masses and how to manipulate them. The purpose was obvious. Hitler's early life as presented in *Mein Kampf* was a departure point for an attack, not just on Jews, Marxists, and Democrats, but also on the respectable and fussy *voelkisch* leaders who wanted to preserve their small organizations from being swallowed up by the NSDAP.

The description of the early years as they appear in *Mein Kampf* is thus purposeful in every sense of the word. Whatever incidents fitted in well with one of his themes, Hitler used. Anything that did not was omitted. A necessary rule to remember in using factual material from *Mein Kampf* is that Hitler's political objectives were far more important than his devotion to accuracy. Any determination of the real importance of a given happening depends upon in-

APPENDIX II 163

formation from other sources rather than upon his own testimony. In addition to *Mein Kampf*, three men who had contact with Hitler in Vienna after he separated from Kubizek have provided descriptions of the later Fuehrer. Here, too, we must consider such complexities as motivation. The question of their contact with one another is also difficult. The man who has had the longest acceptance as an authority is Reinhold Hanisch. Although he is of great value as a source, care must be taken in using his material. Hanisch was a German from Bohemia who went to Berlin at an early age, followed a number of occupations, but worked mainly as a servant. In 1907, he served three months in jail for theft in Berlin, and, in 1908, another six months for falsification of documents. He then took to the road under a false name, Fritz Walter, finally ending up in the Meidling shelter in Vienna at the end of 1909. In August 1910, he was again jailed for carrying false identity papers, a fact which emerged from his squabble with Hitler.[1] Two months later, he was again living under a false name. Shortly after his break with Hitler, he became a gilder and goldworker and managed to struggle by during the next twenty years practicing an assortment of trades on the edge of the world of art. He served in the Austrian army during the war, and was married for a short time in 1918. In 1922 he was jailed for three months in Vienna, and in 1932 he received another three days for a minor offense.

In 1933, when Hitler came to power, Hanisch attempted to make use of his early contacts with the Fuehrer. During that year he provided the information for a pamphlet entitled *"Hitler wie er wirklich ist!"* ("Hitler as he really is!"), which was published by the Verlag Novina in Bratislava. No copies of this pamphlet have been found; from indirect references it seems to have been a wild denunciation of Hitler, based on imprudent exaggerations made by Hanisch. In the years immediately following this publication, he was interviewed by a number of journalists including, apparently, Rudolf Olden, but he was unable to earn much from these contacts. Serious money troubles caused him to work out an arrangement with one Jacques Weiss whereby Hanisch copied paintings and Weiss peddled them as originals in other parts of Eu-

[1] Chapter VII, p. 140.

rope. On November 16, 1936, the Vienna police picked him up because of reports that excessive numbers of Hitler's pictures were going into circulation and that Hanisch was connected with this business. At the time of his arrest, police found postcards in his room which had the same pictures on them as the "Hitler paintings" then appearing. The police quickly built up an overwhelming case to establish that Hanisch had painted the pictures and forged Hitler's signature. Art experts declared the pictures fakes. All the sales were ultimately traced to Hanisch who would not provide information about where he obtained the pictures. Even in the face of this evidence and, after admitting that the pictures were fakes and that he had sold them, he still claimed he had not forged them.

The police believed they had an open-and-shut case, and the evidence certainly indicates it (*HA*, File 1741, Reel 86). By early February, they were merely waiting for evidence on earlier frauds before they brought him to trial. On February 4, 1937, according to the medical report, Hanisch was found dead in his cell, apparently from a heart attack. Soon after this event, when some of Hanisch's writing appeared in America, it was assumed that Hanisch had been killed on orders "from Berlin." Yet it seems unlikely that Hanisch was a victim of a political murder, even though he had earlier made a deposition that on November 24, 1936, he had been roughed up on the way to his cell. The police certainly had no reason to eliminate him; they were almost guaranteed a conviction. Hanisch was then fifty-three. It seems probable that, with almost certain conviction and a substantial sentence ahead of him, he collapsed under the strain.

At the time of his arrest, the police picked up two articles which he had written and apparently had tried to sell without success. They were entitled "Adolf Hitler's Companion in Vienna Speaks," *Adolf Hitlers Weggenosse in Wien Erzaehlt*), and "My Encounter with Adolf Hitler," (*Meine Begegnung mit Adolf Hitler*). Presumably, either one or both of these articles found their way out of Austria and were ultimately published in the *New Republic* in 1939. Later, in 1944, Konrad Heiden made use of the *New Republic* material when he wrote *Der Fuehrer*. The material as it ultimately appeared in the *New Republic* is generally accurate. A few dates are wrong, and some details are undoubtedly inaccurate or exaggerated, but there is external confirmation of important facts. In general, except for Hanisch's obvious attempts to show himself in a better light, the main lines of Hitler's life in the period Hanisch knew him are accurately recorded. A sobering corrective to his occasional flights of fancy is provided in a two-page description of his friendship with Hitler which he wrote for a friend in 1933, (*HA*, File 64, Reel 3).

The case of Josef Greiner is somewhat different. His account is so dotted with serious errors that it would be easy to conclude the whole story was fabricated. Greiner describes his life with Hitler at the Men's Hostel in his book, *Das Ende des Hitler-Mythus*. He confidently provides precise dates for most of the incidents he describes; every one is incorrect by at least two years. Greiner gives wildly exaggerated accounts of his adventures with Hitler in the hostel which are demonstrably incorrect even if one ignores the completely erroneous dating. Yet despite this collection of error piled upon error, Greiner actually knew Hitler, although for a much shorter period than he claimed. When Greiner wrote in 1947, he had to depend nearly exclusively on his own unreliable memory. He had read about Hanisch, but only imprecisely, perhaps in Olden (*Hitler the Pawn*), and in Heiden's early book, *Hitler, a Biography*. He therefore stated that Hanisch had already come and gone when he met Hitler in the hostel for men. Yet, while he dated his own meeting with Hitler as 1907, he also accepted Heiden's date of 1910 for Hitler's contact with Hanisch.

Although Greiner could not remember Hanisch, Hanisch, ironically enough, remembered Greiner. In the *New Republic* article, written in 1936, he specifically mentions Greiner, whom he describes as a former "lamplighter in the Cabaret Hoelle in the Theater an der Wien." Furthermore, in sharp contrast to the picture Greiner was later to paint of himself, Hanisch held that he was a very bad influence on Hitler because he encouraged him in all kinds of wild projects. One of the ideas Hanisch says fascinated Greiner and Hitler emerged from newspaper advertisements of a miraculous hair restorer sold by one Anna Csillag. Greiner and Hitler wanted to use her mildly fraudulent advertisements as a model for some of their own equally questionable projects. When Greiner came to write his book in 1947, he had forgotten Hanisch and much else as well, but he remembered their enthusiasm for the advertisements of Anna Csillag. It is difficult to see how Greiner could have known of the article by Hanisch. It was published in America only five months before the outbreak of war, and was almost certainly inaccessible to him. If Greiner had read it, he could have avoided many of the grave errors in his book. Greiner is not accurate, but his claim of acquaintanceship with Hitler is adequately supported. With the exception of a few documents obtained from Jetzinger, and the hints he was able to glean from Olden and from Heiden's early book, he apparently developed his account independently.

The third individual who knew Hitler in the later Vienna period and wrote about it was Karl Honisch. He was a young clerk who drifted to Vienna just before the war and lived in the *Maennerheim* in the months just prior to Hitler's departure for Munich. With the exception of his term of service during the war, in which he was severely wounded, he continued to reside in Vienna from 1913 until the late 1930's. He was contacted by the *Hauptarchiv* in 1938 and agreed to write his recollections for the Nazis. The 21-page handwritten manuscript may be found in File 17 of the *Hauptarchiv* material. Honisch's account is the only extensive check on Hanisch and it also provides the sole account of the last phase of Hitler's Vienna period. The Honisch statement is naive and understandably cautious. One gains the impression that he is anxious to avoid controversy by working to death relatively unimportant aspects of the association. There are lines of continuity between the Hanisch and Honisch versions and a similarity in treatment which raises the question of possible contact between the two men. However, Hanisch could not have used Honisch's material. It was never released by the Nazis and, more important, Hanisch died two years before Honisch wrote, although Hanisch's *New Republic* article did not appear until 1939, three years after his death.

The possibility that Honisch used other sources seems equally unlikely. He mentions Hanisch, but chiefly to make it clear Hanisch and Honisch were totally different men. In an introductory statement Honisch says he never met Hanisch but had heard he was responsible for articles describing the *Maennerheim* as a kind of "hellhole." Honisch regretted that he had not read the articles and could not answer them in detail, but he indignantly defended the reputation of the *Maennerheim*.

Under the circumstances, it seems reasonable to conclude that Hanisch, Greiner, and Honisch wrote almost completely independent accounts. The only exception is Greiner's use of some marginal Hanisch material. This does not alter the fact that we possess, in addition to *Mein Kampf* and Kubizek's description of the earliest period, three separate personal accounts of Adolf Hitler's life in Vienna.

BIBLIOGRAPHY

I. UNPUBLISHED MATERIALS

A. *Hauptarchiv der NSDAP* (Microfilm copies at the Hoover Institution, Stanford, California):

File 15, Reel 1. Hitler-Prof. Poetsch correspondence.
File 17, Reel 1 and 1A. The chief file of material on Hitler's youth.
File 17A, Reel 1. File of correspondence by and about Alois Hitler.
Files 25-40, Reel 2. Miscellaneous material on Hitler's painting.
File 64, Reel 3. Material on Reinhold Hanisch.
File 65, Reel 13A. Materials on Hitler's youth prepared for a Nazi party display.
File 653, Reel 5. Materials on the Linz *Realschule*.
File 1229, Reel 52. *Ostara* material.
File 1741, Reel 86. Police records on Reinhold Hanisch.
File 1760, Reel 25A. Materials related to the effort to deport Hitler in 1924.

B. The National Archives – Arlington Material:

Micro Copy T-84, Roll 4, File 4. Prof. Huemer letter and Alois Hitler *Meldezettel*.
Micro Copy T-175, Roll 38, File 255. Description of Adolf Hilter correspondence from 1908.
Micro Copy T-175, Roll 67, File 52. SS correspondence on documents from Linz concerned with Hitler's family (August 1942).
Micro Copy T-175, Roll 69, File 51. Notarized statements on Hitler paintings by Reinhold Hanisch and Prof. Leidenroth.

C. The Library of Congress – "German Materials":

German Material, Safe 5, Portfolio 472B. Original Dokumente zur Familiengeschichte Adolf Hitler, (part of this material in *HA* File 17A).
German Materials, Lot 4890. Photo portraits of Hitler family, plus letter Bormann to Himmler in "Supplemental Reference File."

II. MATERIALS DIRECTLY RELATING TO HITLER

A. *Books:*

Brehm, Bruno, *Der Trommler* (Graz, Vienna, Cologne, Verlag Styria, 1960), 362 p.
Bullock, Alan, *Hitler, A Study in Tyranny* (London, Odhams, 1952), 776 p.
Cohen, Elie A., *Human Behavior in the Concentration Camp.* Translated by M. H. Braaksma (New York, The Universal Library, 1953), 295 p.
Daim, Wilfried, *Der Mann, der Hitler die Ideen Gab. Von den religioesen Verirrungen eines Sektierers zum Rassenwahn des Diktators* (Munich, Isar Verlag, 1958), 286 p.
Dietrich, Otto, *Hitler.* Translated by Richard and Clara Winston (Chicago, Henry Regnery, 1955), 277 p.
Domarus, Max, *Hitler. Reden und Proklamationen, 1932-1945.* Vol. I – *Triumph, 1932-1938* (Wuerzburg, Domarus, 1962), 987 p.
Frank, Hans, *Im Angesicht des Galgens. Deutung Hitlers und seiner Zeit auf Grund eigner Erlebnisse und Erkenntnisse* (Munich-Graefelfing, Beck Verlag, 1953), 479 p.
Gilbert, Felix, *Hitler Directs His War* (New York, Oxford University Press, 1950), 187 p.
Gilbert, G. M., *Nuremberg Diary* (New York, Farrar, Straus, 1947). 471 p.
——, *The Psychology of Dictatorship* (New York, Ronald Press, 1950), 327 p.
Goerlitz, Walter, *Adolf Hitler* (Goettingen, Musterschmidt-Verlag, 1960), 145 p.
Goerlitz, Walter and Herbert A. Quint, *Adolf Hitler, eine Biographie* (Stuttgart, Steingrueber-Verlag, 1952), 656 p.
Gosset, Pierre and Renée, *Adolf Hitler.* Vol. I (Paris, Juillard, 1961), 347 p.
Greiner, Josef, *Das Ende des Hitler-Mythus* (Vienna, Amalthea Verlag, 1947), 343 p.
Heiber, Helmut, *Adolf Hitler; eine Biographie* (Berlin, Colloquium Verlag, 1960), 159 p.
Heiber, Helmut (ed.), *Hitlers Lagebesprechungen* (Stuttgart, Deutsche Verlags-Anstalt, 1962), 970 p.
Heiden, Konrad, *Der Fuehrer.* Translated by Ralph Manheim (Boston, Houghton Mifflin, 1944), 788 p.
——, *Hitler, A Biography* (London, Constable, 1936), 415 p.
Heinz, Heinz A., *Germany's Hitler* (London, Hurst and Blackett, 1934), 288 p.
Hilberg, Paul, *The Destruction of the European Jews* (Chicago, Quadrangle Books, 1961), 788 p.
Hitler, Adolf, *Mein Kampf.* Translated by Ralph Manheim (Boston, Houghton Mifflin, 1962), 694 p.
——, *Adolf Hitler's Reden* (Munich, Deutscher Volksverlag Dr. E. Boepple, 1934), 127 p.
——, *The Testament of Adolf Hitler.* Translated by R. H. Stevens (London, Cassell, 1961), 115 p.
Hitler's Table Talk, 1941-1944. Translated by Norman Cameron and R. H. Stevens (London, Weidenfeld and Nicholson, 1953), 746 p.
Hoffman, Heinrich, *Hitler in seiner Heimat* (Berlin, Zeitgeschichte-Verlag, 1938).
——, *Hitler Was My Friend.* Translated by Lt.-Col. R. H. Stevens (London, Burke, 1955), 256 p.

——, *Hitler wie ihn keiner kennt* (Berlin, Zeitgeschichte-Verlag, n.d.), 96 p.
Jetzinger, Franz, *Hitlers Jugend. Phantasien, Luegen – und die Wahrheit* (Vienna, Europa Verlag, 1956), 308 p.
——, *Hitler's Youth*. Translated by Lawrence Wilson (London, Hutchinson, 1958), 200 p.
Kelley, Douglas M., *Twenty-Two Cells in Nuremberg* (New York, Macfadden Books, 1961), 176 p.
Krause, Karl Wilhelm, *Zehn Jahre Kammerdiener bei Hitler* (Hamburg, Hermann Laatzen Verlag, n.d.), 88 p.
Koppensteiner, Rudolf, *Die Ahnentafel des Fuehrers* (Leipzig, Zentralstelle fuer deutsche Personen- und Familiengeschichte, 1937), 154 p.
Krebs, Albert, *Tendenzen und Gestalten der NSDAP. Erinnerungen an die Fruehzeit der Partei* (Stuttgart, Deutsche Verlags-Anstalt, 1959), 245 p.
Kubizek, August, *The Young Hitler I Knew*. Translated by E. V. Anderson (Boston, Houghton Mifflin, 1955), 298 p.
Lenk, Rudolf, *Oberdonau – die Heimat des Fuehrers* (Munich, Verlag F. Bruckmann, 1941), 120 p.
Olden, Rudolf, *Hitler the Pawn* (London, Victor Gollancz, 1936), 439 p.
Picker, Henry, *Hitlers Tischgespraeche im Fuehrerhauptquartier, 1941-42* (Stuttgart, Seewald Verlag, 1963), 546 p.
Price, Ward G., *I Know These Dictators* (New York, Holt, 1938), 305 p.
Rabitsch, Hugo, *Aus Adolf Hitlers Jugendzeit. Jugenderinnerungen eines zeitgenoessischen Linzer Realschuelers* (Munich, Deutscher Volksverlag, 1938), 152 p.
Rauschning, Hermann, *The Voice of Destruction* (New York, Putnam's Sons, 1940), 295 p.
Recktenwald, Johann, *Woran hat Adolf Hitler Gelitten?* (Munich/Basel, Reinhardt Verlag, 1963), 122 p.
Reich, Albert, *Aus Adolf Hitlers Heimat* (Munich, Franz Eher Verlag, 1933), 128 p.
Röhrs, H. D., *Hitler, Die Zerstörung einer Persönlichkeit* (Neckargemünd, Vowinckel, 1965), 151 p.
Roberts, Stephen H., *The House that Hitler Built* (London, Harper and Brothers, 1939), 408 p.
Shirer, William L., *The Rise and Fall of the Third Reich: A History of Nazi Germany* (New York, Simon and Schuster, 1960), 1,245 p.
Trevor-Roper, Hugh, *The Last Days of Hitler* (New York, MacMillan, 1947), 254 p.
Wagner, Ludwig, *Hitler: Man of Strife*. Translated by Charlotte La Rue (New York, W. W. Norton, 1942), 331 p.
Ziegler, Hans, *Adolf Hitler aus dem Erleben dargestellt* (Goettingen, K. W. Schutz, 1964), 300 p.
Zoller, Albert (ed.), *Hitler Privat. Erlebnisbericht seiner Geheimsekretaerin* (Duesseldorf, Droste-Verlag, 1949), 240 p.

B. *Articles:*

Bloch, Dr. Edward, (as told to J. D. Ratcliff). "My Patient Hitler," *Colliers*, Vol. 107, No. 1 (March 15, 1941), 11 and 35-39; No. 2 (March 22, 1941), 69-73.

Deuerlein, Ernst, "Hitlers Eintritt in die Politik und die Reichswehr," *Vierteljahrshefte für Zeitgeschichte*, VII (April 1959), 179-85, 191-205.
Hanisch, Reinhold, "I Was Hitler's Buddy," *New Republic*, Vol. 98, No. 1270 (April 5, 1939), 239-42; No. 1271 (April 12, 1939), 270-72; No. 1272 (April 19, 1939), 297-300.
Heiden, Konrad, "Portrait of the Artist as a Young Man," *Saturday Review*, Vol. 26, No. 49 (December 4, 1943), 6-9.
"Hitler-Kein Ariernachweis," *Der Spiegel*, 11 Year, No. 24 (June 12, 1957), 54-59.
"Hitler vs. Hitler," *Time*, Vol. 33, No. 15 (April 10, 1939), 20.
Hook, Sidney, "Hitlerism: A Non-metaphysical View," *Contemporary Jewish Record*, Vol. 7 (April 1944), 146-55.
Hornick, M. P., "Had Hitler Jewish Blood?" *Contemporary Review*, Vol. 194, No. 1111 (July 1958), 28-31.
Kurth, Gertrud. M., "The Jew and Adolf Hitler," *Psychoanalytic Quarterly*, Vol. 16 (1947), 11-32.
Mann, Klaus, "Cowboy Mentor of the Fuehrer," *Living Age*, Vol. 359 (November 1940), 217-22.
Muehl, Anita, "Factors Influencing Hitler's Life," reprint from the *Transactions of the Medical Guild of St. Luke* (March 1941), 1-18.
Nolte, Ernst, "Eine fruehe Quelle zu Hitlers Antisemitismus," *Historische Zeitschrift*, Vol. 192, No. 3, pp. 584-606.
Phelps, Reginald H., "Hitler and the Deutsche Arbeiter Partei," *American Historical Review*, Vol. LXVIII, No. 4, (July 1963), 974-86
"La première recontre d'Hitler avec la croix gammée, etc.," *Illustration*, No. 186 (November 4, 1933), 322-23.
Wechsberg, Joseph, "Winnetou of der Wild West," *The American West*, Vol. I, No. 3 (Summer 1964), 32-39.

III. AUSTRIA

A. *Books:*

Baedekers *Oesterreich* (Leipzig, Verlag v. Karl Baedeker, 1907), 383 p.
Benedikt, Heinrich, *Die Wirtschaftliche Entwicklung in Franz-Joseph Zeit* (Vienna/Munich, Verlag Herold, 1958), 200 p.
Coldstream, John P., *The Institutions of Austria* (Edinburgh, Arch. Constable, 1895), 127 p.
Coloquhoun, Archibald R. and Ethel, *The Whirlpool of Europe. Austria-Hungary and the Habsburgs* (New York, Dodd Mead, 1907), 349,
Crankshaw, Edward, *The Fall of the House of Habsburg* (New York, Viking, 1963), 459 p.
Drage, Geoffrey, *Austria-Hungary* (London, John Murray, 1909), 846 p.
Eder, Karl, *Der Liberalismus in Altoesterreich: Geisteshaltung, Politik und Kultur* (Vienna, Verlag Herold, 1955), 277 p.
Ferber, Walter, *Die Vorgeschichte der NSDAP in Oesterreich: Ein Beitrag zur Geschichtsrevision* (Konstanz, Verlagsanstalt Merk u. Co., 1954), 40 p.
Franz, Georg, *Liberalismus: Die deutschliberale Bewegung in der Habsburgischen Monarchie* (Munich, Verlag Georg D. W. Callwey, 1955), 531 p.

Hantsch, Hugo, *Die Nationalitaetenfrage im alten Oesterreich: Das Problem der konstruktiven Reichsgestaltung* (Vienna, Verlag Herald, 1953), 124 p.

Hellbling, Ernst C., *Oesterreichische Verfassungs- und Verwaltungsgeschichte* (Vienna, Springer-Verlag, 1956), 552 p.

Jaszi, Oscar, *The Dissolution of the Habsburg Monarchy* (Chicago, University of Chicago Press, 1929), 488 p.

Jenks, William Alexander, *The Austrian Electoral Reform of 1907* (New York, Columbia University Press, 1950), 227 p.

Kann, Robert A., *The Habsburg Empire: A Study in Integration and Disintegration* (New York, Praeger, 1957), 227 p.

———. *The Multinational Empire: Nationalism and National Reform in the Habsburg Monarchy, 1848-1918*. 2 vols. (New York, Columbia University Press, 1950), 444 p. and 423 p.

Kuppe, Rudolf. *Karl Lueger und seine Zeit* (Vienna, Oesterreichische Volksschriften, 1933), 583 p.

May, Arthur J., *The Hapsburg Monarchy, 1867-1914* (Cambridge [Mass.], Harvard University Press, 1951), 532 p.

Mayer-Loewenschwerdt, Erwin. *Schoenerer der Vorkaempfer: Eine politische Biographie* (Vienna/Leipzig, Universitaets-Verlag, 1938), 390 p.

Metnitz, Gustav Adolf v., *Die deutsche Nationalbewegung 1871-1933* (Berlin, Junker u. Duennhaupt Verlag, 1939), 304 p.

Meyer, Henry Cord, *Mitteleuropa in German Thought and Action, 1815-1945* (The Hague, Martinus Nijhoff, 1955), 378 p.

Molisch, Paul, *Geschichte der deutschnationalen Bewegung in Oesterreich von ihren Anfaengen bis zum Zerfall der Monarchie* (Jena, Verlag von Gustav Fischer, 1926), 277 p.

———, *Politische Geschichte der deutschen Hochschulen in Oesterreich von 1848 bis 1918* (Vienna/Leipzig, Wilheim Baumueller Universitaets-Verlag, 1939), 267 p.

Palmer, Francis H. E., *Austro-Hungarian Life in Town and Country* (New York, Putnam's Sons, 1903), 295 p.

Pichl, Eduard, *George Schoenerer*, (6 vols. in 3), (Berlin, Gerhard Stalling Verlag, 1938), Vol. I, 387 and 636 p.; Vol. II, 486 and 674 p.; Vol. III, 500 and 650 p.

Schnee, Heinrich, *Georg Ritter von Schoenerer: Ein Kaempfer fuer Alldeutschland*, 3d edition (Reichenberg, Sudetendeutscher Verlag Franz Kraus, 1943), 275 p.

———, *Karl Lueger: Leben und Wirken eines grossen Sozial- und Kommunal Politikers. Umrisse einer politischen Biographie* (Berlin, Duncker und Humblot, 1960), 123 p.

Schuschnigg, Kurt, *My Austria*. Translated by John Segrue (New York, Knopf, 1938), 354 p.

Sieghart, Rudolf, *Die Letzten Jahrzehnte einer Grossmacht: Menschen, Voelker, Probleme des Habsburger-Reichs* (Berlin, Im Verlag Ullstein, 1932), 475 p.

Skalnik, Kurt, *Dr. Karl Lueger: Der Mann zwischen den Zeiten* (Vienna, Verlag Herold, 1954), 182 p.

Taylor, A. J. P., *The Habsburg Monarchy, 1809-1918: A History of the Austrian Empire and Austria-Hungary* (London, Hamish Hamilton, 1948), 279 p.

Weil, Georges, *Le Pangermanisme en Autriche* (Paris, Albert Fontemoing, 1904), 296 p.
Werner, Lothar, *Der Alldeutche Verband 1890-1918: Ein Beitrag zur Geschichte der oeffentlichen Meinung in Deutschland in den Jahren vor und waehrend des Weltkrieges* (Berlin, Verlag Dr. Emil Ebering, 1935), 294 p.
Whiteside, Andrew G., *Austrian National Socialism Before 1918* (The Hague, Martinus Nijhoff, 1962), 143 p.

B. *Articles:*

Fodor, M. W., "Austrian Roots of Hitlerism," *Foreign Affairs*, Vol. 14, No. 4, (July 1936), 685-91.
Kann, R. A., "German-Speaking Jewry During Austria Hungary's Constitutional Era," *Jewish Social Studies*, Vol. 10, No. 3 (July 1948), 239-56.
Karbach, Oscar, "The Founder of Political Antisemitism: Georg von Schoenerer," *Jewish Social Studies*, Vol. 7, No. 1 (January 1945), 3-30.
Kogan, A. G., "The Social Democrats and the Conflict of Nationalities in Habsburg Austria," *Journal of Modern History*, Vol. 21, No. 3 (September 1949), 204-17.
Kuehnelt-Leddihn, Erik R. von, "The Bohemian Background of German National Socialism: DAP, DNSAP, and NSDAP," *Journal of the History of Ideas*, Vol. 60, No. 3 (June 1948), 339-71.
Skilling, Gordon H., "Austrian Origins of National Socialism," *University of Toronto Quarterly*, Vol. 10, No. 4 (July 1941), 482-92.
Turner, Ewart Edmund, "To Hitler via Two Men," *The American Scholar*, Vol. 6, No. 1 (1937), 3-16.
Whiteside, Andrew G., "The Deutsche Arbeiterpartei 1904-1918: A Contribution to the Origins of Fascism," *Austrian Historical Newsletter*, No. 4 (1963), 3-14.

IV. VIENNA

A. *Books:*

Grunwald, Max, *Vienna*. (Philadelphia, The Jewish Publication Society of America, 1936), 557 p. (Jewish Communities Series).
Jahrbuecher der K. K. Zentral Anstalt fuer Meteorologie und Geodynamik (Vienna, 1911 [Jahrgang 1909], Vienna, 1912 [Jahrgang 1910], n/p.).
Jenks, William Alexander, *Vienna and the Young Hitler* (New York, Columbia University Press, 1960), 252 p.
Levetus, A. S., *Imperial Vienna* (London and New York, John Lane, 1905), 431 p.
Mayer, Sigmund, *Ein Juedischer Kaufmann, 1831 bis 1911 Lebenserinnerungen* (Leipzig, Duncker u. Humblot, 1911), 400 p.
——, *Die Wiener Juden, 1700-1900*, 2d ed. (Vienna/Berlin, R. Loewit Verlag, 1918), 531 p.
The Newest Guide Through Vienna and Environs, 13th ed. (Vienna, R. Lechner, 1912), 163 p.
Sedgwick, Henry Dwight, *Vienna: Biography of a Bygone City* (New York, Bobbs-Merrill, 1939), 336 p.
Statistisches Jahrbuch der Stadt Wien, 1908-1913, 6 vols. (Vienna, Verlag des Wiener Magistrates, 1910-1916), pages vary.

Tietze, Hans, *Die Juden Wiens: Geschichte – Wirtschaft – Kultur* (Leipzig/ Vienna, E. P. Tal, 1933), 301 p.
Wassermann, Jacob, *My Life as German and Jew*. Translated by S. N. Brainen (New York, Coward-McCann Inc., 1933), 282 p.
Zweig, Stefan, *The World of Yesterday* (New York, The Viking Press, 1943), 455 p.

B. *Articles:*

de Battaglia, Otto Forst, "Wien, das Anlitz einer Stadt im Wandel der Zeit," *Universitas*, Vol. 10 (October 1953), 1019-30.
Gruenberg, A. and A. Freund, "Die Assanierung Wiens vom medizinal-statistischen Standpunkte," *Forschritte der Ingenieurwissenschaften*, Vol. 2, No. 9 (1902), 129-93.

V. HITLER'S PSYCHOLOGY, YOUTH DEVELOPMENT, AND ADJUSTMENT

A. *Books:*

Achille-Delmas, F., *Adolf Hitler: Essai de biographie psycho-pathologique* (Paris, Libraire Marcel Riviere et Cie, 1946), 256 p.
Adorno, T. W., Else Frenkel-Brunswik, *et. al.*, *The Authoritarian Personality* (New York, Harper and Brothers, 1950), 990 p.
Aichhorn, August, *Wayward Youth* (New York, Viking Press, 1951), 236 p.
Bettelheim, Bruno, *The Informed Heart: Autonomy in a Mass Age* (New York, Free Press of Glencoe, 1962), 309 p.
Cole, Luella, *Psychology of Adolescence* (New York, Rinehart, 1959), 731 p.
Erikson, Erik, *Childhood and Society* (New York, Norton, 1950), 397 p.
——, *Identity and the Life Cycle* (New York, International Universities Press, 1959), 171 p.
——, *Young Man Luther: A Study in Psychoanalysis and History* (New York, Norton, 1958), 288 p.
Freud, Anna, *The Ego and Mechanisms of Defence*. Translated by Cecil Baines (New York, International Universities Press, 1950), 196 p.
Friedenburg, Edgar, *The Vanishing Adolescent* (New York, Dell, 1962), 223 p.
Mussen, Paul Henry; John J. Conger; Jerome Kagan, *Child Development and Personality* (New York, Harper and Row, 1963), 631 p.
Muus, Rolf E., *Theories of Adolescence* (New York, Random House, 1962), 184 p.
Seidman, Jerome M. (ed.), *The Adolescent: A Book of Readings* (New York, Holt, Rinehart and Winston, 1960), 870 p.

B. *Articles:*

Erikson, Erik, "Hitler's Imagery and German Youth," *Psychiatry*, Vol. 5 (1942), 475-93.
Wallace, Anthony F. C., "Revitalization Movements," *American Anthropologist*, Vol. 58, No. 2 (1956), 264-81.
——, "Stress and Rapid Personality Changes," *International Record of Medicine*, Vol. 169, No. 12 (December 1956), 761-74.

VI. POVERTY AND TRAMP LIFE

Books:

Anderson, Nels, *The Hobo: The Sociology of the Homeless Man* (Chicago, Phoenix Books, 1961), 296 p.

Brown, Edwin A., *"Broke": The Man Without the Dime* (Boston, The Four Seas Co., 1920), 370 p.

Flynt, Josiah, *Tramping with Tramps* (New York, The Century Co., 1907), 398 p.

Orwell, George, *Down and Out in Paris and London* (New York, Berkeley Books, 1959), 155 p.

Solenberger, Alice Willard, *One Thousand Homeless Men: A Study of Original Records* (New York, Charities Publication, 1911), 374 p.

VII. ANTI-SEMITISM AND *VOELKISCH* IDEOLOGY

A. *Books:*

Ackermann, Nathan W. and Marie Jahoda, *Anti-Semitism and Emotional Disorder: A Psychoanalytic Interpretation* (New York, Harper, 1950), 135 p.

Adler, H. G., *Theresienstadt, 1941-1945: Das Anlitz Einer Zwangsgemeinschaft, Geschichte, Soziologie, Psychologie* (Tuebingen, J. C. B. Mohr, 1955), 773 p.

Arendt, Hannah, *Origins of Totalitarianism* (New York, Meridian Books, 1958), 520 p.

Bernstein, Peretz F., *Jew Hate as a Sociological Problem*. Translated by David Saraph (New York, Philosophical Library, 1951), 300 p.

Leschnitzer, Adolf, *The Magic Background of Modern Anti-Semitism: An Analysis of the German-Jewish Relationship* (New York, International Universities Press, 1956), 236 p.

Loewenstein, Rudolph M., *Christians and Jews: A Psychoanalytic Study* (New York, International Universities Press, 1952), 224 p.

Massing, Paul, *Rehearsal for Destruction: A Study of Political Anti-Semitism in Imperial Germany* (New York, Harper and Brothers, 1949), 341 p.

Mosse, George L., *The Crisis of German Ideology* (New York, The Universal Library, 1964), 373 p.

Pinson, Koppel S. (ed.), *Essays on Antisemitism* (New York, Conference on Jewish Relations, 1946), 269 p.

Pulzer, P. G., *The Rise of Political Anti-Semitism in Germany and Austria*, (New York, John Wiley and Sons, 1964), 364 p.

Reichmann, E. G., *Hostages of Civilization: The Social Sources of National Socialist Anti-Semitism* (London, Gollancz, 1950), 281 p.

Sartre, Jean-Paul, *Anti-Semite and Jew*. Translated by George J. Becker (New York, Grove Press, 1962), 153 p.

———, *Portrait of the Anti-Semite*. Translated by Mary Guggenheim (New York, Partisan Review, 1946), 27 p.

Simmel, Ernst (ed.), *Anti-Semitism: A Social Disease* (New York, International Universities Press, 1946), 140 p.

Stern, Fritz, *The Politics of Cultural Despair* (New York, Anchor Books, 1965), 426 p.

Trachtenberg, Joshua, *The Devil and the Jews: The Medieval Conception of the Jew and Its Relation to Modern Antisemitism* (Cleveland and New York, Meridian Books, 1961), 278 p.

B. *Articles:*

Bettelheim, Bruno, "The Dynamism of Anti-Semitism in Gentile and Jew," *Journal of Abnormal and Social Psychology.* Vol. 42, No. 2 (April 1947), 153-68.

Fenichel, Otto, "Psychoanalysis of Antisemitism," *American Imago*, Vol. I, No. 2 (March 1940), 24-39.

Frenkel-Brunswik, Else and R. Novitt Sanford, "Some Personality Factors in Anti-Semitism," *Journal of Psychology*, Vol. 20, No. 2 (1945), 271-91.

Loeblowitz-Lennard, Henry, "The Jew as Symbol," *The Psychoanalytic Quarterly*, Vol. 16 (1947), 33-37.

Loewenstein, Rudolph M., "The Historical and Cultural Roots of Anti-Semitism," in *Psychoanalysis and the Social Sciences*, Vol. I (New York, International Universities Press, 1947), pp. 313-56.

Rose, Arnold, "Anti-Semitism's Root in City-Hatred: A Clue to the Jew's Position as Scapegoat," *Commentary*, Vol. 6 (October 1948), 374-78.

Tarachow, Sidney, "A Note on Anti-Semitism," *Psychiatry*, Vol. 9, No. 2 (May 1946), 131-32.

INDEX

Alldeutsche, 81-85, 125. *See also* Pan-Germanism
Alldeutsche Blaetter, 82
Altenberg, Jacob, 141, 149
Anschluss, 152, 155
Anti-Semitism, 86-88, 107, 124-125, 147-150, 154

Badeni language decrees, 59-60, 81
Bloch, Edmund (Dr.), 98 f, 105-107, 111
Boer War, 66, 83-84
Breitender, Johann, 29

Christian Socialist Party, 59, 138-139, 145
Cichini (family), 95-96
Cooper, James Fenimore, 66
Csillag, Anne, 165-166

Decker, Eva Maria, 19. *See also* Heidler, Eva Maria
Deutsche Fortschrittspartei, 81
Deutsche Volksblatt, 86
Deutsche Volkspartei, 81, 85 f
Dirnhofer, Edgar, 37

Eckhart, Dietrich, 153, 153 f
Encephalitis, epidemic, 73-75

Frank, Hans, 157-160
Frankenberger, 157, 159

Glassl, Anna, 28-29, 32-33, 47
Goldbacher, Gregor, 96, 98
Greiner, Josef, 137, 140, 165-167

Grill (ex-priest), 137
Groeber (professor), 100
Groag (professor), 95
Gustav - - - -, 96
Gymnasium, 68-70

Hanisch, Magdalena, 113
Hanisch, Reinhold, 129-133, 135-138, 140-141, 145, 163-167
Heiden, Konrad, 164-166
Heidler. *See also* under Hitler
Heidler, Anna Maria, 19-21, 28
Heidler, Eva Maria, 19-20, 28
Heidler, Johann Georg, 18-22, 29-31, 159
Hiedler, Johann Nepomuk, 19-23, 28-31, 35, 39, 48, 157
Hiedler, Johanna, 20, 22. *See also* Poelzl, Johanna (mother)
Hiedler, Josefa, 20, 22, 39
Hiedler, Lorenz, 31
Hiedler, Maria Anna. *See* Schickelgruber, Maria Anna
Hiedler, Walburga, 20, 22, 30, 39
Hitler (family name), 18, 29, 29 f, 31-32. *See also* under Hiedler
Hitler, Adolf
—, Politics: on anti-semitism, 86-88, 126, 147-150, 154; on Boer War, 66; on Habsburgs, 84-85; on Pan-Germanism, 84 f, 145, 147; on Christian Socialism, 139, 145; on Social Democrats, 123-124, 139; influence of *Ostara* on, 124-125; on nationalism, 80-81, 83-86, 120, 146-147; political development, 80-81,

107, 120-121, 125-126, 138-139, 152-155; class consciousness, 102, 102 f
—, Family: origin, 17, 50-51, 157-159; family life, 53-57, 62, 64; on siblings, 51, 94-94 f, 121; on mother, 51-51 f, 101, 110-111; on father, 53-54, 58, 61-64, 70-73, 75, 84-85, 91-92, 139; Jewish grandfather story, 157-160; legacies, 91, 111-112
—, Health: 73-75, 97-98
—, Acquaintances: Greiner, 165; Hanisch, 133-135; Kubizek, 101-103, 105, 116-117, 119, 121; Neumann, 138; *Maennerheim* society, 144-145; childhood peers, 65-66
—, Education: 55-56, 61, 63, 65, 69-73, 75, 79, 89, 92-100; *Art Academy*, 108-109, 113, 114, 117, 122, 140-141, 150; *Volksschule*, 65, 67-69, 71, 75-76; *Oberrealschule*, 96-98; *Realschule*, 68-71, 75-81, 84-85, 88-89, 94-96, 98-99, 107, 109, 117, 155, 162
—, Employment: early unemployment, 101, 107-108, 113, 117, 119 f, 119-120, 123, 126-131, 142-144; employment as artist, 132, 135-137, 141-142; military service, 150-151
—, Character: interest in painting, 70-71, 73, 78, 100-101, 108-109, 113-114; interest in architecture, 102-103, 108-109, 117-118; on civil service, 72; on religion, 61, 85, 85 f, 93-95, 139; on sex, 94, 104, 120, 142; on *Maennerheim*, 144-145; on Vienna, 104, 115, 118, 161; influence of Karl May, 66-68; his self-image, 161-163; creates fantasy world, 56, 61, 65-66, 75, 80, 92, 103-104, 107-108, 137; withdraws from society, 77-78, 93, 93 f; slow maturation, 75-77, 104, 153-156; temperament, 56, 72, 100, 110, 119-124, 140-142, 152-153; disdains manual labor, 113; takes music lessons, 105-106

Hitler, Alois: paternity and name change, 29-31, 35-36, 157, 159; marriage to Anna Glassl, 32; marriage to Franziska Matzelburger, 32-33; marriage to Klara Poelzl, 33-39, 42-43; on religion, 42, 59, 61-63, 85, 85 f, 88-89; career, 32, 34, 43-44, 52-53; beekeeping, 45-46, 51, 58; social life, 44; role as husband and father, 43-45, 51-54, 57-59, 61-64, 69, 72, 75, 85; financial condition, 46-49, 53, 55; retirement, 55-58, 62-63; drinking "problem," 57, 57 f, 60; political beliefs, 59-60, 84-85, 85 f; on Adolf's education and career, 60, 69-73, 75; died, 89-93, 111. See also Schickelgruber, Alois

Hitler, Alois, Jr., 33, 38, 46, 51, 53-54, 58, 72, 91, 106, 158-159

Hitler, Angela, 33, 38, 46, 51, 53-54, 61, 91, 94, 106-107, 111, 112, 114, 121, 131, 143

Hitler, Anna. See Glassl, Anna

Hitler, Edmund, 54-56, 61, 64, 69, 74 f, 78

Hitler, Franziska. See Matzelburger, Franziska

Hitler, Gustav, 40-41

Hitler, Ida, 40-41

Hitler, Klara: marries Alois, 38-43, 47-48; bears Adolf, 49-51; re Alois' death, 90-92, 105-108, 110-111; role in family, 52, 60-61, 63-64; relation to Adolf, 78, 97-101, 104, 108; pregnancies, 54, 57; financial condition, 94, 97, 143. See also Poelzl, Klara

Hitler, Otto, 41

Hitler, Paula, 57, 61, 91, 101, 106-107, 111-112, 121, 143

Hitler, William Patrick, 158-159

Hoerl, Rosalia, 26, 26 f. See also Schichtl

Hoezl, Ludwig, 33, 37

Honisch, Karl, 145, 166-167

Huemer (professor), 79, 79 f, 80 f, 95

Huettler, 18. See Hitler

Jetzinger, Franz, 157, 159, 166

Keiss, Dr., 97, 97 f

INDEX

Kostplatz, 92
Kubizek, August, 101-105, 107, 111, 113-123, 148-149, 163, 167

Landsberger (art dealer), 141
Lanz von Liebenfels, 124-125, 147
Ledermueller, Herr, 21
Linzer Fliegende Blaetter, 82
List, Guido von, 125
Los von Rom movement, 82, 85, 86
Lueger, Karl, 59, 120, 138-139
Lugert, Emmanuel, 94-95
Maennerheim, 132-135, 137-138, 140-142, 144-145, 148-151, 154-156, 166
Matzelberger, Alois, 32-33
Matzelberger, Franziska, 28, 32-33, 35, 38, 40-41, 47-48, 91
Matzelberger, Maria, 40-41, 50
May, Karl, 66-68
Mayerhofer, Josef, 63, 91, 112-113, 143
Mein Kampf, 161-163, 167
Motlach, Frau, 113

Neumann (art dealer), 137-138, 149
National Socialist Party, 146-147, 152
Nationalism, German, 59, 80-83, 120, 125, 146

Obdachlosenheim, 128
Olden, Rudolf, 163, 165, 166
Ostara, 124-125, 147

Pan-Germanism, 81-84, 87, 107, 145-148. See also Alldeutsche
Parkinsonism (Parkinson's disease), 73-74
Paukh, Engelbert, 29
Poelzl, Johann, 22, 35, 39-40
Poelzl, Johanna (mother of Klara), 35, 39, 93, 105. See also Hiedler, Johanna.
Poelzl, Johanna (sister of Klara), 37, 39-41, 46-48, 50, 93, 106-107, 111, 114, 131, 143
Poelzl, Klara, 28, 32-37. See also Hitler, Klara
Poelzl, Theresia. See Schmidt, Theresia
Poetsch (professor), 79-80

Pommer, Josef, 37
Preisinger (blacksmith), 60
Prevratsky, Josef, 105
Prinz, Johann, 40, 50
Prinz, Johanna, 40, 50

Raubal, Leo, 94, 94 f, 113
Rauscher Gut, 55, 58
Ritschel (professor), 140
Roller (professor), 113-114
Romeder, Josef, 22, 29-31, 39
Romeder, Walburga. See Hiedler, Walburga
Rosenberg, Alfred, 153

Sailer, Josefa, 39. See Hiedler, Josefa
Sailer, Leopold, 22
Schichtl, Rosalia, 36-39. See also Hoerl
Schickelgruber (family name), 17, 39, 157-158
Schickelgruber, Alois: childhood, 17-19; raised by Heidlers, 19-21; early career, 23-25; on his legitimacy and name change, 20-22, 29-30; character, 24-27; on religion, 21 f, 27; on education, 26-27; personal life, 27-29. See also Hitler, Alois
Schickelgruber, Betti, 39
Schickelgruber, Franz, 17-18, 47
Schickelgruber, Johann, 17-19
Schickelgruber, Josef, 17-18
Schickelgruber, Josefa, 18
Schickelgruber, Leopold, 18
Schickelgruber, Maria Anna, 17-19, 28
Schmidt, Anton, 39-40, 93, 105
Schmidt, Johann, 97
Schmidt, Theresia, 39, 40, 93
Schoenerer, Georg von, 81-83, 85 f, 87, 125, 146, 148
Schulvereine, 81
Schutzvereine, 81
Sekira, Frau, 92
Semper, Gottfried, 137
Social Democratic Party, 123, 139

Trummelschlager, Johann, 18
Tunnel, The, 138-139

Urban, Karl, Dr., 105

Veit, Josef, 25, 39 f
Veit, Josefa, 26
Voelkisch, 84, 84 f, 126, 149, 162

Wagner, Richard, 78, 80, 83, 101, 103-104, 108, 113, 119, 136
Walter, Fritz, 140, 163

Weiss, Jacques, 163, 164
Wendt, Josef, 105
Wesseley, Karl, 32, 33, 85 f
"Wieland the Smith," 118-119, 119 f
Wolf, Karl, 82, 146

Zakreys, Maria, 108, 116, 121-122
Zoebl (miller), 60